ENVIRONMENTAL LAW

IN A NUTSHELL

SEVENTH EDITION

By

ROGER W. FINDLEY
Professor of Law and Fritz B. Burns
Chair of Real Property
Loyola Law School, Los Angeles

DANIEL A. FARBER
Sato Sho Professor of Law
University of California, Berkeley

Mat #40556114

COPYRIGHT © 1983, 1988, 1992, 1996 WEST PUBLISHING CO.
© West, a Thomson business, 2000, 2004
© 2008 Thomson/West
        610 Opperman Drive
        St. Paul, MN 55123
        1–800–313–9378

Printed in the United States of America

ISBN: 978–0–314–17720–9

TEXT IS PRINTED ON 10% POST
CONSUMER RECYCLED PAPER

For my children, Sheila and Steve, and my grandchildren, D.J., Annabelle, and Gracie, who will inherit our environment.

R.W.F.

To the memory of Sam Hamick.

D.A.F.

*

OUTLINE

Page

TABLE OF CASES

References are to Pages

ENVIRONMENTAL LAW

IN A NUTSHELL

SEVENTH EDITION

*

CHAPTER 1

JUDICIAL REVIEW OF GOVERNMENT DECISIONS

Environmental litigation often involves disputes with governmental agencies rather than between private parties. Thus, an understanding of administrative agencies and their relationship with the courts is important. In this chapter, we will begin by discussing the general rules governing judicial review of agency decisions. Those rules are mostly derived from the Administrative Procedure Act (APA). We will then consider the special procedures imposed on federal agencies by the National Environmental Policy Act (NEPA).

A. THE JUDICIAL ROLE IN ENVIRONMENTAL LAW

Apart from the political process, the only check on agency action is found in the courts. Because of the importance of government agencies in environmental law, it is crucial to understand the circumstances under which courts will intervene in environmental decisionmaking. We can break this problem down into three issues. First, when will a court hear a case challenging agency action? Sec-

1

ond, if the court does hear the case, what standards will it apply in reviewing the agency's action? And third, what remedies will the court provide?

We will begin with the first of these issues, the limits of a court's ability to hear environmental cases. It is quite possible to conceive of a legal system in which any individual could bring suit to halt any government action that violated the law. It is also possible to conceive of a system in which the only redress against illegal government action would be at the ballot box. American law has taken an intermediate position. Courts can hear some, but not all, claims that a government agency has acted illegally. A plaintiff who seeks to bring such a claim must demonstrate that she is a proper individual to challenge the government action and that she is raising issues a court is authorized to consider. The requirement that the suit be brought by the proper individual is known as the doctrine of "standing." The requirement that the issues be suitable for judicial resolution is the doctrine of "reviewability." The standing issue has given rise to a great deal of litigation in environmental cases.

1. STANDING

In the past thirty-five years, the Supreme Court has considered the standing issue in eight major environmental cases. The first of these cases was Sierra Club v. Morton, 405 U.S. 727 (1972). This case challenged a plan by Walt Disney Enterprises to build a $35 million resort in the Mineral King

Valley, which the Court described as "an area of great natural beauty nestled in the Sierra Nevada Mountains." The Sierra Club argued that approval of the plan by the Forest Service had violated several federal statutes. The Sierra Club did not base its lawsuit on the claim that its members would be directly injured by the construction of the resort. Instead, it invoked its status as a public interest group with a long-standing focus on preservation of the environment.

Although some lower courts had indicated a willingness to confer standing based on similar allegations, the Supreme Court refused to do so. Instead, it relied on earlier cases establishing a general test for standing under the APA. This test, known as the *Data Processing* test, requires that the plaintiff seeking judicial review of agency action show two things: (1) an "injury in fact"; and (2) an interest "arguably within the zone of interests to be protected or regulated" by the statute that the agency is claimed to have violated. (Later decisions make it clear that the plaintiff must be within the zone of interests of the particular provision involved in the case, not of the statute as a whole.) The "injury in fact" requirement has proved to be the more important of these two elements of the *Data Processing* test.

In *Sierra Club* the Court held that a mere allegation of a sincere interest in a problem, even if the interest has been active and long-standing, is not enough to constitute injury in fact. The practical importance of this holding, however, was diminished by the Court's assertion that the Sierra Club could establish injury in fact merely by alleging that some of its members used the area in question for recreational purposes. The aesthetic injury suffered by these members, who would no longer be able to hike through an unspoiled wilderness if the project was built, was sufficient to constitute an injury in fact not only as to themselves, but also as to the organization to which they belonged. Obviously, there was little doubt that the Sierra Club could satisfy this requirement, so the ultimate effect of the Court's holding was simply to require an amendment to the pleadings.

The next Supreme Court case suggested that it would be easy to satisfy the *Sierra Club* requirements. United States v. Students Challenging Regulatory Agency Procedures, 412 U.S. 669 (1973) (*SCRAP I*) involved a challenge to a decision by the Interstate Commerce Commission (ICC) in a railroad rate case. (Both the ICC and the system of rate regulation were later abolished.) The railroads had sought permission for a rate increase to expand their revenues and to cover expenses. The ICC had not given final approval for the increase, but did allow it to go into effect pending investigation. The plaintiffs, who had formed an association in order to bring the case, alleged that the existing rate schedule unfairly discriminated against recycled goods. As a result of this rate discrimination, they alleged, recycled goods were used in lower amounts than they otherwise would be. The plaintiffs' theory was that the situation would only be made worse by an across-the-board rate increase. They alleged that the result of this increase would be to discriminate against recycled goods, further diminishing the use of recycling, thereby increasing the amount of litter on a nationwide basis, and thus causing an increase in the amount of litter in the parks near the plaintiffs' homes. They also alleged that the decrease in recycling would cause an increase in mining and logging in the region. Despite the somewhat tenuous chain of causation alleged by the plaintiffs, and the fairly minimal injury that they claimed as a result of this chain of causation, the Supreme Court held that they did have standing to challenge the ICC's action.

The *SCRAP* decision clarified two elements of standing law. First, the Court made it clear that standing "is not to be denied simply because many people suffer the same injury." As the Court pointed out, to deny standing to individuals who are injured simply because many others are also injured would mean that the "more injurious Government actions could be questioned by nobody." Second, the Court held that the test for standing was qualitative, not quantitative. Thus the magnitude of the injury in fact makes no difference so long as some injury exists.

The Supreme Court's next decision also took a generous approach to environmental standing. That case, Duke Power Co. v. Carolina Environmental Study Group, Inc., 438 U.S. 59 (1978), involved a chain of causation almost as extended as that in the *SCRAP* case. The plaintiffs in *Duke*

Power challenged the constitutionality of the Price-Anderson Act. That statute limits the liability of the nuclear industry for damages resulting from a single nuclear accident. The plaintiffs claimed that without this limitation on liability, reactors would not be built, and that this in turn would spare them immediate environmental injuries such as injury to fishing.

Despite the tenuousness of the chain of causation, the Court held that there was a "substantial likelihood" that the nuclear plants near the plaintiffs' homes would not be completed or operated without the statute. This was held to be a sufficient basis for standing. The defendants had also attacked the plaintiffs' standing because the injury they were using to establish their standing had no logical relationship to their claims on the merits. The Court held, however, that such a nexus between the plaintiffs' injury for standing and the claim on the merits was unnecessary. (The nonconstitutional status of the zone of interests test was reaffirmed in Bennett v. Spear, 520 U.S. 154 (1997), in which the Court upheld the power of Congress to grant standing to anyone suffering an injury in fact, without regard to whether that person was within the zone of interests of the statute.)

In *Duke Power* and earlier decisions, the Supreme Court took a liberal approach to standing in environmental cases. In 1990, however, the Court signaled a change in direction. The first indication of this new attitude was a reference, in an non-environmental opinion, to *SCRAP I* as involving "[p]robably the most attenuated injury" ever to confer standing, with the additional comment that *SCRAP I* "surely went to the very outer limit of the law." Whitmore v. Arkansas, 495 U.S. 149 (1990). A second, more serious signal followed later the same year, in Lujan v. National Wildlife Federation, 497 U.S. 871 (1990).

National Wildlife Federation involved a Bureau of Land Management (BLM) review of past executive orders protecting many public lands from resource development. (These "withdrawals" are discussed in Chapter 6.) In 1976, Congress directed BLM to review existing withdrawals in eleven western states and decide whether the lands should be re-opened for development. The plaintiff alleged that BLM had violated the required statutory procedures in numerous respects, and that BLM's action would open up the lands involved to mining. The Court held that the plaintiff lacked standing.

Justice Scalia's opinion for the Court held that the plaintiff's claims were invalid in two respects. First, plaintiff had attempted to comply with *Sierra Club* by filing affidavits attesting to use of the affected lands by some of its members. The affidavits were defective, the Court held, because they only alleged that these members used federal lands "in the vicinity" of those locations affected by the order. Justice Scalia concluded that actual presence, not merely vague proximity, was required. Second, even if those affidavits had been adequate, they would have established the plaintiff's right only to litigate about the specific lands used by those individuals, not to challenge the entire BLM program. Unless a statute specifically permits broad regulations to be directly reviewed, a plaintiff can challenge only some "concrete action applying the regulation to the claimant's situation in a fashion that harms or threatens to harm him." The opinion then pointed out that exceptions exist when provided by statutes such as the Clean Air Act or when a rule "as a practical matter requires the plaintiff to adjust his conduct immediately."

Justice Scalia continued his campaign to restrict standing in Lujan v. Defenders of Wildlife, 504 U.S. 555 (1992). The ultimate issue in *Defenders*, which the Court never reached, was whether the Endangered Species Act (ESA) applies only to actions within the United States. The plaintiffs alleged that they would be harmed in various ways by federally supported actions taking place in Egypt and Sri Lanka. The Court held that they lacked standing, in the process striking down the ESA's citizen suit provision, which authorized the suit. Without any injury in fact, the plaintiffs could only be suing to vindicate the abstract interest in administrative compliance with the law—but that interest, the Court said, is properly the concern not of the courts but of the President, who is constitutionally obligated to "take care that the laws be faithfully executed."

The plaintiffs had unsuccessfully alleged several forms of injury. Two members alleged that they had visited the relevant areas of Egypt and Sri Lanka in the past and hoped to do so again in the future. "Such 'some day' intentions—without any description of concrete plans, or indeed even any specification of *when* the some day will be," were not enough to support standing. Justice Scalia was no more impressed with what he described as the plaintiffs' more novel standing theories. The first of these theories was called ecosystem nexus, under which "anyone who uses any part of an affected ecosystem has standing even if the activity is located a great distance away." Although the ESA is aimed in part at the protection of ecosystems, Justice Scalia found no basis for concluding that it created a cause of action on behalf of people who use parts of the ecosystem "not perceptibly affected" by the government's action.

Justice Scalia was equally unimpressed by the plaintiffs' other two theories. One, which they called the animal nexus, would have conveyed standing on anyone who studies or observes an endangered species. The other theory, the vocational nexus, would grant standing to anyone with a professional interest in the animal. To say that Justice Scalia was unpersuaded is an understatement. "It goes beyond the limit," he said, "and into pure speculation and fantasy, to say that anyone who observes or works with an endangered species, anywhere in the world, is appreciably harmed by a single project affecting some portion of that species with which he has not had more specific connection."

A concurrence by Justice Kennedy, who joined by Justice Souter, attempted to stake out a

middle ground.   The Kennedy concurrence deserves
careful attention because he and Souter were the
swing voters.   Kennedy entered two caveats to the
Scalia opinion.   First, he agreed that the record in
Defenders was inadequate to support the plaintiff's
nexus theories, but was not willing to foreclose
them as a matter of law in some future case.   Second, he saw a greater role for Congress in defining
the perimeter of injury in fact:

> As government programs and policies become
> more complex and far-reaching, we must be sensi-
> tive to the articulation of new rights of action
> that do not have clear analogues in our common-
> law tradition. . . .   In my view, Congress has the
> power to define injuries and articulate chains of
> causation that will give rise to a case or contro-
> versy where none existed before. . . .   In exercis-
> ing this power, however, Congress must at the
> very least identify the injury it seeks to vindicate
> and relate the injury to the class of persons
> entitled to bring suit.   The citizen-suit provision
> of the Endangered Species Act does not meet
> these minimal requirements. . . .

Defenders and *National Wildlife Foundation*
seemed to signal a sharply restrictive attitude toward standing.   This trend seemed to be confirmed
by Steel Company v. Citizens for a Better Environment, 523 U.S. 83 (1998).   *Steel Company* stressed
another prong of standing: the redressability requirement.   The plaintiffs sued to recover civil penalties and for other relief against a company that
had failed to make toxic emission disclosures re-

quired by federal law. The civil penalties, being payable to the government, were held not to redress any injury to the plaintiff. Because the statutory violation had no prospect of recurring, the Court held that the other claimed relief was unavailable. Hence, the plaintiffs had no available redress for their injury and therefore lacked standing. Justice Scalia, the author of the opinion, had seemingly won another battle in his campaign to restrict standing.

But in the Court's first standing decision of the new century, Friends of the Earth, Inc. v. Laidlaw Environmental Services (TOC), Inc., 528 U.S. 167 (2000), yet another change in direction seemed to occur. *Laidlaw* involved a citizen suit under the Clean Water Act against a company that had repeatedly violated the mercury limits in its permit. Although the lower court had held that the discharges had not actually caused any environmental harm, the Court nonetheless found standing. The plaintiffs had alleged that they lived in the area but did not use the river for recreational purposes because of concerns about pollution. Quoting *Sierra Club*, the Court said that "environmental plaintiffs adequately allege injury in fact when they aver that they use the affected area and are persons 'for whom the aesthetic and recreational values of the area will be lessened' by the challenged activity." Because the plaintiffs' "reasonable concerns" about the effects of the discharge "directly affected" their recreational and aesthetic interests, they had standing. This holding, as Justice Scalia complained in dissent, seemed to take a more generous attitude toward injury in fact than had *Defenders* and similar cases.

Laidlaw also cut back on *Steel Company*'s redress-ability holding. Read broadly, *Steel Company* would seem to suggest that private parties never have standing to seek civil penalties payable to the government. In *Laidlaw*, however, the violations had continued through the filing of the lawsuit. Consequently, the Court said, civil penalties would redress potential future injury to the plaintiffs by deterring further violations. Whether *Laidlaw*'s more generous attitude toward standing marks a doctrinal turning point remains to be seen.

In Massachusetts v. E.P.A., 127 S.Ct. 1438 (2007), the Court took a generous view of the state's standing to challenge the federal government's failure to respond to global climate change. The plaintiffs challenged EPA's refusal to initiate a rulemaking to regulate greenhouse gas emissions from vehicles. A key issue was standing. Indeed, Chief Justice Roberts' dissent seemed to suggest that federal courts could never hear cases involving climate change, because the "very concept of global warming seems inconsistent with this particularization requirement," since climate change affects the entire human race. Nevertheless, writing for a five-Justice majority, Justice Stevens concluded that standing was present.

Because some of the plaintiffs were state governments, the Court suggested that their standing claim should be treated with particular generosity. Having surrendered some of their sovereign abilities to protect their environments when they entered the union—for example, the ability to negotiate for greenhouse gas reductions with foreign powers—states were now reliant on Congress to help protect their "quasi-sovereign interests." This special solicitude for states may encourage them to become more deeply involved in judicial review of agencies.

The Court also found, however, that the plaintiffs had satisfied the normal three-part test for standing. The Court noted that the effects of climate change posed a particular threat to the state's interests: "If sea levels continue to rise as predicted, one Massachusetts official believes that a significant fraction of coastal property will be 'either permanently lost through inundation or temporarily lost through periodic storm surge and flooding events.'" As to causation, EPA did "not dispute the existence of a causal connection between man-made greenhouse gas emissions and global warming." EPA did contend, however, that the particular government action that the plaintiffs sought would not have a significant impact, because automobiles are only one source of greenhouse gases and because the United States as a whole accounts for only a portion of these gases. The Court rejected this "erroneous assumption that a small incremental step, because it is incremental, can never be attacked in a federal judicial forum." Finally, the Court was untroubled by the remedial issues.

"While it may be true that regulating motor-vehicle emissions will not by itself *reverse* global warming, it by no means follows that we lack jurisdiction to decide whether EPA has a duty to take steps to *slow* or *reduce* it."

Massachusetts v. EPA was a 5–4 decision and may have relied to some extent on the special status of the state government as a plaintiff. Thus, it is unclear whether it portends a long-term expansion in standing. Nevertheless, it clearly confirms the indication in *Laidlaw* that the Court currently has no enthusiasm for Justice Scalia's campaign to contract standing.

Although the Court is obviously divided in how strictly to apply the standing requirements, it does seem united in its understanding of the basic test. To summarize the law of standing, the Supreme Court has required plaintiffs to prove that they have suffered an injury in fact. In environmental cases, the plaintiff must allege the existence of a chain of causation between the allegedly illegal government action and an injury to some portion of the environment used by the plaintiff. The plaintiff need not allege any health injury or any economic damage; aesthetic or recreational impairment is enough. To obtain standing, the plaintiff need only demonstrate a "substantial likelihood" that judicial relief against the illegal government action would reduce the extent or likelihood of the plaintiff's environmental injury.

2. REVIEWABILITY

The existence of standing does not mean that the plaintiff will necessarily get a hearing on the merits. Standing involves the relationship between the plaintiff and the issues in the case. Although the plaintiff may stand in the proper relationship to an issue, the issue itself may not be suitable for judicial resolution. If *anyone* could litigate the issue, the plaintiff would be the proper person to do so, but some issues simply cannot be litigated by anyone at all. The question of whether an issue is subject to judicial resolution is called "reviewability."

Fortunately, virtually all issues that might arise in an environmental case are subject to judicial review. This was made clear by the Supreme Court in Citizens to Preserve Overton Park, Inc. v. Volpe, 401 U.S. 402 (1971). *Overton Park* involved a dispute over the use of federal highway funds to finance the construction of an interstate highway through Overton Park, a 342-acre city park in Memphis. The applicable statute prohibited the Secretary of Transportation from using federal funds to finance the construction of highways through a public park if a "feasible and prudent" alternative route existed. The plaintiffs contended that the Secretary had violated this restriction. The Supreme Court held that the plaintiffs were entitled to judicial review on this issue.

The Court found the key to the reviewability problem in section 701 of the Administrative Procedure Act, 5 U.S.C.A. § 701. Section 701 provides that an action by any administrative agency is subject to judicial review except (1) where there is a statutory prohibition on review or (2) where "agency action is committed to agency discretion by law." In order to find the first exception applicable, a court must find "clear and convincing evidence" that Congress intended to restrict access to judicial review. Such evidence is rarely available. The second exception, action "committed to agency discretion," is not easy to understand, inasmuch as even discretionary agency actions can be reviewed by a court to determine if the agency has abused its discretion. In *Overton Park*, the Court concluded that the "committed to agency discretion" exception is very narrow and applies only where statutes are drawn in such broad terms that "there is no law to apply." Thus, this exception really applies only in cases in which a statute gives an agency such broad powers, subject to so few restrictions, that a court could never reasonably conclude in any given case that the agency had exceeded its powers. This seems to be another way of saying that judicial review is pointless because we can conclude without even considering the specific facts of the case that the agency could not possibly have acted illegally. Thus, holding that a question is "committed to agency discretion" comes very close to a holding on the merits that whatever the agency has done is necessarily lawful. In the specific case before it, the *Overton Park* Court concluded that the decision was not committed to agency discretion because the statute provided specific criteria that the Secretary of Transportation was supposed to apply.

In a few exceptional cases, the issue of reviewability has proved to be troublesome. Generally, these cases have involved statutes that provide either no limitations on administrative action or limitations that are so broad as to be almost nonexistent. Occasionally, administrative action may be held to be unreviewable because it involves some special area in which courts are hesitant to become involved, such as foreign affairs or military decisions. In the typical environmental law case, however, reviewability is unlikely to be a serious issue.

3.   STANDARD OF REVIEW

We have seen that the plaintiff in an environmental law case must establish that she has standing and that the issues involved in the case are reviewable. Making this showing gets the plaintiff through the courtroom door. Of course, getting into the courtroom is not an end in itself; it is merely a means of getting a decision on the merits of the case. Thus, for many plaintiffs, the important question is not whether a court will be willing to hear the case, but rather what kind of hearing the court will provide. In particular, a great deal turns on the degree to which the court is willing to second-guess the administrative agency as opposed to deferring to the agency's expertise.

Before considering the scope of judicial review, it is helpful to understand the basics of administrative procedure. What follows is a brief sketch of the various forms of administrative procedure, which should help the reader understand the judicial review process more fully.

Under the Administrative Procedure Act, there are three important categories of administrative actions. The first category consists of adjudications. This form of procedure normally applies whenever the specific statute governing the agency requires an issue to be "determined on the record after opportunity for an agency hearing." The procedures required are essentially similar to those of a civil trial. The second category of administrative action is rulemaking. With the limited exception of a few situations in which a "formal rulemaking" is required, the procedure is relatively simple. The initial step is the publication of a notice in the Federal Register describing the proposed rule. The agency must then allow interested parties an "opportunity to comment" for at least thirty days. Then, the agency must issue, in conjunction with its promulgation of the rule, a "concise general statement" of the rule's basis and purpose. (There are a limited number of exceptions to these requirements.) The third category of administrative action consists of a vast number of government decisions that neither impose sanctions on individuals, grant licenses to them, nor impose rules governing future conduct. The APA does not specify any procedures for these actions.

The extent of judicial review generally depends on the kind of issues involved in the case. In particular, it is useful to distinguish between issues relating to pure questions of law, issues involving the factual basis for the agency's action, and issues relating to the agency's procedures. Courts apply a different level of scrutiny to each type of issue.

The first kind of issue involves only questions of law. Several practical reasons exist for giving some degree of deference to the administrative agency's view of the law. In a highly technical area, the agency has more experience than any particular judge in applying the statute. Also, Congress has given the agency, rather than the court, primary responsibility for carrying out the law. Furthermore, it is often important that private individuals or local governments be able to rely immediately on an agency's view of the statute. If the agency's view of the statute were given no credence at all by the courts, it would be unsafe to depend on the agency's position until the issue had been litigated all the way to the Supreme Court. Thus, giving deference to the agency's view serves the purpose of expediting compliance with the law.

The Supreme Court has also emphasized an additional reason for deferring to administrative agencies on statutory interpretation issues. In Chevron U.S.A., Inc. v. NRDC, 467 U.S. 837 (1984), which is discussed in greater detail on pages 126–127, the Court stressed that policy choices should be made by the political branches of government, rather than the courts. Where Congress has delegated regulatory authority to an administrative agency, that agency should decide upon public policy in the

area, not federal judges. Of course, the agency
must act within the scope of the authority delegated
by Congress. Thus, the Court still plays an important role in assuring that the agency decision is
consistent with the statutory mandate. Nevertheless, while *Chevron* does not give agencies unlimited
discretion with respect to statutory interpretation,
their decisions are entitled to a high level of deference. Agency interpretations that lack the force of
law generally receive a lower level of deference than
agency rulemaking or adjudication.

With respect to factual issues, the standard of
review also depends on the type of proceeding. In
an adjudicative action, the standard for review of
factual issues is the "substantial evidence" test.
The agency's action must be upheld by the court
unless there is no substantial evidence in the record
to support the agency ruling. With respect to other
forms of administrative action, the leading authority on review of factual issues is *Overton Park*. In
that case, the Court held that the standard of
review for non-adjudicative administrative decisions
was the "arbitrary and capricious" test. In applying this test, a court must examine the record
considered by the administrative agency. On the
basis of that record, the court must decide whether
the agency considered all of the relevant factors and
whether the agency made a clear error of judgment.
In practice, this standard of review may involve
either a very cursory examination of the administrative action or an intense scrutiny of the reasons
given for the administrative decision to determine

whether adequate support exists in the record. In environmental cases, some courts apply the "arbitrary and capricious" test in a way that closely resembles the application of the "substantial evidence" test. This has become known as the "hard look" approach. Thus, agencies may face intensive judicial scrutiny of their factual determinations. Yet courts have not forgotten that many of these determinations involve highly technical matters with which judges have little familiarity. Hence, some tendency toward deference to the agency exists, but less than one might expect from the phrase "arbitrary and capricious."

Judges sometimes have felt uncomfortable about attempting to assess an agency's technical judgment on factual issues. Feeling more comfortable in assessing procedural issues, some of these judges, led by Judge Bazelon of the D.C. Circuit, imposed procedural requirements on some administrative agencies beyond those contained in the APA. While this approach had some arguable merit, it was rejected by the Supreme Court in Vermont Yankee Nuclear Power Corp. v. NRDC, 435 U.S. 519 (1978), a case involving rulemaking about nuclear waste disposal. The lower court had faulted the NRDC for relying heavily on a conclusory statement by one of its own staff members, which had not been subject to cross-examination. In *Vermont Yankee* the Court held that judges normally lack the authority to impose any additional procedures on agencies beyond those required by statute, the Constitution, or the agency's own rules. The decision leaves open the possibility that in extremely compelling circumstances some additional procedures might be imposed. Fundamentally, the Court's rationale was that the agency itself is in the best position to decide on procedures.

Lower courts have found, however, that *Vermont Yankee* does leave them some room for maneuver. One exception to the *Vermont Yankee* rule is that courts may reverse agency actions when the agency has violated statutory procedural requirements. Some lower courts responded to *Vermont Yankee* by giving an expansive reading to statutes relating to agency procedures. For example, the APA on its face requires only a brief explanation of the agency's rule and an opportunity to comment by outsiders. Lower courts have held that the opportunity to comment is not "adequate" unless the agency has fully disclosed in advance the technical data it is considering. In effect, these courts have required an additional procedure on the part of agencies. Although courts applying this rationale have stopped short of requiring agencies to allow oral presentation of testimony or cross-examination, they have required procedures that have been aptly described as involving a "paper hearing." In addition, it should be remembered that many individual statutes such as the Clean Air Act contain detailed provisions concerning agency procedures in certain kinds of cases. These provisions often go well beyond the minimum requirements of the APA.

4. REMEDIES

Once the court decides that an agency has violated the law, the plaintiff is clearly entitled to some form of relief, if only an order directing the agency to give further consideration to the issue before acting. It has sometimes been argued that a court should withhold any remedy from the plaintiff if granting relief would be "unreasonable." The Supreme Court has clearly rejected that position. In TVA v. Hill, 437 U.S. 153 (1978), the Court authorized an in-junction against the completion of a multimillion dollar dam because the dam would threaten an endangered species of fish known as the snail darter. The Court found that completion of the dam would violate the Endangered Species Act. Having reached this conclusion, the Court held that it had no choice but to issue an injunction against completion of the dam. An enormous amount of money had already been spent on the dam, and little work remained to be done, but the Court held that these factors were simply irrelevant. In passing the statute, Congress had weighed the importance of saving endangered species against other government policies and had found the policy of saving endangered species to be paramount. The Court held that it was not its function to reassess a congressional balancing of these policies.

Courts do retain some discretion, however. In a later case, Weinberger v. Romero-Barcelo, 456 U.S. 305 (1982), the Court held that a statutory violation need not always lead to an injunction against the activity. The violation in question was the Navy's failure to get a permit under the Clean Water Act before a training exercise. The permit was technically required because munitions would fall in the water, but the lower court found that no harm to the coastal waters would in fact result. Under the circumstances, the Court held that ordering the Navy to apply for a permit was a sufficient remedy.

Remedial discretion was also an issue in Amoco Production Co. v. Village of Gambell, Alaska, 480 U.S. 531 (1987). *Gambell* involved a grant of oil and gas leases covering tracts offshore of Alaska. The environmental effects on Alaskan lands allegedly required the use of special procedures designed to protect the interests of Alaskan Natives. The Court found *Weinberger* controlling because only a procedural violation, rather than an actual environmental injury, was present. If an actual environmental injury had been present, however, the result would probably have been different. As the Court said:

Environmental injury, by its nature, can seldom be adequately remedied by money damages and is often permanent or at least of long duration, i.e., irreparable. If such injury is sufficiently likely, therefore, the balance of harms will usually favor the issuance of an injunction to protect the environment.

The Court stressed that injury to the environment was unlikely in *Gambell* and that the countervailing

interest in oil exploration was itself the goal of
another federal statute.

The Court has not clearly explained how these
three cases fit together. One way of harmonizing
the cases is as follows. In issuing relief, a court's
primary duty is to effectuate the goals of the statute. In *TVA v. Hill*, the statutory purpose was to
protect endangered species at virtually any cost;
the only way to effectuate that intent was to enjoin
the dam. In *Weinberger*, the goal of the statute was
to eliminate water pollution to the extent practicable. That goal was not compromised by the district
judge's order, which had directed the Navy to apply
for a permit but had allowed the military exercises
to continue in the meantime. Similarly, in *Gambell*, a preliminary injunction was not required to
accomplish the statutory goal of environmental protection. On the other hand, as the *Gambell* Court
pointed out, where a procedural violation results in
environmental harm, generally an injunction will be
required to effectuate federal policy. Thus, the
choice of a remedy is neither mechanical nor left to
the district judge's unguided discretion; rather, the
judge must effectuate congressional policy.

Another important remedial issue relates to attorneys' fees. Much of the most important environmental litigation is brought by public interest
groups. Their ability to bring these suits, thereby
acting as private attorneys general policing agency
compliance with federal statutes, is dependent on
their access to funding. One of the most important
sources of funding for these groups consists of the

awards of attorneys' fees provided by many environmental statutes. The availability of fee awards and their size have been the subject of tremendous litigation, both in the environmental area and elsewhere. Two basic rules are that (1) fees are available only to "prevailing parties," and (2) the fee is usually calculated by multiplying a reasonable hourly rate times the number of hours reasonably invested in the suit.

Many of the issues we have been discussing are considered in far more depth in an administrative law class. The discussion given here, however, should be enough to enable the reader to understand how courts function in environmental law cases.

B.   THE NATIONAL ENVIRONMENTAL POLICY ACT

Like the APA, NEPA imposes environmental responsibilities on all agencies of the federal government. Most of our discussion of NEPA will relate to § 102(2)(c), which concerns the environmental impact statement (EIS). Before turning to the EIS requirement, however, it is worth reviewing some of the other provisions of NEPA.

Section 101 of NEPA makes it the policy of the federal government to use all practicable means to administer federal programs in the most environmentally sound fashion. Section 102(1) requires that the laws and regulations of the United States be "administered in accordance with the policies set forth in this chapter." Prior to NEPA, some agencies contended that they lacked the statutory authority to consider environmental issues even if they wanted to do so. For example, the Atomic Energy Commission (now the Nuclear Regulatory Commission) contended that the thermal pollution caused by nuclear power plants was beyond its jurisdiction. One important result of NEPA is to ensure that every agency has the authority to consider the environmental consequences of its actions. Of course, granting agencies the authority to consider the environment does not guarantee that they will actually do so, but it does open the door for those agencies that are willing to take this step.

Section 102(2) contains several provisions that are intended to force agencies to take environmental issues seriously. Subsections (a) and (b) require new agency procedures to ensure that the decision-making process takes into account environmental factors. When a proposal involves conflicts between alternative uses of available resources—which is likely to be true of any important government decision—subsection (e) requires the agency to develop alternatives to recommended courses of action. These provisions supplement the EIS requirement and provide a basis for judicial intervention where the EIS requirement does not apply. Another important aspect of NEPA was the establishment of the Council on Environmental Quality (CEQ), which is primarily charged with advising the President about environmental matters.

The most significant provision of NEPA is undoubtedly § 102(2)(c). The primary purpose of this provision is to force agencies to take environmental factors into consideration when making significant decisions. The crucial language of this subsection reads as follows:

The Congress authorizes and directs that, to the fullest extent possible: ... (2) all agencies of the federal government shall—

. . .

(c) include in every recommendation or report on proposals for legislation and other major Federal actions significantly affecting the quality of the human environment, a detailed statement by the responsible official on—

(i) the environmental impact of the proposed action,

(ii) any adverse environmental effects which cannot be avoided should the proposal be implemented,

(iii) alternatives to the proposed action,

. . .

The subsection goes on to require the federal agency to consult other agencies with jurisdiction over or special expertise concerning the environmental problem involved. Copies of the EIS are to be circulated among federal, state, and local agencies, to the President, to the CEQ, and to the public.

The EIS is also supposed to "accompany the proposal through the existing agency review processes."

In essence, the statute requires the agency to prepare a detailed explanation of the environmental consequences of its actions and to make that report available to higher-level agency officials, other agencies, and the public. The EIS provision in NEPA makes no reference to judicial enforcement. Indeed, the drafter of the provision apparently did not have such enforcement specifically in mind. Nevertheless, soon after the statute was passed, it became clear that courts would become actively involved in enforcing it.

With this background in mind, we turn to a detailed consideration of the EIS requirement. For convenience, we divide our inquiry into two parts. The first issue to be considered is whether an agency needs to prepare any EIS at all. If the answer is affirmative, it is then necessary to consider the scope, timing, and content of the EIS.

1. THRESHOLD REQUIREMENTS

We will begin by discussing the threshold question: Is an EIS necessary? A reading of the statute indicates that three requirements must be met before an EIS is necessary. The proposed action must (1) be federal, (2) qualify as "major," and (3) have a significant environmental impact. There has been considerable litigation about these requirements.

We can begin with the first issue. In general, a proposed action is considered "federal" if some federal agency has the power to control the action. Thus, building a nuclear reactor involves a federal action because a federal license is required. Sometimes federal control takes the form of licensing, sometimes of funding, and sometimes of direct federal involvement, as in projects constructed by the Army Corps of Engineers. Occasionally, problems arise when an attempt is made to structure a project so as to "defederalize" all or part of it. Nevertheless, in most cases the "federal" requirement poses little difficulty.

The second requirement, that the project be "major," has proved to pose few problems. Any substantial commitment of resources, whether monetary or otherwise, is enough to qualify a project as "major." Indeed, it is unclear whether any project having a significant environmental impact could ever be considered "minor." In any event, neither of the first two requirements poses serious conceptual problems, although there are problems of line-drawing.

The final requirement, "significant environmental impact," is analytically more difficult. It poses two questions. First, what counts as an "environmental" impact? Second, when is such an impact "significant"? There is a temptation to assume that "environmental" refers only to the natural environment (wilderness areas, rivers, beaches, etc.). Nevertheless, the statute itself indicates that Congress had broader concerns. Section 101 of NEPA speaks of the need to assure all Americans "safe, healthful, productive, and esthetically and culturally pleasing surroundings." The same section speaks of the need to preserve the important historical and cultural aspects of our national heritage, to enhance the quality of renewable resources, and to achieve a balance between population and resource use. These goals extend beyond undisturbed natural areas.

Judicial decisions confirm that NEPA is not limited to the natural environment. For example, in Hanly v. Mitchell, 460 F.2d 640 (2d Cir.1972), the Second Circuit held that the construction of a new jail in Manhattan potentially involved significant environmental impact. In addition to air pollution, among the impacts considered were the possibility of increased crime in the area, the aesthetic impact of the building, and other socioeconomic effects. Given this reading, the scope of NEPA could be virtually unlimited. Almost everything the federal government does has some effect on the quality of life. Yet, the drafters of NEPA presumably did not intend that the government issue an EIS for every decision about foreign policy, medicaid, or tax law, even though these decisions presumably do affect the quality of human life.

The problem of defining the meaning of "environmental impact" reached the Supreme Court in Metropolitan Edison Co. v. People Against Nuclear Energy, 460 U.S. 766 (1983). The question before the Court was whether the NRC was required to prepare an EIS before allowing Metropolitan Edison to resume operation of one of the reactors at Three Mile Island. (Three Mile Island had been the site of a significant reactor breakdown.) The D.C. Circuit held that an EIS was required because the psychological stress caused by reopening the plant would have a significant health effect on residents of the surrounding communities. The Supreme Court apparently agreed with the lower court that "effects on human health can be cognizable under NEPA, and that human health may include psychological health." Generally speaking, however, the Court believed that in NEPA "Congress was talking about the physical environment—the world around us, so to speak."

Under *Metropolitan Edison*, an effect qualifies as environmental only if it has a "reasonably close causal relation" to a change in the physical environment. NEPA requires consideration of the direct effects of present physical actions and of the possible effects should future risks materialize. It does not, however, require consideration of the immediate psychological impact that the mere existence of a risk may have before that risk has materialized. Similarly, as the Court pointed out, in cases involving the construction of a new jail or other public facility, "the psychological health damage to neighboring residents resulting from unrealized risks of crime is too far removed from that event [the operation of the facility] to be covered by NEPA."   In short, a psychological effect can qualify as environmental only if it is proximately caused by a physical event.

In addition to the problem of deciding what impacts count as "environmental," there is also the problem of deciding when an environmental impact is sufficiently serious to be "significant." Courts have taken various approaches to this problem. The Second Circuit in Hanly v. Kleindienst, 471 F.2d 823 (2d Cir.1972) (*Hanly II*) adopted a two-part test involving the degree of change from current land use and the absolute quantity of the impact. Formulations adopted by other courts include "significant degradation of the environment" and "arguably adverse environmental impact," as well as other attempts to paraphrase the statute. The CEQ regulations, which are made binding by a Presidential order, instruct agencies to consider factors such as impact on public health, unique features of the geographic area, the precedential effect of the action, and whether the action is highly controversial. Even after considering these factors, a determination must be made about their magnitude. This is a "judgment call" about which very little can be said, except to observe that courts seem to have some tendency to resolve close cases in favor of requiring an impact statement.

Before 1989, the lower courts were sharply divided regarding the proper scope of review when an agency decides not to prepare an EIS. The Supreme Court resolved the issue in Marsh v. Oregon Natural Resources Council, 490 U.S. 360 (1989). The plaintiffs in *Marsh* claimed that a dam required a supplemental EIS (SEIS) because of two new documents: a report from the state department of fish and wildlife suggesting that the dam would have more effect on downstream fishing than the

original EIS suggested, and a federal soil survey
that implied greater downstream turbidity. Although the issue was whether a supplemental EIS
was needed, rather than the threshold requirements
for an initial EIS, the Court stressed that the two
issues are similar. If new information shows that a
federal action will affect the environment "in a
significant way or to a significant extent not already
considered," a supplemental EIS is required. This
is obviously very similar to the threshold requirement for an EIS. In both situations, the Court
said, NEPA requires an agency to take a "hard
look" at the environmental effects of its proposal.
The Court held the proper standard for review is
the arbitrary and capricious test, because the agency's decision whether to issue an EIS or SEIS
involves "a factual dispute, the resolution of which
implicates substantial agency expertise." After
Marsh, the same standard should apply to review of
an agency's decision to forego an EIS entirely, although some confusion on this point remains in the
lower courts.

As noted earlier, the "arbitrary and capricious"
test can result in either cursory or searching review
of the agency decision, depending on how the court
applies the standard. *Marsh* calls for fairly careful
review of the agency decision. Lower court judges,
the Court said, "should not automatically defer to
the [agency] without carefully reviewing the record
and satisfying themselves that the agency has made
a reasoned decision...." On the other hand,
where experts disagree, the agency may "rely on

the reasonable opinions of its own qualified experts even if, as an original matter, a court might find contrary views more persuasive." In applying this test, the Court reviewed the record in great detail before upholding the agency decision. Thus, the Court's embrace of the "arbitrary and capricious" test does not free the agency's decision from serious scrutiny on review.

2. SCOPE AND TIMING

This brings us to the most important set of issues relating to NEPA. If an EIS is necessary, *what* must it contain and *when* must it be prepared? As we shall see, the Supreme Court has addressed repeatedly the issues relating to the scope and content of the EIS.

Before considering the EIS's *content*, it may be helpful to review briefly the procedure used in preparing an EIS. The CEQ regulations contain detailed procedural requirements for the entire EIS process. The process begins with an "environmental assessment" (EA), which is a brief analysis of the need for an EIS. The EA must also consider alternatives to the proposed action, as required by § 102(2)(E) of NEPA. If the agency decides not to prepare an EIS, it must make a "finding of no significant impact" (FONSI) available to the public. Under *Marsh*, this finding is subject to judicial review using the arbitrary and capricious standard.

If the agency does decide to prepare an EIS, the first step in the EIS process is called "scoping."

Scoping is intended to obtain early participation by other agencies and the public in planning the EIS, to determine the scope of the EIS, and to determine the significant issues to be discussed in the EIS. The actual preparation of the EIS itself involves a draft EIS, a comment period, and a final EIS. Agencies with jurisdiction or special expertise relating to the project are required to comment. Major interagency disagreements are to be referred to CEQ for its recommendation. When an agency reaches a final decision on the project, it must prepare a "record of decision" summarizing its actions and explaining why it rejected environmentally preferable alternatives and mitigation measures.

As reflected by the CEQ regulations, one of the most important issues relating to the content of an EIS is its scope. This is the reason CEQ included a special stage in the procedure focusing on this issue. *Segmentation* of a project is one means of evading NEPA. For example, suppose the Department of Transportation planned to fund construction of a highway through an environmentally sensitive area such as a wildlife preserve. If it did not wish to give full consideration to this environmental impact, it might proceed as follows: first, it could prepare an environmental impact statement on the highway segment terminating on one side of the preserve. Since this segment of the highway would not involve any environmentally sensitive areas, the agency would then conclude that that segment was environmentally sound. It could then do the same for the segment terminating near the other side of the preserve. Finally, when it got to the segment involving the preserve, it would simply note the obvious fact that millions of dollars spent on the other segments would go to waste unless the segments were connected. Thus, by the time it got around to considering the environmental impact of the final segment, the decision would be a foregone conclusion. At no stage in the process would the agency really have given consideration to the overall environmental costs and countervailing benefits of the project. This would defeat the purpose of NEPA. In order to prevent such evasion of NEPA's purpose, courts must be prepared to determine the proper scope of an EIS. In this hypothetical, for example, a court must have some means of determining whether the scope of the EIS can be restricted to these individual segments, considered one by one, or whether a single EIS must be prepared covering the entire project.

The Supreme Court has considered three cases involving the scope and timing issues. The first case involved rather unusual facts and attracted little notice at the time. This case was Aberdeen & Rockfish Railroad Co. v. Students Challenging Regulatory Agency Procedures, 422 U.S. 289 (1975) (*SCRAP II*), a continuation of the lawsuit discussed in connection with the doctrine of standing on pages 4–5. After the Supreme Court's standing decision, the case was remanded to the district court, which held that the ICC had failed to comply with NEPA. On appeal, the Supreme Court reversed. In deciding both the scope and the timing of the EIS, the Court used a relatively mechanical test. According to the Court:

> Under ... the statute, the time at which the agency must prepare the final "statement" is the time at which it makes a recommendation or report on a *proposal* for federal action. Where an agency initiates federal action by publishing a proposal and then holding hearings on the proposal, the statute would appear to require an impact statement to be included in the proposal and to be considered at the hearing. Here, however, [until its actual decision], the ICC had made no proposal, recommendation, or report. The only proposal was the proposed new rates filed by the railroads. Thus, the earliest time at which the *statute* required a statement was the time of the ICC's report....
>
> In order to decide what kind of an environmental impact statement need be prepared, it is necessary first to describe accurately the "federal action" being taken.
>
> Having defined the scope of the "federal action" being taken ... our decision of this case becomes easy.

Thus, in *SCRAP II*, the Court used a fairly mechanistic test. Under *SCRAP II*, the key to determining the scope and timing of the EIS is simply to identify carefully the "proposal" in question. The EIS is due at the same time, and not before, the proposal is issued. Moreover, the scope of the EIS is simply determined by the scope of the proposal itself. The scope, impact, and alternatives to *that* proposal must be discussed, not some broader set of issues.

Despite this relatively clear language in *SCRAP II*, it failed to receive careful attention from either federal agencies or the lower federal courts. The reason is that much of the other language in the Court's opinion seemed more specifically related to the special characteristics of ICC law.

The Supreme Court's next decision on this issue made it clear that *SCRAP II* was intended to have a broader effect. That decision, Kleppe v. Sierra Club, 427 U.S. 390 (1976), remains the Court's definitive statement on the scope and timing issues. *Kleppe* involved the leasing of coal reserves on public lands to private mining companies. The D.C. Circuit held that individual leasing proposals in an area identified as the "Northern Great Plains region" involved such interrelated environmental effects that a single EIS was necessary for the entire region. The Supreme Court faulted the lower court for creating a balancing test to decide the issue rather than focusing on the language of the statute. Looking to the language of the statute, the Court found it clear that an EIS is required only if there has been a report on a formal proposal for major federal action. On examining the record, the Court concluded that no proposal existed with respect to the Northern Great Plains region; instead, there were only proposals for actions of either local or national scope. The Court noted that an EIS was plainly required both for the local issuance of a lease and for the adoption of a national coal-leasing program. But, according to the Court, there was "no evidence in the record of an action or a proposal for an action of regional scope." Hence, the Court applied the *SCRAP* test and concluded that no regional EIS was necessary.

Having disposed of the argument adopted by the lower court, the Supreme Court then turned to an additional argument made by the Sierra Club. The Sierra Club stressed the interrelated environmental impacts of individual mining operations in this region. The Court rejected this argument also. The Court pointed out that this argument could be viewed in two different ways. First, it could be viewed as an attack on the sufficiency of the EISs already prepared by the government on those projects already approved. As such, the Court held that the issue was not properly before it, since the case was not brought as a challenge to any particular EIS. Second, the argument could also be viewed as an attack on the decision not to prepare one comprehensive impact statement on all proposed projects in the region. The Court conceded that when several proposals are pending before an agency at the same time, and when those proposals have cumulative or synergistic environmental impacts, their environmental consequences must be considered together. This apparent concession was undermined by qualifications. The Court indicated that this consideration could be made as part of the issuance of the individual EIS governing each site. That is, a discussion of the general program could be tacked onto the EIS about each specific mine. Also, the Court held that judicial review of the interrelatedness issue would be based on the arbitrary and capricious standard. So long as the agency does not act arbitrarily in deciding on the scope of the impact statement, the Court held that judicial interference was inappropriate.

Two important criticisms can be made of the *Kleppe* opinion. To begin with, the opinion indicates little sympathy with the purposes of NEPA. The Court exhibits little concern over whether its test would advance or frustrate the underlying statutory purpose—which is ensuring that agencies seriously consider environmental factors, not simply prepare additional paperwork in the course of making a decision. Under the *Kleppe* Court's view, the statute seems to require only the preparation of an additional report at the time a decision is announced, rather than serious consideration by the agency of the environmental factors discussed in the report. This seems to substantially undermine the purposes of NEPA.

This brings us to the other major criticism of the Court's opinion. The Court seems to have believed that it was adopting a clear, almost mechanical test. In fact, however, there is no talismanic significance to the word "proposal." In the course of the development of a major federal program, there are often dozens and perhaps even hundreds of major memoranda prepared by various agency officials either sketching possible courses of action or attempting to evaluate those courses of action. Some reports are made at higher levels within the agency than others, and some seem to reflect a more definitive disposition of the issues than others. Nevertheless, no bright line divides those memoranda that are merely evaluations of possible courses of action from those that constitute "recommendations or reports on proposals for action," to use the statutory language. For this reason, as discussed below, the CEQ regulations call for a more functional analysis, in order to determine the existence and scope of a proposal.

The *Kleppe* test surfaced again in an unexpected context. In Weinberger v. Catholic Action of Hawaii, 454 U.S. 139 (1981), the issue before the Court was how to apply the EIS requirement when the government's action involved classified information. Specifically, the government established "nuclear capable" storage facilities, but would neither admit nor deny (for security reasons) that nuclear weapons were actually stored there. The Court held that if nuclear weapons were indeed stored at the facilities, an EIS had to be prepared. But this duty was not judicially enforceable. The plaintiffs were unable to prove the existence of a specific proposal to store nuclear weapons (because any such proposal would be classified)—so under *Kleppe* they were unable to prove that an EIS was required. Consequently, the suit was dismissed for the plaintiffs' failure to prove their cause of action, but with an admonition to the agency that a classified EIS had to be prepared if the military actually was storing nuclear weapons. Thus, both the need for an EIS and the actual contents of the EIS were committed solely to the agency's good faith. Whatever else might be said about it, this case does little to clarify any ambiguities in the *Kleppe* test.

The CEQ has attempted to clarify both the timing and scope issues. The current regulation defines the term "proposal" as follows:

"Proposal" exists at that stage in the development of an action when an agency subject to the Act has a goal and is actively preparing to make a decision on one or more alternative means of accomplishing that goal and the effects can be meaningfully evaluated.

This definition essentially captures the functional approach formerly used by the D.C. Circuit but restates that test in terms of the Supreme Court's emphasis on the determination of whether a "proposal" exists. Other CEQ regulations make it clear that the EIS should be "prepared early enough so that it can serve practically as an important contribution to the decisionmaking process," not simply "to rationalize or justify decisions already made." The CEQ regulations also require the EIS to consider (a) connected actions that are closely related, (b) actions that may have a cumulative effect with the proposed action under consideration, and (c) similar actions that should be considered together in view of other "reasonably foreseeable or proposed agency action." This seems to reflect an expansion of the *Kleppe* test by requiring agencies to consider other foreseeable actions even if there has been no formal proposal as to those actions.

3.   CONTENT OF THE EIS

Determining the scope of the EIS essentially decides what the precise subject-matter of the EIS will be.   The next important question, of course, is what must be said about that subject-matter.   In particular, what alternatives and environmental impacts must be discussed?

The leading case on the issue of what alternatives must be included in the EIS is NRDC v. Morton, 458 F.2d 827 (D.C.Cir.1972).   This case involved the lease of eighty tracts of submerged land off eastern Louisiana.   These tracts included about 10% of the total leased area.   The purpose of the suit was to enjoin sale of oil and gas leases pending compliance with NEPA.   The sale was a part of President Nixon's energy program.   The plaintiffs attacked the EIS for failing to consider a number of alternative approaches to the energy problem, such as relaxing oil quotas.   The plaintiffs argued that the need to discuss such alternatives was especially acute in view of the impact of the project.   The lease area was adjacent to the greatest estuary and marsh area in the United States.   It was agreed that if substantial oil pollution resulted from offshore operations, serious damage to the biological community in the area could occur.

The D.C. Circuit held that the test in determining which alternatives must be discussed in the EIS is the "rule of reason." The court rejected the argument that the Interior Department was required to discuss only alternatives that were within its own jurisdiction. Instead, the court held that the Interior Department must discuss all reasonable alternatives within the jurisdiction of *any* part of the federal government. The court also held that the EIS must discuss the environmental effects of all the reasonable alternatives. The less likely an alternative is to be implemented, however, the less need there is to discuss it in detail. Alternatives that are extremely implausible need not be discussed at all. The test for deciding these issues is whether a reasonable person would think that an alternative was sufficiently significant to warrant extended discussion.

The *Morton* test was endorsed by the Supreme Court in the *Vermont Yankee* case. In addition to the rulemaking procedure discussed earlier, *Vermont Yankee* also involved a challenge to the issuance of a particular license. In attacking the issuance of the license, the plaintiffs argued that the AEC failed adequately to discuss energy conservation as an alternative to building new nuclear plants. Applying the "rule of reason" approach, the Supreme Court rejected this argument for several reasons. First, energy conservation had not become an important subject of discussion at the time this particular license was issued. It was only shortly thereafter, with the advent of a middle-Eastern oil embargo, that conservation became highlighted. Second, the plaintiffs involved in this aspect of the litigation had failed to participate adequately in the proceedings before the agency. They had filed a list of objections to the grant of the license, but only 17 out of 119 of these objections related to the general topic of energy conservation. This group participated in none of the hearings in the final stage of the proceedings. The Court stressed that the plaintiffs should have structured their participation so that it would alert the agency to their position. This was "especially true when [the plaintiffs] are requesting the agency to embark upon an exploration of uncharted territory, as was the question of energy conservation in the late 60's and early 70's." The Court also stressed that the deceptively simple phrase "energy conservation" involves a vast number of possible actions that might in one way or another ultimately reduce projected demands for electricity. The plaintiffs had done nothing to specify which of these alternatives should be considered. The Court emphasized the need for a reasonable approach to the question of inclusion of alternatives:

Common sense also teaches us that the "detailed statement of alternatives" cannot be found wanting simply because the agency failed to include every alternative device and thought conceivable by the mind of man. Time and resources are simply too limited to hold that an impact statement fails because the agency failed to ferret out every possible alternative, regardless of how uncommon or unknown that alternative may have been at the time the project was approved.

For this reason, the Court adopted the "rule of reason" test promulgated in *Morton*.

Under the CEQ regulations, one alternative that must always be discussed is the alternative of doing nothing. The momentum of decisionmaking often creates a desire on the part of the agency to take action about a particular problem. Often, however, the most important alternative to the agency's projected form of action is not some modification in the agency action, but rather a decision to take no action at all. For this reason, the regulations require that the agency explain why it has not chosen the alternative of "no action."

If the EIS is to be more than a checklist of alternative actions, the consequences of each alternative must be discussed in detail. One frequently litigated issue is whether the discussion of the environmental impacts of the alternatives was adequate. In deciding which impacts must be discussed, the test once again is the "rule of reason." Speculative impacts need not be discussed. Unfortunately, courts have not done well in deciding what impacts are too speculative to require discussion. For example, in Carolina Environmental Study Group v. United States, 510 F.2d 796 (D.C.Cir.1975) the D.C. Circuit held that the possibility of a Class Nine accident to a nuclear reactor was too unlikely to require discussion in an environmental impact statement. The NRC staff later classified the accident at Three Mile Island (TMI) as a Class Nine accident. Following TMI, but before Chernobyl, the D.C. Circuit held again that NEPA does not require discussion of Class Nine accidents in an EIS, although the NRC had voluntarily decided to require such discussion in future impact statements. The court reasoned that the chance that a Class Nine accident would actually cause any environmental damage was negligible. The Third Circuit, however, rejected that view.

Often, the consequences of an agency action are highly uncertain due to lack of scientific information. Under a previous CEQ regulation, agencies were required to deal with this problem by including a "worst case scenario" in the EIS. Although the regulation was later rescinded by CEQ, some lower courts held that the "worst case" discussion was still required by the statute. In Robertson v. Methow Valley Citizens Council, 490 U.S. 332 (1989), however, the Court rejected the "worst case" requirement. The plaintiffs claimed the agency should have considered the "worst case" impact of a planned ski resort on a herd of mule deer. The Court held that CEQ's decision to repeal the worst case regulation was entitled to judicial deference. The Court also upheld CEQ's replacement for the worst case regulation. The amended regulation requires agencies, in the face of "unavailable information concerning a reasonably foreseeable significant environmental consequence," to prepare "a summary of existing credible scientific evidence" and present an "evaluation of such impacts based upon theoretical approaches or research methods generally accepted in the scientific community."

The preceding discussion gives only an overview of the general issues likely to arise in an EIS case. Courts are often forced to engage in extensive factual inquiries concerning the agency's evaluation of the seriousness of the various impacts and its explanations of the countervailing benefits of the project. Agencies often engage in slipshod cost-benefit analysis of their proposals, frequently biasing their results in favor of their projected course of action. Courts have proved capable on a number of occasions of perceiving the unreliability of the agency's analysis and have not hesitated to require the agency to redo its work. Very little can be said in the way of general rules governing the disposition of these issues, because the issues are generally tied to the specific facts of each individual case.

4. REVIEW ON THE MERITS

Thus far, we have been concerned with the contents of and necessity for an EIS. The reader may well be asking a question which goes beyond the EIS itself: What happens if the EIS is perfect, the project is clearly a senseless environmental disaster, and the agency decides to go ahead anyway? Is NEPA only a procedural requirement imposing additional paperwork on agencies, or does it also impose substantive limits on agency decisions? The courts of appeals were split on this issue. The majority view was apparently that NEPA does impose substantive limits on agencies and that agency action is subject to judicial review if it transgresses

these limits. However, except for a single Second
Circuit decision, which was reversed by the Supreme Court in Strycker's Bay Neighborhood Council, Inc. v. Karlen, 444 U.S. 223 (1980), no court of
appeals actually overturned an agency for violating
NEPA's substantive limits.

Strycker's Bay involved construction of a housing
project in a middle income area. The Second Circuit held that the agency's choice of site was unjustifiable. According to the Second Circuit, when the
agency considers such projects, "environmental factors, such as crowding low-income housing into a
concentrated area, should be given determinative
weight." The Supreme Court summarily reversed
the Second Circuit decision. The Court stated:

> [I]n the present case there is no doubt that [the
> agency] considered the environmental conse-
> quences of its decision to redesignate the pro-
> posed site for low-income housing. NEPA re-
> quires no more.

This statement by the Court implies that NEPA
imposes no substantive duties on agencies, or at
least that violation of such duties is not subject to
judicial review. An accompanying footnote, however, seemed to leave the door open to review under
the arbitrary and capricious standard.

That door was seemingly shut in *Robertson*.
Apart from the need for a "worst case" discussion
in the EIS (discussed above), the plaintiffs also
argued that the agency had failed to adopt an
adequate mitigation plan. In rejecting that argu-

ment, the Court made clear its view that NEPA is purely procedural:

> If the adverse environmental effects of the proposed action are adequately identified and evaluated, the agency is not constrained by NEPA from deciding that other values outweigh the environmental costs. In this case, for example, it would not have violated NEPA if the Forest Service, after complying with the Act's procedural prerequisites, had decided that the benefits to be derived from downhill skiing at Sandy Butte justified the issuance of a special use permit, notwithstanding the loss of 15 percent, 50 percent, or even 100 percent of the mule deer herd. Other statutes may impose substantive environmental obligations on federal agencies, but NEPA merely prohibits uninformed—rather than unwise—agency action.

In concluding that NEPA is purely procedural, the Court referred to the statement of environmental policies in § 101 as "precatory." This description seems to fly in the face of the language of § 102(2) of NEPA, which "directs that, to the fullest extent possible: (1) the policies, regulations, and public laws of the United States shall be interpreted and administered in accordance with the policies set forth in this chapter. . . ." Section 102(2) seems never to have come to the Court's attention.

Given the language of § 102(2), the Supreme Court's rejection of substantive review under NEPA seems unjustifiable in principle. Nevertheless, it probably does not make much practical difference. Even if substantive review were allowed, the arbitrary and capricious test would require only that the agency present a "reasoned explanation" for its decision. Review of the EIS provides an alternative method of ensuring that the agency has a reasoned explanation for its decision. (Only in law professors' hypotheticals does the agency candidly announce that it is planning to cause a total environmental disaster for no good reason!) So in practice, substantive review and review of the EIS may amount to much the same thing—an agency that is making an arbitrary and capricious decision will be hard pressed to prepare an EIS that a court will uphold.

5.   EVALUATION OF NEPA

We have not considered the question of whether NEPA has served a useful purpose. There seems to be no objective way of answering this question, and opinions by experts differ. Very few federal projects have actually been halted by permanent injunctions based on NEPA. NEPA litigation does cause substantial delays in a significant number of projects. Not infrequently, projects are halted at some point after initiation of the NEPA litigation, most often because either a local agency or a federal agency decides to withdraw from the project. It is unclear how often such decisions to abandon projects result from the delays caused by the NEPA litigation. It is also impossible to know the extent to which agencies have refrained from taking controversial actions because of the desire to avoid the expense and delay of NEPA litigation. At least some environmentally unjustifiable projects surely have either been abandoned or never begun because of NEPA. In addition, a number of other projects have been modified to reduce their environmental impact. The unanswered question is whether the benefits thus attained are sufficient to justify the expense and delay created in all those instances in which the project ultimately proceeds.

If it turns out that NEPA has not made a major contribution to preserving the environment—a matter that is itself hotly disputed—perhaps some of the blame should go to the Supreme Court. Since NEPA was passed, the Court has decided twelve NEPA cases on the merits. It has never upheld a NEPA claim. Indeed, it has never taken a case for review in which the lower court rejected a NEPA claim. Only lower courts that upheld NEPA claims have found their decisions subjected to Supreme Court review. A cynical observer might say that the Court's sole interest in NEPA is rebuking lower court judges who exhibit undue enthusiasm for the statute. Perhaps that is an unfair interpretation, but the fact remains that the Court's attitude toward the statute can hardly have increased NEPA's effectiveness.

It may be useful at this point to summarize briefly the discussion of NEPA. As we have seen, NEPA requires an EIS when an agency has made a report on a proposal for a major federal action with a substantial environmental impact. In deciding whether any EIS is required, the most difficult question to answer has been whether there will be a substantial environmental impact. Once it has been concluded that an EIS is required, the next question is the scope of the EIS. The answer to this question is to be found by determining the precise scope of the agency "proposal" under consideration. The alternatives to that proposal, and the environmental impacts of the proposal and the alternatives, must be discussed in detail. In deciding which alternatives and which environmental impacts must be discussed, the applicable standard is the "rule of reason." This statutory scheme, whatever uncertainties may exist about its cost-effectiveness, has now stood the test of time. Indeed, it has been emulated by many states and by many other countries.

CHAPTER 2

FEDERALISM AND THE ENVIRONMENT

The United States is divided into fifty states along with the District of Columbia. Environmental problems pay no heed to these geographic lines. Frequently, an environmental problem in one state is caused by conduct in another. Hence, any one state may be effectively unable to protect its own environment. On the other hand, when a state does attempt to engage in environmental regulation, its actions may well have repercussions elsewhere. The regulating state may fail to take into account the costs imposed by its regulations on individuals or firms in other jurisdictions. Moreover, it is commonly believed, the ability of individual states to regulate may be frustrated by a "race to the bottom," in which states are forced to lower their standards to retain and attract industry. Thus, problems inevitably result from the division of governmental power into units that do not correspond with sharp divisions in either the environment or the economy.

In compensation for these problems, however, we obtain the benefits of fuller local government. Individual states in which the public is more strongly motivated to deal with environmental problems may do so without being held back by the less interested citizens of other states. This allows the government to be more responsive to the desires of the population. States also may act as laboratories, in which various forms of environmental regulation may be tried out before being used on a nationwide scale. These advantages are illustrated by the wave of state climate change efforts prior to any federal action. In short, federalism is both a problem and a useful tool.

To a great extent, the idea of federalism has its impact through the political process. Congress may be reluctant to enact legislation that infringes the traditional prerogatives of the states. The discussion in this chapter, however, will be limited to the constitutional dimensions of federalism. In the first part of the chapter we will consider constitutional limits on environmental regulation by the federal government. Then we will consider the extent to which the Constitution limits environmental regulation by states.

A. SCOPE OF FEDERAL POWER

One of the basic assumptions of American constitutional law is that Congress has limited powers. The federal government does not necessarily have the power to take any action it deems in the public interest. Instead, it is a government of limited, delegated powers. Environmental regulation by the federal government must utilize one of a list of specific powers. In environmental law, the most important of these specific powers are the power to regulate interstate commerce, the power to tax and spend, the power to enter into treaties, and the power to regulate the use of public lands. Together, these specific powers form an imposing arsenal of authority.

1. THE COMMERCE POWER

In practice, the most important of these federal powers is the power to regulate interstate commerce. The breadth of this power is illustrated in Hodel v. Virginia Surface Mining and Reclamation Association, Inc., 452 U.S. 264 (1981). *Hodel* involved the Surface Mining and Reclamation Act, 30 U.S.C.A. § 1201 et seq. The Act imposes a detailed series of restrictions on strip mining. In particular, the Act requires restoration of the land to approximately its original state. A mining association argued that the Act's principal goal was regulating the use of private lands rather than regulating the effects of coal mining on interstate commerce. Thus, the association contended, the ultimate issue was whether land use as such was subject to regulation under the commerce clause. The Court rejected the attempt to frame the question in this manner. According to the Court:

The task of a court that is asked to determine whether a particular exercise of congressional power is valid under the Commerce Clause is relatively narrow. The court must defer to a congressional finding that a regulated activity affects interstate commerce, if there is any rational basis for such a finding. . . .

Judicial review in this area is influenced above all by the fact that the Commerce Clause is a grant of plenary authority to Congress. This power is "complete in itself, may be exercised to its utmost extent, and acknowledges no limitations other than prescribed in the constitution." Moreover, this Court has made clear that the commerce power not only extends to "the use of channels of interstate or foreign commerce" and to "protection of the instrumentalities of interstate commerce . . . or persons or things in commerce," but also to "activities affecting commerce." As we explained in Fry v. United States, 421 U.S. 542, 547 (1975), "[e]ven activity that is purely intrastate in character may be regulated by Congress, where the activity, combined with like conduct by others similarly situated, affects commerce among the States or with foreign nations."

Applying this test to the Surface Mining Act, the Court found a rational basis for the congressional determination that surface mining affects interstate commerce. The effect of mining on water pollution was especially significant. The Court also noted that uniform national standards were necessary because of the difficulties encountered by attempts of individual states to regulate the problem.

The Court considered it irrelevant whether land use is properly considered a "local" activity. So long as Congress rationally determines that regulation is necessary to protect interstate commerce from adverse effects, characterization of the activity as local is irrelevant. The Court also rejected the argument that the Act was unnecessary because various other federal standards already adequately addressed the federal interests in controlling the environmental effects of surface mining. According to the Court, the "short answer to this argument is that the effectiveness of existing laws in dealing with the problems identified by Congress is ordinarily a matter committed to legislative judgment."

In the companion case of Hodel v. Indiana, 452 U.S. 314 (1981), the Court rejected another attack on the same statute. The district court in this case had struck down the provisions of the Act that attempted to protect prime farmland. The district court had found that only .006% of the total prime farmland in the nation was affected annually by mining. It termed the effect on interstate commerce "infinitesimal." The Supreme Court rejected this quantitative test. According to the Court, the "pertinent inquiry therefore is not how much commerce is involved but whether Congress could rationally conclude that the regulated activity affects interstate commerce." The Court found an ample basis for this conclusion. There was testimony before Congress about the effects of strip mining on agricultural productivity. The Court noted that even given the district court's finding concerning the amount of land affected, the amount of grain production involved would still be in the neighborhood of $56 million per year, which "surely is not an insignificant amount of commerce."

Until recently, it could be safely said that the commerce power was effectively unlimited. Cases such as *Hodel* gave such a high degree of deference to Congress that almost any imaginable statute seemed likely to be upheld. For this reason, the Court's decision in United States v. Lopez, 514 U.S. 549 (1995) surprised many observers. A majority of the Court in *Lopez* departed from almost sixty years of past practice by ruling that Congress had exceeded its powers under the commerce clause in a regulation of private activity. Specifically, the Court struck down a federal statute prohibiting the possession of firearms in the vicinity of schools. The implications of *Lopez* remain unclear even a decade later, but the opinion probably does not jeopardize previous cases such as the *Hodel* decisions.

Chief Justice Rehnquist's opinion for the five-Justice majority in *Lopez* attempts to erect a limit on the commerce power, without overruling any cases or imperiling any well-entrenched federal programs. The opinion begins by invoking the original understanding that federal powers are "few and defined," while state powers are "numerous and indefinite." Rehnquist emphasized that the original function of this division of powers was to assist in preserving liberty. Admittedly, he added, the scope of federal power had greatly increased in the post-New Deal era, partly because of "great changes" in the economy and partly because of a desire to eliminate what were considered "artificial" restraints on federal power. Having analyzed the post-New Deal case law, however, Rehnquist concluded that the school gun law did not fall squarely within the previously recognized scope of congressional power, and he declined to expand that scope further. In reaching this conclusion, he noted that the statute related to education, traditionally a core area of state concern; that Congress had made no findings at the time about the effect of the prohibited activity on interstate commerce; and that the statute required no proof of any nexus between the defendant's activity and interstate commerce.

Justice Kennedy, joined by Justice O'Connor, agreed that the statute "upsets the federal balance to a degree that renders it an unconstitutional assertion of the commerce power." But Justice Kennedy's concurrence is more tentative than the majority opinion. It repeatedly suggests that the Court's role is to police against disturbance of the *existing* balance of regulatory power between the states and the federal government, rather than to begin a roll-back of federal power. Justice Kennedy concluded that the statute intruded on state sovereignty. In the absence of a stronger link with commercial activities, "that interference contradicts the federal balance the Framers designed and that this Court is obliged to enforce."

Both the majority opinion and the Kennedy concurrence emphasize the noncommercial nature of the regulated activity, which was simply to be present in the vicinity of a school while in possession of a firearm. A later decision struck down a federal law concerning violence against women, also emphasizing the completely noncommercial character of the problem. In contrast, environmental statutes are heavily focused on regulating commercial activities such as industry, agriculture, and logging. Moreover, the interstate repercussions of pollution are more obvious than those of gun possession. For these reasons, *Lopez* probably does not pose a threat to the current federal regulatory regime as a whole. It may, however, have some impact on marginal applications of environmental statutes to seemingly local, noncommercial activities. In particular, *Lopez* cast doubt on the application of federal wetlands and endangered species regulation in some borderline situations, particularly when the regulated party is not engaged in a commercial enterprise.

The Court alluded to these constitutional difficulties in Solid Waste Agency of Northern Cook County [SWANCC] v. U.S. Army Corps of Engineers, 531 U.S. 159 (2001). The question before the Court was whether SWANCC needed a federal permit before filling an abandoned gravel pit. Under the statute, federal jurisdiction covers "navigable waters," further defined as the "waters of the United States." The government asserted jurisdiction over the gravel pit under the Army Corps' "migratory bird" regulation, which claimed jurisdiction over intrastate waters that can be used by migratory birds. The Supreme Court held that the regulation went beyond the Corps' statutory authority. The

Court expressed considerable doubt about whether the commerce clause would support the migratory bird rule, and construed the statute to avoid this constitutional doubt. Finding "nothing approaching a clear statement from Congress," the Court rejected what it viewed as a "significant impingement of the States' traditional and primary power over land and water use." As we will see in Chapter 6, the scope of federal statutory authority over wetlands has remained contested.

The scope of *Lopez* remains unclear. In Gonzales v. Raich, 545 U.S. 1 (2005), the Court placed an important limitation on *Lopez* by reaffirming that Congress can regulate purely local activities if they are part of a class of activities that have a substantial cumulative effect on interstate commerce, where excluding the local activities from regulation might undermine the regulation of the interstate market. Justice Scalia emphasized in a concurring opinion that the regulation in *Lopez* had not been part of a larger regulation of economic activity. This decision augurs well for the constitutionality of the major federal pollution statutes, even as applied to localized or non-commercial activities.

Even before *Lopez*, congressional power had already been placed in question in the special context of federal regulation of the activities of state governments. The Tenth Amendment has often served as the basis for efforts to protect state sovereignty. On occasion, the Supreme Court has struck down such a federal statute on federalism grounds, even while conceding that the statute was otherwise within Congress's power under the commerce clause. The Tenth Amendment had served as one basis of important federalism rulings before the New Deal, but was widely considered defunct after 1937. For almost forty years, the Tenth Amendment was considered to be nothing more than a truism stating that "all is retained which has not been surrendered." United States v. Darby, 312 U.S. 100 (1941). In 1976, however, the Court resurrected the Amendment in National League of Cities v. Usery, 426 U.S. 833 (1976), striking down an extension of the federal minimum wage to cover state employees.

Largely as a result of *League of Cities*, some important federal statutes were challenged on Tenth Amendment grounds. The result was considerable confusion about the limits of congressional power. For example, the lower courts disagreed about whether Congress could force the states to administer inspection programs for automobiles. Although the Supreme Court never resolved that issue, it did reject Tenth Amendment challenges to other important environmental legislation. In the *Hodel* cases, the Court upheld the Surface Mining Act against a Tenth Amendment challenge. The Court unanimously rejected the claim that land-use regulation is an inherently state concern beyond federal power under the Tenth Amendment. Only when Congress directly imposes duties on state officers, the Court held, does the Tenth Amendment come into play. Even then, the statute might still pass muster under the *League of Cities* test. In

FERC v. Mississippi, 456 U.S. 742 (1982), a sharply divided Court upheld portions of a 1978 energy conservation act, even though the statute imposed some affirmative duties on state administrative agencies.

Justice Blackmun had been the swing vote in *League of Cities*. In Garcia v. San Antonio Metropolitan Transit Authority, 469 U.S. 528 (1985), he changed his mind and became the decisive vote to overrule *League of Cities*. Like the earlier case, *Garcia* involved the federal minimum wage law, this time as applied to public transit workers. Despairing of the effort to distinguish integral state functions from other state activities, the Court held that the political process is the states' primary shield against Congress. At least in the absence of a clear breakdown in the political process, courts should not intervene when Congress regulates state activities.

If *League of Cities* is defunct as a constitutional rule, it lives on as a guide to statutory interpretation. Gregory v. Ashcroft, 501 U.S. 452 (1991) involved application of the federal age discrimination act (ADEA) to state judges. Because the case involved a core aspect of state sovereignty, the Court concluded that the statute had to be read narrowly. "Indeed," Justice O'Connor wrote for the Court, "inasmuch as this Court in *Garcia* has left primarily to the political process the protection of the States against intrusive exercises of Congress' Commerce Clause powers, we must be absolutely certain that Congress intended such an exercise." After reviewing the statute, she concluded that it was "at least ambiguous whether Congress intended" the ADEA to cover appointed judges. "In the face of such ambiguity, we will not attribute to Congress an intent to intrude on state governmental functions...." Similarly, in *SWANCC*, supra page 62, the Court refused to defer to an agency's interpretation of its own statute where that interpretation would raise "significant constitutional and federalism questions."

It is one thing for Congress to restrict the state's activities; it is another to impose affirmative duties on state officials. In New York v. United States, 505 U.S. 144 (1992) the issue was whether Congress could force states to establish programs for disposing of low-level radioactive waste, at penalty of "taking title" to the waste if they failed to enact such a program on schedule. The statute was obviously designed to deal with the NIMBY (Not in My Back Yard) syndrome: every state wanted to generate low-level waste in local medical facilities, but every state wanted some other state to take the responsibility of providing a site for disposal. While it did not quarrel with the purpose of the statute, the Court rejected the "take title" provision as an unprecedented effort to mandate affirmative legislative activity by the states. Justice O'Connor ruled that the immunity of states from such federal coercion is so fundamental that it can never be allowed—even if state officials initiate the federal legislation (as they had in *New York*) and regardless of the strength of the government's regulatory interest. The latter holding, notably, elevated state sovereignty above such less substantial interests as racial equality and freedom of speech, both of which can be impaired on the basis of a sufficiently compelling government interest. It should be noted, however, that the statute also provided a number of other incentives for states to legislate, which the Court upheld.

Beginning in 1937, the Supreme Court has been careful to give Congress broad leeway in regulating, particularly with respect to commercial activities. Currently, however, congressional power is suspect in two areas. First, with respect to regulation of private individuals, congressional power is subject to question if a statute focuses on an activity that is noncommercial, takes place in a field of traditional state concern, and has no apparent interstate connection. Second, regulations that impinge directly on state government have been under a cloud since 1976, when *League of Cities* was decided. Although *League of Cities* has been replaced by *Garcia*, the current trend seems to be back toward the protection of state rights. Perhaps the only safe prediction that can be made about the future is that federalism will remain a dynamic and uncertain area of the law, in sharp contrast to most of the past half century when federal power was at its apex. These developments seem unlikely, however, to threaten the core of federal environmental law.

2.   OTHER FEDERAL POWERS

Perhaps the most important of the other federal powers arises from the property clause of the Constitution.   This clause provides that "Congress shall have Power to dispose of and make all needful Rules and Regulations respecting the Territory or other Property belonging to the United States." This clause is important because of the vast amount of land owned by the federal government, which comprises an area nearly the size of India.   Almost 180 million acres have been reserved for national forests and parks.   These enormous tracts of land contain much of the nation's remaining wilderness. It is the property clause that gives Congress the power to protect these lands.

The leading case on congressional power under the property clause is Kleppe v. New Mexico, 426 U.S. 529 (1976).   *Kleppe* involved the Wild Free-Roaming Horses and Burros Act.   The Act protects all unbranded horses and burros on public lands from capture.   If the animals stray onto private land, the landowner may require the government to retrieve them.   In *Kleppe,* state game wardens entered public land to remove wild horses.   The state argued that the statute could not be supported by the property clause.   According to the state, the clause grants Congress only the powers to dispose of federal land and to protect federal land.   The first power was allegedly not broad enough to support legislation protecting wild animals that live on federal land, while the second power was not implicated because the Act allegedly was designed to protect only the animals, which are not themselves federal property. The Court rejected the narrow reading of the property clause implicit in these arguments. According to the Court, the clause is not limited to rules regarding disposal, use, and protection of federal lands. Rather, Congress possesses the powers of both a proprietor and a legislature over the public domain. With respect to public lands, Congress has the same regulatory power that each state has with respect to its own lands. Thus, Congress may regulate for any public purpose concerning activities on public lands.

It is less clear how much regulatory power the property clause gives Congress over private lands adjoining public lands. In one early case, the Supreme Court held that Congress had the power to order the removal of a fence built on private land that limited access to public land. Camfield v. United States, 167 U.S. 518 (1897). The Court held that the fence constituted a nuisance and that Congress had the power to abate this nuisance. The Court remarked more generally that Congress has the power to protect the public lands without being required to seek the aid of state legislatures. Following the logic of these remarks, some lower court opinions have read the property clause quite broadly to allow Congress to prevent any activity on private lands that would interfere with Congress's goals respecting the public lands. See Minnesota v. Block, 660 F.2d 1240 (8th Cir.1981); United States v. Brown, 552 F.2d 817 (8th Cir.1977). Thus, if

Congress sets aside public lands for quiet, peaceful enjoyment, it may prevent activities on adjoining private lands that would produce excessive noise. This reading of the property clause seems to be correct. If the Constitution gives Congress the power to dedicate public lands to a particular purpose, it must surely give Congress the power to effectuate that decision by preventing interference from private parties.

Some lower courts construed *Kleppe* to mean that federal power over public lands was not only broad but exclusive, so that any state laws dealing with public lands would be preempted. In California Coastal Commission v. Granite Rock Co., 480 U.S. 572 (1987), however, the Court made it clear that the congressional power over public lands is not necessarily exclusive. Applying the standard preemption analysis discussed in Part C of this chapter, the Court upheld a state law requiring a permit for mining on public lands. (Note that the mining was being done by private parties; state power to regulate the activities of the federal government itself is sharply limited by federal sovereign immunity.)

Two other sources of federal power deserve at least brief mention. One is the treaty power. Congress has broad powers to make treaties with foreign nations on matters of international concern. Thus, the Court in Missouri v. Holland, 252 U.S. 416 (1920) upheld a treaty restricting the hunting of migratory birds. Today, legislation on this subject would be upheld under the commerce clause.

The Court in *Missouri v. Holland* held, however, that even if Congress' power under the commerce clause did not extend to the subject of migratory birds, a treaty on the subject was still a proper basis for implementing congressional legislation.

A final source of congressional power is the spending clause. The Constitution authorizes Congress to spend money in pursuit of the public interest. The Supreme Court has generally held that Congress has free rein in determining where that public interest lies. This clause rarely gives rise to litigation but has vast importance to the economy. It has been used, for example, to authorize the spending of vast amounts of money to enable local governments to build municipal wastewater treatment works. The spending clause also allows Congress to place conditions on federal grants, giving it considerable leverage over state governments.

As we have seen, congressional power in the environmental area is extremely broad. The commerce clause reaches virtually any economic activity that has significant environmental consequences. That power, broad as it is, is augmented by the other broad powers to protect public property, to deal with matters of international concern, and to spend money in the public interest.

The Constitution not only grants powers to the federal government but also limits the activities of state governments. In the next section we will consider those limitations as they are relevant in the environmental area.

B. COMMERCE CLAUSE RESTRICTIONS ON STATE POWER

In a unified national economy, the existence of a multitude of differing state environmental laws can impede the flow of commerce. Yet the states have often been in the lead in the environmental area because of pressing local problems. The conflict between the local interest in regulation and the economic interest of other states cannot be resolved effectively by the courts of any of the states involved. Obviously, neither the state that is engaging in regulation nor the states that are affected by the regulation can provide a completely neutral forum. For this reason, the federal courts have emerged as the tribunals in which these conflicting interests can be assessed.

Balancing the need for environmental regulations against their economic impact on outsiders is not a uniquely American problem. The European Court of Justice has also attempted to strike such a balance within the European Union. In the broader international arena, World Trade Organization (WTO) rules regarding free trade can also call local environmental regulations into question. Under Article III of the General Agreement on Tariffs and Trade (GATT), regulations that discriminate against imports are prima facie illegal. They can be defended, however, on the basis of Article XX, which authorizes regulations tied to certain crucial governmental interests. One particularly controversial area has been the extent to which a government can exclude imports in order to prevent harm to the environment relating to the production of those goods. For example, can the United States exclude tuna caught in a way that poses an undue threat to dolphins? WTO issues can also arise with respect to more mundane environmental regulations when they have the effect of favoring domestic products over imports. WTO tribunals are only now beginning to analyze these knotty issues which U.S. courts have struggled with since the days of John Marshall.

The basis for federal court involvement in these issues is the commerce clause of the Constitution. The commerce clause, on its face, is a grant of power to Congress, not a grant of power to the federal courts or a restriction on state legislation. Yet since the early 19th century, the Supreme Court has construed the commerce clause as preventing certain kinds of state legislation even when Congress has not spoken. Various doctrinal explanations have been utilized in an effort to support judicial intervention. Moreover, the restrictions have been subject to changing formulations. For present purposes, however, we can ignore the rather tangled history of commerce clause theory and concentrate on the theory as it exists today.

At present, there are three strands to dormant commerce clause theory. One test governs state legislation that discriminates against interstate commerce. Such legislation is virtually *per se* unconstitutional. A second test applies to a state's proprietary activities. Such activities are virtually immune to attack under the dormant commerce clause. The third test applies to the remaining forms of state legislation. These forms of legislation are covered by a balancing test.

1. DISCRIMINATORY LEGISLATION

The first strand is illustrated by City of Philadelphia v. New Jersey, 437 U.S. 617 (1978). This case involved a New Jersey statute prohibiting the import of most waste originating outside the state. The Supreme Court struck down this restriction. The parties in the case disputed whether the purpose of the restriction was economic favoritism toward local industry or environmental protection of the state's resources from overuse. The Court found it unnecessary to resolve this dispute. According to the Court, "the evil of protectionism can reside in legislative means as well as legislative ends." Thus, "whatever New Jersey's ultimate purpose, it may not be accomplished by discriminating against articles of commerce coming from outside the State unless there is some reason, apart from their origin, to treat them differently." Having found that the statute was discriminatory, the Court found it easy to resolve the case:

The New Jersey law at issue in this case falls squarely within the area that the Commerce Clause puts off-limits to state regulation. On its face, it imposes on out-of-state commercial interests the full burden of conserving the State's remaining landfill space. It is true that in our previous cases the scarce natural resource was itself the article of commerce, whereas here the scarce resource and the article in the commerce are distinct. But that difference is without consequence. In both instances, the State has overtly moved to slow or freeze the flow of commerce for protectionist reasons. It does not matter that the State has shut the article of commerce inside the State in one case and outside the State in the other. What is crucial is the attempt by one State to isolate itself from a problem common to many by erecting a barrier against the movement of interstate trade.

The Court conceded that certain quarantine laws have not been considered forbidden by the commerce clause even though they were directed against out-of-state commerce. The Court distinguished those quarantine laws, however, on the ground that in those cases the "very movement" of the articles risked contagion and other evils. According to the Court, "[t]hose laws thus did not discriminate against interstate commerce as such, but simply prevented traffic of noxious articles, whatever their origin." Subject to this very narrow exception, legislation that on its face distinguishes out-of-state items from domestic items will be struck down in the absence of compelling justification.

As it turned out, *Philadelphia v. New Jersey* was simply the first in a series of cases in which the Court thwarted efforts by states to control the flow of garbage. In two 1992 cases, the Court struck down two variations on the New Jersey statute. One variation was to impose a tax on garbage imports rather than banning them. In Chemical Waste Management v. Hunt, 504 U.S. 334 (1992), the Court struck down a special tax imposed on waste generated outside the state. A second variation was to delegate import controls to the local level. In Fort Gratiot Sanitary Landfill, Inc. v. Michigan Department of Natural Resources, 504 U.S. 353 (1992), the Court struck down a state law forbidding landfills from accepting garbage generated elsewhere unless the county's landfill plan authorized them to do so.

A later decision in this series involved the converse of *Philadelphia v. New Jersey*: rather than attempting to exclude garbage *imports*, the government was trying to ban garbage *exports*. Many municipalities adopted flow control ordinances that required all waste generated in the locality to be sent to a designated facility. The main reason for the requirement was to assure a sufficient flow of waste in order to finance new state-of-the-art waste disposal facilities. A five-Justice majority in C & A Carbone, Inc. v. Town of Clarkstown, 511 U.S. 383 (1994) found that flow control was facially discriminatory and struck it down under the *Philadelphia v. New Jersey* test. The majority pointed to several alternatives to flow control, including the use of property taxes to subsidize the local disposal facility. Justice O'Connor concurred in the result. She considered the ordinance to be nondiscriminatory but invalid as an undue burden on commerce under the balancing test discussed below. Applying the same balancing test, Justice Souter and two other dissenters would have upheld the local ordinance. He argued that none of the alternatives to flow control were as desirable, and that the locality should be free to impose on its own residents the increased costs caused by flow control. As *Carbone* illustrates, what constitutes "discrimination" is sometimes in the eye of the beholder: what five Justices considered to be patent discrimination, the other four did not find to be discriminatory at all.

2.   PROPRIETARY ACTIVITIES

The second class of state regulations involves proprietary or quasi-proprietary activities by states. Here, the leading case is Hughes v. Alexandria Scrap Corp., 426 U.S. 794 (1976). This case involved a Maryland bounty system for old, abandoned cars ("hulks"). Prior to 1974, no title certificate was needed by the scrap processor in order to claim the bounty. After 1974, Maryland processors needed only to submit an indemnity agreement in which their suppliers certified their own rights to the hulks. In contrast, out-of-state processors were required to submit title certificates or police certificates. The legislation was challenged by a Virginia processor. The Court held that this statute was valid because the state was not exercising a regulatory function but rather had itself entered the market in order to bid up prices. As Justice Stevens noted in his concurrence, the interstate commerce at issue would never have existed except for the state's bounty system. Because the state's failure to create such commerce would have been unobjectionable under the commerce clause, Justice Stevens believed that out-of-state processors could not complain if they were excluded from this commerce. Justice Brennan filed a strong dissent. Because *Hughes* came down on the same day as *National League of Cities*, Justice Brennan apparently feared that the Court was creating tremendous loopholes in the commerce clause in the name of state sovereignty.

In a later decision, the Court extended this rationale by holding that South Dakota could refuse to sell cement from a state-owned plant to out-of-state buyers during a shortage. Reeves, Inc. v. Stake, 447 U.S. 429 (1980). This decision seems to be a recognition that quasi-proprietary state activities are not subject to normal commerce clause restrictions. As the Court held in Hughes v. Oklahoma, 441 U.S. 322 (1979), however, the state's theoretical title in wild animals does not justify discrimination against out-of-state businesses.

3.   BALANCING TEST

Most state legislation is neither proprietary nor discriminatory, and thus falls into the third class. State legislation of this kind is not as suspect as legislation that is discriminatory on its face. Nevertheless, there is a real risk that the state may pass legislation without adequately considering its impact elsewhere in the country. The risk also exists that a state will use what appears to be nondiscriminatory legislation as a covert means of burdening out-of-state businesses. In order to guard against these risks, the Court subjects non-discriminatory state legislation to a balancing test. Under this test, the impact of a statute on interstate commerce is balanced against the state's justifications for the statute.

The Seventh Circuit decision in Procter & Gamble Co. v. Chicago, 509 F.2d 69 (7th Cir.1975) is a good illustration of the balancing test. The case involved a Chicago ordinance banning the use of detergents containing phosphates. Due to the warehousing methods used in the industry, the Chicago ordinance would restrict sales of phosphate detergents in a wide area including parts of Wisconsin, Indiana, and Michigan. Nevertheless, the court found that the possible contribution of the ordinance to controlling the growth of algae in the Illinois River and in Lake Michigan was sufficiently great to justify the burden placed on commerce.

Balancing tests are not always predictable in their application. This one is no exception. On the whole, however, environmental laws have fared well in commerce clause litigation. For example, the Supreme Court found that the burden on commerce created by a Minnesota container law was not "clearly excessive," even though the Minnesota Supreme Court had found the supposed benefits of the statute to be illusory. Minnesota v. Clover Leaf Creamery Co., 449 U.S. 456 (1981).

The Supreme Court's most recent dormant commerce clause decision illustrates some of the perplexities of this area. It involved an ordinance that was functionally close to the one struck down in *Carbone*, but the result was quite different. In United Haulers Ass'n, Inc. v. Oneida–Herkimer Solid Waste Management Authority, 127 S.Ct. 1786 (2007), a city ordinance required all local waste haulers to bring their waste to a city-owned facility. The Court found this distinction from *Carbone* (where the facility had been privately-owned) to be critical. According to the Court, "[d]isposing of trash has been a traditional government activity for years, and laws that favor the government in such areas-but treat every private business, whether in-state or out-of-state, exactly the same-do not discriminate against interstate commerce for purposes of the Commerce Clause." The Court then upheld the regulation under the balancing test. The Court explained the reasons for drawing this distinction as follows:

> The contrary approach of treating public and private entities the same under the dormant Commerce Clause would lead to unprecedented and unbounded interference by the courts with state and local government. The dormant Commerce Clause is not a roving license for federal courts to decide what activities are appropriate for state and local government to undertake, and what activities must be the province of private market competition.... The citizens could have left the entire matter for the private sector, in which case any regulation they undertook could

not discriminate against interstate commerce. But it was also open to them to vest responsibility for the matter with their government, and to adopt flow control ordinances to support the government effort.

Yet, the result was very similar to the flow control ordinance struck down in *Carbone*, except that title to the facility was held by the state.

The use of this balancing test has been attacked by Justice Scalia, some lower court judges, and several scholars. These critics make several arguments against a balancing test. If a state law does not discriminate against interstate commerce, they argue, the federal courts should not second-guess the state legislature about the balance between a statute's costs and benefits. Moreover, ill-advised but nondiscriminatory statutes are subject to a built-in political check, because the adversely affected local industry will lobby for repeal. Thus, these laws can be handled by the political process without judicial intervention. Finally, these critics argue, the judicial balancing in these cases is unhappily reminiscent of the era when courts routinely overturned statutes they considered unwise—an approach that has long since been repudiated in other contexts. Although these arguments against the balancing test have some force, so far they have failed to make much headway on the Court. On the other hand, perhaps in response to these concerns, most judges have applied the balancing test cautiously, tending to defer strongly to state environmental policies.

C. FEDERAL PREEMPTION

The preceding section dealt with the validity of state regulation in the absence of federal regulation. In this section we will be concerned with the validity of state regulations in areas where Congress has acted. In cases of direct conflict, the state statute must give way. The Supremacy Clause of the Constitution provides:

This Constitution, and the Laws of the United States which shall be made in Pursuance thereof; and all Treaties made, or which shall be made, under the authority of the United States, shall be the Supreme Law of the Land; and the Judges in every State shall be bound thereby, any Thing in the Constitution or Laws of any State to the Contrary not withstanding.

Sometimes, statutes contain express preemption provisions. But preemption may exist even without such provision.

The Supreme Court has set forth various factors that are to be considered in preemption cases. First, the federal regulatory scheme may be so pervasive and detailed as to suggest that Congress left no room for states to supplement it. Or the statute enacted by Congress may involve a field in which the federal interest is so dominant that enforcement of all state laws is precluded. Other aspects of the regulatory scheme imposed by Congress may also support the inference that Congress has completely foreclosed state legislation in a particular area. This is often called "field" preemption.

Second, even where Congress has not completely foreclosed state regulation, a state statute is void to the extent that it actually conflicts with a valid federal statute. Such a conflict can be found where compliance with both the federal and state regulations is impossible, or more often, where the state law interferes with the accomplishment of the full objectives of Congress.

These factors are obviously rather vague and difficult to apply. The Supreme Court has done little to create any more rigorous framework for analysis. Therefore, the only way to grasp preemption is to examine particular cases to see what kinds of situations have been found appropriate for application of the preemption doctrine.

One recurrent preemption issue involves nuclear energy. In a 1971 case, Northern States Power Co. v. Minnesota, 447 F.2d 1143 (8th Cir.1971), the court held that the state lacked the authority to impose conditions on nuclear waste releases stricter than those imposed by federal regulations. The court relied heavily on a provision of the Atomic Energy Act that allows the federal government to delegate regulatory authority over certain categories of nuclear materials to the states. Radioactive releases from nuclear power plants did not fall within any of these categories, which the court considered the exclusive areas in which states may regulate with respect to radiation hazards. The court concluded that state regulation would interfere with the congressional objectives expressed in the 1954 Act:

Thus, through direction of the licensing scheme for nuclear reactors, Congress vested the AEC with the authority to resolve the proper balance between desired industrial progress and adequate health and safety standards. Only through the application and enforcement of uniform standards promulgated by a national agency will these dual objectives be assured. Were the states allowed to impose stricter standards on the level of radioactive waste releases discharged from nuclear power plants, they might conceivably be so overprotective in the area of health and safety as to unnecessarily stultify the industrial development and use of atomic energy for the production of electric power.

In contrast, the Supreme Court upheld a California nuclear moratorium in a later decision, Pacific Gas & Electric Co. v. State Energy Resources Conservation & Development Commission, 461 U.S. 190 (1983). In an opinion by Justice White, the Court upheld a California statute prohibiting nuclear plant operation until the federal government approved a permanent method of waste disposal. The Court found that the state statutes were aimed not at radiation hazards, but instead at economic problems posed by the failure of the federal government to approve a permanent method of waste disposal. The Court concluded that Congress had not intended to promote nuclear power at all costs. Rather,

Congress had decided to leave the choice as to the necessity or economic benefits of a nuclear plant to the states through its utility regulatory powers. Apparently, if a state casts its legislation in the form of utility regulation, it may indirectly accomplish what federal law would not allow it to do directly—that is, impose its own views as to the safety of nuclear reactors under various circumstances. So long as it can reasonably be argued that a possible safety risk would have repercussions on the economic desirability of nuclear energy, the Supreme Court would apparently allow the state to regulate.

A year after the *PG&E* case, the Court again displayed a permissive attitude toward state laws dealing with the nuclear industry. In Silkwood v. Kerr-McGee Corp., 464 U.S. 238 (1984), the Court upheld an award of punitive damages against a utility for an employee's radiation injuries. As the dissent pointed out, the jury was told it could impose punitive damages even if the defendant had complied with all federal regulations. Thus, the state was allowed to hold the defendant to higher standards of conduct in the handling of radioactive materials than those imposed by the federal government. Together with *PG&E*, *Silkwood* signaled that the Court's enthusiasm for preemption in the nuclear area had waned considerably since it summarily affirmed *Northern States Power* in 1972.

Every preemption case in a sense is unique. Apart from some vague and usually unhelpful maxims, little can be said about this area of law that is of much help in deciding individual cases. The Court has articulated a presumption against preemption, but seems to apply the presumption fitfully. The question before the court in each case is whether Congress in passing a particular statute would have been willing to allow the state to impose certain kinds of regulations in the same area. This is essentially an issue of statutory construction. It can only be resolved by close attention to the language of the federal statute, to its legislative history, and to its purposes. Thus, the best advice in analyzing preemption problems is to carefully scrutinize the text and to probe the legislative materials and the extent to which the state statute would have a practical effect on the implementation of the federal statute.

Even when a federal statute itself does not preempt state law, the federal administrative agency implementing the statute may issue a regulation that preempts state law. The Court is reluctant to infer preemption merely from the presence of comprehensive federal regulations. The state law will stand unless it directly conflicts with the federal regulation. This reluctance to infer preemption makes sense, because the agency can readily adopt an express preemption regulation. Congress, on the other hand, must overcome considerably more inertia to respond to a state law that interferes with a federal statute. Hence, there is less reason for courts to apply preemption doctrines expansively when agency regulations are involved.

In this chapter, we have seen that the federal regulatory power in the environmental area is broad indeed. Questions about the scope of this power arise only when Congress directly attempts to regulate the activities of state government, or when legislation focuses on noncommercial activities that are traditionally state concerns and have no apparent interstate implications. The vast majority of federal regulations fall outside of these gray zones and are clearly constitutional. When the federal government has acted, the Supremacy Clause invalidates any state legislation that interferes with the accomplishment of the congressional purpose or the operation of the regulatory scheme. Even when Congress has not acted, a state statute may run afoul of the dominant federal interest in the free flow of interstate commerce. Thus, while federalism imposes only relatively minor restraints today on the national government, it continues to circumscribe the actions of state governments.

*

CHAPTER 3

POLLUTION CONTROL

Consider the problem of a common pasture, posed by Garrett Hardin in his classic article, "The Tragedy of the Commons." Even as the number of cattle begins to exceed the pasture's carrying capacity, each herder benefits from increasing his own herd. The marginal utility of adding one more animal always seems positive, since the herder receives all the benefits from the animal, while most of the resulting costs of overgrazing are borne by other herders. Since the herders all act in the same way, freedom in the commons brings ruin to all.

Similarly, the market may not strike a proper balance between economic output and environmental quality because the costs of pollution are borne by someone besides the polluter. As a result, these "externalized" costs will not be taken into account by polluters. Without the incentive to reduce the amount of pollution, insufficient resources are devoted to this objective. Insofar as pollution costs are not borne by polluters or their customers, some of the total welfare resulting from economic activity is redistributed away from the victims of pollution to other groups in the society. In a sense, the polluter is subsidized by others who bear the environmental costs of his activities. Because of this subsidy, the polluter's conduct is not economically efficient: total social wealth (without regard for its distribution) is not maximized.

An economic activity may also confer external *benefits*. For example, renovation of a deteriorated building improves aesthetic and property values for nearby landowners. External benefits, like external costs, usually are not reflected in the producer's balance sheet. Closely related to the concept of external benefits is that of collective or public goods, commodities that cannot efficiently be supplied to one person without enabling others to enjoy them. Examples are national defense and clean air. Consumption of such goods is collective, because enjoyment by any one person does not diminish the enjoyment available to others. The nonexcludability that characterizes collective goods causes underproduction by the market, even though their total value may substantially exceed the production costs.

Theoretically, as Professor Coase demonstrated, even these problems could be surmounted by the free market. Without barriers to transactions, such as imperfect knowledge, limited rationality, or negotiation expenses, individuals could enter into enforceable bargains to produce public goods or to refrain from producing externalities such as pollution. Indeed, Coase argued, absent impediments to bargaining, individuals would bargain their way to the same levels of public goods or externalities regardless of the legal rule. This analysis has become known as the Coase Theorem and has had a powerful impact on law-and-economics scholarship.

Although Coase used pollution as an example, he acknowledged that the large number of victims of pollution would make a contractual solution impossible. The idea of using market transactions to control pollution, however, has proved useful. Later in this chapter, we will examine possible ways for the government to utilize market forces to help control pollution. The Coase Theorem also may be relevant to analyzing situations involving relatively small numbers of individuals, such as some nuisance cases. It does not, however, eliminate the need for government intervention in the pollution area.

Because the free market provides inadequate incentives, government must intervene to limit external costs and facilitate production of external benefits and collective goods. The following basic approaches are available:

Liability. The common law doctrine of nuisance offers injured landowners the remedies of damages and injunctions against polluters. Litigation, however, is ill-suited to resolving widespread environmental problems involving highly technical issues or difficult trade-offs between conflicting interests. Usually government resorts to the other approaches described below, or it provides collective goods itself, using tax revenues.

Direct Regulation. The principal method of controlling pollution has been to prohibit emissions beyond prescribed limits. When the method of enforcement is imposition of financial penalties, rather than injunctions or jail sentences, the boundary between direct regulation and effluent charges (the last method below) becomes blurred.

Subsidies.   Another approach is for government to subsidize private activities that reduce external costs or produce collective goods.   Examples are special tax deductions and credits for installation of pollution control equipment, and federal grants to municipalities for construction of waste treatment facilities.

Charges.   Besides the foregoing approaches, government can require payment of penalties or fees for private activities that generate external costs or fail to provide collective goods.   Relating the amount of the charge to the estimated cost (to the producer) or benefit (to the public) can create a market incentive for the producer to alter his activities.   Rather than setting the level of charges itself, the government can use market mechanisms to price pollution.   For example, it can auction off pollution rights.

The following sections discuss methods of controlling pollution through application of nuisance law, by regulation under the federal Clean Air and Clean Water Acts, and through creation of economic incentives.   Special emphasis is given to the consideration of economic and technological feasibility in a regulatory system.

A. COMMON LAW REMEDIES

Boomer v. Atlantic Cement Co., 257 N.E.2d 870 (N.Y.1970) involved a classic nuisance. Defendant operated a large cement plant, and neighbors incurred damages from dirt, smoke, and vibration emanating from the plant. The neighbors sought an injunction and compensatory damages for past injuries. The court found that the total damages to plaintiffs' properties were relatively small compared with the value of defendant's plant, and that enjoining further pollution would force closure of the plant. The plant was the core of the local economy and already employed the best available pollution control.

In such situations, most courts "balance the equities" and deny injunctions, on the ground that the hardships on defendants and the community would be greater than the harm suffered by plaintiffs left to their damage remedies. In New York, however, a line of cases had held that once a nuisance was found and substantial damage was shown by the plaintiff, an injunction would be granted notwithstanding any disparity in economic consequences between the effect of the injunction and the effect of the nuisance.

In *Boomer* that rule finally was disavowed. The court considered granting the injunction but postponing its effect to a specified future date to allow the defendant to develop the technology to eliminate the nuisance. But the court was uncertain of defendant's ability to achieve such advances, which it believed were the responsibility of the entire cement industry rather than one company. Furthermore, the court believed that the state's extensive regulatory scheme covering air pollution provided a better mechanism for addressing this problem than a nuisance action.

The New York court deviated from the usual path of awarding compensatory damages only for past injuries (leaving plaintiffs free to sue again for future injuries). Instead, the court ordered that the injunction issue unless defendant paid permanent damages to plaintiffs, which would include compensation for the total economic loss to their properties, present and future, caused by defendant's operations. A dissenting judge said that the decision was in effect "licensing a continuing wrong [by] saying to the cement company, you may continue to do harm to your neighbors so long as you pay a fee for it." The dissenter likened the result to conferring the power of eminent domain—the power to condemn an easement—upon a private corporation, to be used for private gain rather than for public use.

The courts' tendency to balance hardships and deny injunctions is not the only factor that has made nuisance law inadequate to control widespread pollution. Another is lack of standing to sue. The common law distinguished public and private nuisances. A public nuisance was one that damaged a large number of persons. Only the attorney general or local prosecutor could sue to abate a public nuisance, unless a private individual could show "special" damage, distinct from that of the public generally. While today some states do allow private suits to abate public nuisances, lack of standing remains a problem elsewhere. Still another difficulty can be the plaintiff's burden of proof. Frequently pollutants derive from many sources, none of which alone would produce the alleged damage. It may be impossible to prove any particular polluter responsible for the poor air or water quality. Also, attempts to join multiple defendants and allocate damages among them can pose difficult procedural problems. Finally, nuisance law fails to provide a systematic mechanism for supervising pollutant discharges. Just as the common law has been supplemented in most communities by land use planning and zoning, so it also has had to be supplemented by legislative intervention in the area of pollution control.

Nevertheless, nuisance law sometimes remains a useful tool. An interesting example is Spur Industries, Inc. v. Del E. Webb Development Co., 494 P.2d 700 (Ariz.1972). In 1957, Del Webb began construction of a retirement community called Sun City, west of Phoenix. By 1967, the development had moved close to Spur's feedlot, which had been in operation for several years before Webb came into the area. Webb complained that Spur's feeding operation was a nuisance because of the flies and the odor. Some residents were unable to enjoy the outdoor living that Webb had advertised, and Webb was faced with sales resistance from prospective purchasers. If Webb alone had been injured, the court said, the doctrine of "coming to the nuisance" would have barred relief. But the court found that Webb was entitled to injunctive relief because of the harm to people who had purchased homes in Sun City. However, the court also concluded that Webb itself should not be free of liability to Spur. Having brought people to the nuisance, to the foreseeable detriment of Spur, Webb was required to indemnify Spur for a reasonable amount of the cost of moving or shutting down, as a condition to obtaining the injunction.

Interstate air and water pollution formerly were governed by a federal common law of nuisance. Thus, in Georgia v. Tennessee Copper Co., 206 U.S. 230 (1907), the State of Georgia obtained an injunction against a Tennessee company whose sulfur oxide emissions were causing wholesale destruction of forests, orchards, and crops in Georgia. However, in Milwaukee v. Illinois, 451 U.S. 304 (1981) (*Milwaukee II*), the Supreme Court held that the comprehensive regulatory system established by the federal Clean Water Act had completely preempted federal common law. The Clean Air Act probably has also displaced the federal common law pertaining to interstate air pollution.

The decision in *Milwaukee II* is open to serious criticism. The Clean Water Act expressly provides that it does not preempt more stringent state laws. Indeed, the Supreme Court has more recently held that federal courts *can* hear nuisance suits arising under state law, so long as they apply the nuisance law of the state where the discharger is located.

International Paper Co. v. Ouellette, 479 U.S. 481 (1987). Moreover, the Court's desire to give sole regulatory authority to the discharging state has been undermined by later regulatory developments. EPA now requires that permits issued by upstream states ensure compliance with the water quality standards set by downstream states. This requirement was upheld in Arkansas v. Oklahoma, 503 U.S. 91 (1992). Thus, the original rationale for *Milwaukee II* now seems to have evaporated.

B. REGULATION UNDER THE CLEAN AIR ACT

Five main classes of air pollutants are widespread. (In addition to these five, greenhouse gas emissions are now regulated by federal law.) *Carbon monoxide* (CO) is a colorless, odorless, poisonous gas, slightly lighter than air, that is produced by the incomplete burning of carbon. The main sources are internal combustion engines, mostly in motor vehicles. *Particulates* are solids or liquids in a wide range of sizes, produced primarily by stationary fuel combustion and industrial processes. Control techniques include filtering, washing, centrifugal separation, and electrostatic precipitation. These work well for most of the particles, but complete removal, especially of the very finest particles, is difficult. *Sulfur oxides* (SO_x) are corrosive, poisonous gases produced when fuel containing sulfur is burned. Electric utilities and industrial plants are the principal producers. *Nitric oxides*

(NO_x) are produced when fuel is burned at very high temperatures. The main sources are vehicles and combustion plants. Sulfur dioxide and nitric oxides, after being emitted into the atmosphere, can be chemically converted into sulfates and nitrates, which may return to earth as components of rain or snow, known as acid precipitation. *Hydrocarbons* (HC), like carbon monoxide, represent unburned and wasted fuel. Unlike carbon monoxide, gaseous hydrocarbons at the concentrations normally found in the atmosphere are not toxic. They are a major pollutant, however, because they combine with NO_x under the influence of sunlight to form photochemical oxidants (or smog), a complex mixture of secondary pollutants including ozone (an unstable, toxic form of oxygen) as well as nitrogen dioxide. They can cause eye and lung irritation, damage to vegetation, offensive odor, and thick haze.

The most important effect of air pollution is its threat to human health. Some acute episodes have been marked by dramatic increases in death and illness rates, especially among the elderly and those with preexisting respiratory or cardiac conditions. Of much greater significance for the general population are the subtle, long-range effects of exposure to low-level, long-lasting pollution. Such pollution contributes to chronic diseases like emphysema, bronchitis, and other respiratory ailments. Air pollution is also linked to higher mortality from other causes such as cancer and arteriosclerosis. Smokers in polluted cities have a much higher rate of lung cancer than smokers in rural areas.

These health effects of air pollution are not known to possess meaningful thresholds or safe levels. For example, scientists cannot demonstrate that exposure to one hundred parts per million of a pollutant for twenty-four hours is "safe" while exposures above that level are "dangerous." It is not even possible to establish that effects of exposure become rapidly more serious around some particular exposure level.

1. OVERVIEW OF THE CLEAN AIR ACT

In 1955, Congress began to respond to the problem of air pollution by offering technical and financial assistance to the states. Amendments in the 1960s authorized federal agencies to expand their research, to intervene directly to abate *interstate* pollution in limited circumstances, to control emissions from new motor vehicles, and to exercise certain powers of supervision and enforcement of state controls. By the end of the decade states had made little progress, and Congress responded with the Clean Air Amendments of 1970. The Environmental Protection Agency (EPA) also was created in 1970, by an executive order of President Nixon combining preexisting units from various federal departments.

The 1970 amendments sharply increased federal authority. For example, § 111 mandated uniform national standards of performance for new sources of air pollution. ("New" sources included preexisting sources subsequently modified by any physical change or change in the method of operation that increased emissions of any pollutant.) Similarly, § 112 provided for uniform national emission standards for hazardous air pollutants likely to cause an increase in mortality or in serious illness. Nevertheless, § 107(a) still provided that each state "shall have the primary responsibility for assuring air quality within the entire geographic area comprising such state." But states no longer were given a choice as to whether they would attain air quality of specified standards.

Section 109 directed the EPA Administrator to establish national ambient air quality standards (NAAQSs) for pollutants that endanger public health or welfare. Each pollutant is subject to two types of standards: *primary* standards that, "allowing an adequate margin of safety, are requisite to protect the public health"; and *secondary* standards "to protect the public welfare from any known or anticipated adverse effect." Within nine months of promulgation of an NAAQS, each state was required to submit to EPA a plan to implement that standard within its boundaries. § 110(a)(1). EPA, in turn, was required to approve a state implementation plan (SIP) if it had been adopted after public hearings and satisfied the conditions specified in § 110(a)(2). The most important condition was that the SIP provide for attainment of primary NAAQSs "as expeditiously as practicable" but no more than three years later. Secondary standards were to be achieved within "a reasonable time." A SIP had to include "emission limitations, schedules, and timetables for compliance with such limitations," as well as assurances of appropriate resources to enforce the plan.

As with many other deadlines set in environmental statutes, the goals set in 1970 were never attained in many areas. Special provisions were added to the statute in 1977 and further strengthened in 1990 to deal with these "nonattainment areas." In nonattainment areas where pollutant concentrations exceed NAAQSs, § 172 requires at a minimum that SIPs impose "reasonably available control technology" (RACT) on existing sources. If EPA determines that state standards are not sufficient to attain primary NAAQSs on schedule or to attain secondary NAAQSs within a "reasonable time," under § 110 it must issue a federal implementation plan within two years that will assure timely attainment. The fact that compliance may be difficult or even impossible for some sources does not excuse promulgation of the required implementation plans.

Once EPA approves a state plan, it is enforceable not only as state law but also as federal law under § 113. If EPA finds a proposed SIP to be inadequate to attain any NAAQS in any region of a state, and if the state fails to make adequate amendments, § 110(c)(1) directs the agency to issue amendments that are binding on the state.

EPA has established NAAQSs for carbon monoxide, particulates, sulfur dioxide, nitrogen dioxide, hydrocarbons, ozone, and lead. Initially, the NAAQSs were the driving force behind EPA's control strategy, since all emissions contributing to violation of the standards were to be eliminated by 1975. This did not happen, however, and the Act has been amended to extend the deadlines, thereby reducing the "absolute" nature of the standards. In 1982, EPA rescinded the hydrocarbon standard as unnecessary, but the remaining NAAQSs continue to play an important role in air pollution policy. EPA has sometimes approved or promulgated SIP provisions that for economic or political reasons were unlikely to be enforced, such as an EPA mandate to reduce automobile traffic in Los Angeles by 70–80% in 1975. In 1990, Congress enacted major amendments intended to accelerate attainment of the standards, as well as to deal with other major problems such as acid rain and toxic pollutants.

As the foregoing indicates, the basic approach of the 1970 Clean Air Act with respect to existing stationary sources and motor vehicles was that EPA would establish uniform NAAQSs, and the states would adopt emission limitations necessary to meet the ambient standards by the statutory deadlines. However, with respect to new vehicles, new stationary sources, and hazardous air pollutants, EPA was required to establish nationally uniform emission standards.

For new motor vehicles, the aim was to reduce 1970 emission levels by 90% by 1975. The Act was later amended, however, extending the deadline to 1983-model vehicles and to 1985 models for NO_x emissions. The 1990 amendments further tightened vehicle emission standards. By 1998, hydrocarbon emissions had to be cut 30% below the prior standard, while nitrogen oxides had to be cut 60%. The standards were phased in during 1994–98. Unless EPA determined that tougher standards are unnecessary or infeasible, a second tier of reductions cutting emissions by about another 50% was required by 2003. States had the option of adopting the even tougher California emission standards.

The 1970 Act also addressed new stationary sources. New source performance standards (NSPSs) for stationary sources reflect best available control technology, taking into account the costs of compliance. The NSPSs normally specify how many pounds of a pollutant may be emitted per unit of plant input or output, leaving each source to decide what combination of technological measures and fuel changes to use.

A 1977 amendment to § 111 directed EPA to take a different approach to setting NSPSs for three pollutants from combustion of fossil fuels—sulfur dioxide, nitrogen dioxide, and particulates. Emissions were to be reduced by a specified *percentage* below what they would be without technological control measures—changes in fuel to reduce emissions were not sufficient. The political intent of these amendments was not only to reduce total pollutant emissions but also to reduce the economic incentive for eastern industries to use low-sulfur western coal instead of high-sulfur eastern coal.

The 1990 amendments took a new approach to this issue. In place of the "percentage reduction" provision, the amendments rely on a complex system of sulfur dioxide "allowances" to control emissions. These allowances are discussed in the materials on acid rain in the final section of this chapter. Plants using scrubbers were able to postpone compliance with the new acid rain requirements until 1997, and the statute also grants additional emission allowances to those plants. To cushion the impact of the new requirements, the amendments authorized $250 million in "transition assistance" for workers fired or laid off because of compliance with the Clean Air Act.

With respect to hazardous air pollutants, § 112 initially required that EPA establish emission standards with "an ample margin of safety to protect public health." The 1990 amendments added complex new regulatory requirements to § 112, which are discussed in Chapter 5.

For geographic areas with superior air quality, where pollutant levels are substantially below an NAAQS, the 1977 amendments asserted a congressional commitment to the principle of prevention of significant deterioration (PSD). A region that complies with the NAAQS is put into one of three classes. Large national parks and wilderness areas are Class I areas, where very little deterioration of air quality is allowed. All other areas are Class II, where moderate increases in ambient concentrations are allowed (but not to exceed the NAAQS). A governor has the power to reclassify a Class II area in his state as Class I, or as Class III, where larger increments are allowed, usually to permit new industry. This power has rarely been exercised. To establish a major new source in any PSD area, the owner must apply for a permit. (The 1990 amendments expanded the permit requirement to include all major sources and all new plants.) The permit requires that the new emissions remain within the allowed increments, and that the source use "best available control technology" (BACT) for *all* pollutants, quite apart from the allowable increments.

The following section focuses on probably the most important issue, economically and politically, in implementing the Clean Air Act: the extent to which the difficulty of compliance is considered in establishing and enforcing limits on pollutant emissions by individual sources. Different categories of sources and pollutants recognized by the Act are discussed in separate subsections.

2.   CONSIDERATION OF ECONOMIC AND TECHNOLOGICAL FEASIBILITY

In setting national ambient air quality standards, EPA cannot consider the feasibility of attaining them. Under § 109 of the Act, NAAQSs must be fixed at levels necessary to protect the public health (with an "adequate margin of safety"), as well as public welfare. If EPA has evidence that primary standards are necessary to protect the health of substantial numbers of people (including sensitive segments of the population, such as the elderly and persons with respiratory diseases), the standards will not be overturned judicially.   Lead Industries Association, Inc. v. EPA, 647 F.2d 1130 (D.C.Cir. 1980).

Air pollutants do not generally exhibit thresholds. Thus, there is no cutoff level, above which there is a known risk of harm and below which there is some assurance of harmlessness.   Instead, at any given level, there is at least some possibility of risk.   Cost-benefit analysis, or simply consideration of the feasibility of compliance, could help draw the line, but the statute precludes these considerations.   Hence, EPA is faced with a considerable difficulty in setting NAAQSs.   In Whitman v. American Trucking Ass'ns, Inc., 531 U.S. 457 (2001), the lower court had held that EPA's discretion was so broad as to be an unconstitutional delegation of legislative power.   The Court rejected this argument, but also rejected any use of cost-benefit analysis to set NAAQSs.   The Court interpreted the statute to require standards "requisite" to protect the public health, with "requisite" defined as "sufficient, but not more than necessary."   Thus, the Court left the EPA with broad discretion to protect public health, but no discretion to consider non-health factors.

Despite EPA's inability to consider feasibility when setting an NAAQS, it would be a mistake to view the CAA as a whole as being oblivious to cost. In fixing emission standards and timetables applicable to various pollution sources and pollutants, EPA is sometimes required to consider economic and technological difficulties of compliance.

a.   New Motor Vehicles

Section 202(b) provided that, beginning with the 1975 model year, exhaust emissions of hydrocarbons and carbon monoxide from "light duty vehicles" must be reduced at least 90% from the permissible emission levels in 1970. As noted by Judge Leventhal in International Harvester Co. v. Ruckelshaus, 478 F.2d 615 (D.C.Cir.1973), Congress was aware that these standards were "drastic medicine," designed to "force the state of the art." Because of doubts whether manufacturers would be able to comply, Congress provided a "realistic escape hatch": the automakers could petition EPA for a one-year suspension of the 1975 requirements. EPA could grant the suspension only if the applicant proved that "effective control technology, processes, operating methods, or other alternatives are not available or have not been available for a sufficient period of time" to achieve timely compliance. In 1972, International Harvester, Ford, Chrysler, General Motors, and Volvo applied for suspensions. EPA denied the applications because it could not make the required finding that technology was unavailable. Although no car had conformed to the standard in actual tests, EPA adjusted the auto companies' test data by use of several assumptions and predicted that the necessary technology would be available by the 1975 model year.

The court in *International Harvester* agreed with EPA that the proper question was whether technology would be available in time for 1975 models, not whether it was already available when the manufacturers applied for suspensions in 1972. But the court reversed EPA's determination that technology would permit compliance without the one-year suspension. The court cited EPA's "unexplained assumptions," the "absence of an indication of the statistical reliability" of the prediction that technology would be available by the 1975 model year, and the "economic and ecological risks inherent in a 'wrong decision.'" Realistically, if the prediction of availability proved wrong, the court did not expect an enforced shutdown of one or more auto companies. Instead, the likely response would be last-minute congressional or administrative forgiveness of noncompliance, imposing a competitive disadvantage on companies able to comply (because their vehicles would cost more and be less fuel-efficient). On the other hand, the court believed that the environmental risks of suspension were small, especially given EPA's authority to prescribe special interim emission standards for 1975 model vehicles. The court concluded that EPA had failed to produce a reasoned basis supporting the reliability of its methodology for predicting the availability of technology.

In so holding, the court seems to have overlooked the statutory provision placing the burden of proof regarding technological availability on the industry rather than on EPA. Under the terms of the statute, if the availability of the technology was unclear, EPA should have prevailed; the burden was on industry to furnish a reliable prediction of unavailability. Presumably, Congress felt the risk of an erroneous denial of suspension to be less severe, or the urgency of pollution control to be greater, than did Judge Leventhal.

Following the court's decision, the Administrator granted the extension and imposed interim standards more lenient than the 90% reduction. As noted earlier, the industry later received additional extensions of time from Congress. Using its special exemption from preemption under § 209(b), California has often taken the lead in imposing stricter standards.

In the absence of a proper exercise of California's exemption, state regulatory authority can be quite limited. In the *Engine Manufacturers* case [Engineer Manufacturers Ass'n v. South Coast Air Quality Management District, 541 U.S. 246 (2004)], the California agency with authority over air pollution in the L.A. region had issued "fleet rules" that required certain operators of vehicle fleets, such as street sweepers and taxi companies, to purchase alternative fuel vehicles and low or zero emissions vehicles already approved for sale in California and commercially available. A provision of the Clean air Act prohibits any state or political subdivision from a adopting a "standard relating to the control of emissions from new motor vehicles or new motor vehicle engines." Because the state had not applied to EPA for a waiver, the California exemption did not apply, so the case was covered by this blanket preemption provision. In an opinion by Justice Scalia, the Court held that the Southern California rule was invalid on the basis of the plain statutory language: the rule related to emission characteristics of a vehicle or engine, which thus constituted a "standard" preempted by the federal statute. The Court was unmoved by the fact that mobile source emissions were the leading contributor to air toxic and air pollution in the region. It also considered irrelevant the fact that the local rule merely required a specific choice among vehicles that were already on the market, rather than requiring a new type or level of pollution control.

Although Congress set specific numerical targets for reducing certain vehicle emissions, the Clean Air Act also provides for the listing of additional pollutants. The test is similar to that used in designating criterion pollutants for stationary sources. This provision became very important in the context of global climate change.

In *Massachusetts v. EPA*, the Court reviewed EPA's refusal to conduct a rule making to determine whether carbon dioxide from vehicles endangers human health or welfare because of its effect on climate. (We considered the standing dimension of this case in Chapter 1). EPA had argued that CO_2 is not a "pollutant" within the meaning of the Clean Air Act. The Court found this view incompatible with the plain language of the statute:

The statutory text forecloses EPA's reading. The Clean Air Act's sweeping definition of "air pollutant" includes "any air pollution agent or combination of such agents, including any physical, chemical ... substance or matter which is emitted into or otherwise enters the ambient air. . . . " On its face, the definition embraces all airborne compounds of whatever stripe, and underscores that intent through the repeated use of the word "any." Carbon dioxide, methane, nitrous oxide, and hydrofluorocarbons are without a doubt "physical [and] chemical . . . substance[s] which [are] emitted into . . . the ambient air." The statute is unambiguous.

The Court also found that EPA had considered impermissible extraneous factors in making its determination, such as the possibilities that the problem could be better resolved through voluntary industry efforts or through international negotiation:

Although we have neither the expertise nor the authority to evaluate these policy judgments, it is evident they have nothing to do with whether greenhouse gas emissions contribute to climate change. Still less do they amount to a reasoned justification for declining to form a scientific judgment. In particular, while the President has broad authority in foreign affairs, that authority does not extend to the refusal to execute domestic laws.

The Court remanded so that the agency could make a finding regarding endangerment, and if the finding was affirmative, to move forward with regulating tailpipe emissions.

b. Existing Stationary Sources

The Act does not preclude a state from adopting an implementation plan exceeding national ambient standards, i.e., producing ambient air even cleaner than that mandated by NAAQSs. In Union Electric Co. v. EPA, 427 U.S. 246 (1976), an electric utility petitioned EPA to disapprove Missouri's SIP, on the ground that compliance by its coal-fired generating plants in St. Louis was economically and technologically infeasible. Union Electric argued that an infeasibly strict state plan should be rejected under § 110 as not "practicable" or "reasonable." However, the Court upheld EPA's position that claims of economic and technological infeasibility are irrelevant to EPA consideration of a SIP.

Union Electric does not mean that claims of infeasibility are never relevant. As the Court pointed out, the most important forum for consideration of feasibility is the state agency that initially formulates the SIP. So long as NAAQSs and PSD requirements will be met, the state generally may select any mix of controls it desires for existing stationary sources (subject since 1977 to the RACT requirement in nonattainment areas). Industries with particular economic or technological problems may seek special treatment in the plan. Moreover, once a SIP is in place, individual plants within the industry may be able to obtain a revision of the provisions applying to those plants (a variance), providing the revised plan still complies with § 110.

If denied variances, sources may also assert claims of infeasibility in the state courts. State courts cannot, however, provide polluters with a complete screen from liability. Even if a state court has enjoined or invalidated a SIP, it is still enforceable as a matter of federal law. Thus, EPA may still be able to obtain a federal court order enforcing the plan even if the state courts have held the plan invalid as a matter of state law. See United States v. Ford Motor Co., 814 F.2d 1099 (6th Cir.1987). EPA does not, however, frequently exercise this power.

A state does not have complete freedom to select any mix of controls that will result in attainment of NAAQSs. For example, one requirement is that the SIP mandate "continuous" emission limitations where possible, rather than "intermittent" and "dispersion" techniques. Prior to 1990, § 110(a)(2)(B) required each SIP to include "emission limitations, schedules, and timetables for compliance with such limitations, and such other measures as may be necessary to insure attainment and maintenance" of NAAQSs. In Kennecott Copper Corp. v. Train, 526 F.2d 1149 (9th Cir.1975), the court struck down portions of Nevada's SIP. The SIP required that Kennecott's smelter reduce SO_2 emissions by 60% through installation of a plant to convert SO_2 to sulfuric acid, i.e., by continuous controls. Further emission reductions, required when weather conditions threatened maintenance of the ambient standard, were to be achieved by reducing temporarily the production level at the smelter, i.e., by intermittent controls. EPA rejected the Nevada plan on the ground that noncontinuous controls (also including use of a tall stack, a dispersion technique) were acceptable only after Kennecott employed continuous controls to the limit of

economic and technological feasibility. The court
agreed with EPA that the phrase "as may be necessary" in § 110(a)(2)(B) modified only "such other
measures," and not "emission limitations." Thus,
noncontinuous emission limitations were appropriate only when continuous controls were infeasible.
The court noted that the reliability and enforceability of intermittent control systems were questiona-
ble, since they may not be implemented when needed, and that dispersion techniques do not reduce
emissions but only spread out the pollution geo-
graphically, threatening other clean air areas.

In 1990, § 110(a)(2)(B) was rephrased in a way
that undercuts the court's reading of that section.
In the meantime, however, *Kennecott* had been codified elsewhere in the Act. Section 123, the "tall
stacks" provision added after *Kennecott* in 1977,
provides that the "degree of emission limitation
required for control of any air pollutant" under a
SIP "shall not be affected in any manner" by (1)
stack height in excess of "good engineering practice," or (2) any other dispersion technique. "Good
engineering practice" means the height necessary
to ensure that emissions from the stack do not
result in "excessive concentrations" of any pollutant in the "immediate vicinity" of the source.
Ordinarily, such height may not exceed two and a
half times the height of the source. Section 123(b)
treats intermittent controls as a form of dispersion
technique.

Variances from SIP-prescribed emission standards are granted by state agencies subject to ap-

proval by EPA. Such variances are treated as "revisions" of the SIP. Under § 110(a)(3)(A), EPA was required to approve any revision if it did not jeopardize timely attainment and subsequent maintenance of NAAQSs, if it required continuous emission controls to the maximum extent feasible, and if it satisfied the other requirements of § 110(a)(2). Train v. NRDC, 421 U.S. 60 (1975). This provision was repealed in 1990, but § 110(k) now requires EPA to approve revisions if they are properly documented and meet the requirements of the Act.

Having exhausted the statutory and administrative possibilities for an extension of time, a firm may then be faced with an EPA enforcement proceeding or a citizen suit under § 304. At that point, the firm may seek to invoke the equitable discretion of the federal court to obtain a further delay. As we saw in the previous chapter, the extent of equitable discretion to delay compliance with federal statutes is somewhat unclear. When Congress has so carefully structured the statutory mechanisms for considering feasibility, however, a free-wheeling exercise of discretion by the courts is surely out of place. Thus, as the Third Circuit has said, any remaining judicial discretion to delay compliance must be narrow indeed. United States v. Wheeling-Pittsburgh Steel Corp., 818 F.2d 1077 (3d Cir.1987).

The foregoing paragraphs have focused on the feasibility of individual sources' compliance with emission limitations. But what if an entire air quality control region is unable to achieve timely attainment of an NAAQS? Section 172, as amended in 1977, authorized postponement of the date for compliance with primary standards until 1982, or 1987 for oxidants and carbon monoxide, if that was "as expeditiously as practicable." Under §§ 110(a)(2)(I), 172, and 173, the main sanction for nonattainment of primary NAAQSs by the statutory deadlines was a moratorium on construction and operation of new or modified major stationary sources. Section 176 also contemplated denial of federal grants for highway construction and various other purposes. Early in 1983, EPA designated more than 100 counties nationwide as probable noncompliance areas and announced procedures for making final determinations, prior to imposing sanctions. EPA was able to avoid imposing stringent sanctions by approving unrealistic SIP amendments for some states and granting "conditional approval" of others, subject to a requirement that states revise them later to assure attainment.

The arrival of the 1987 deadline placed EPA in an even more uncomfortable position. More than 70 cities missed the deadline for the ozone and carbon monoxide standards. One response was a series of attempts by states to carve attainment areas out of larger nonattainment areas. This tactic, however, at best reduced but did not eliminate a state's noncompliance problem. In Abramowitz v. United States EPA, 832 F.2d 1071 (9th Cir.1987), the court rejected the California SIP because it would not result in attainment of the standards by the statutory deadline. EPA had attempted to temporize by allowing California to take "reasonable extra efforts" to comply. In Delaney v. EPA, 898 F.2d 687 (9th Cir.1990), the court again rebuffed EPA's efforts to give states more time to comply.

Nonattainment was one of the central concerns of the 1990 amendments. The amendments limited the ability of states to carve up nonattainment areas. A nonattainment area now must include the entire metropolitan area, unless the state can show that some sub-area does not contribute significantly to the nonattainment problem. The relatively simple noncompliance provisions of the 1977 amendments are replaced by a far more elaborate scheme.

The amendments require another round of SIP amendments to achieve compliance. In this connection, it is worth noting some changes in the procedures governing plan revisions. EPA must issue minimum standards that a plan revision must meet in order to be considered a "complete" submission. Within sixty days of a plan submission, EPA must consider whether the submission is complete. If not, EPA may treat it in whole or in part as a nullity; if the submission is complete, EPA must approve or disapprove the plan within twelve months. (EPA's failure to meet this deadline arguably may affect its ability to collect penalties from some noncomplying sources. The Supreme Court ducked this issue under the pre-1990 version of the Act.) See General Motors Corp. v. United States, 496 U.S. 530 (1990). EPA may issue a conditional approval if the state commits itself to adopt specific enforceable measures within a year.

If a SIP for a nonattainment area is inadequate, EPA must issue a federal implementation plan within two years. The amendments provide several other sanctions, including a cutoff of federal highway funds. Another important sanction is an upward adjustment of the "offset" requirements, which are discussed later in this chapter. The effect of the adjustment is to limit economic growth in the offending region. Areas that fall behind schedule may be "bumped up" to higher categories, resulting in more stringent requirements. Finally, depending on the severity of the nonattainment problem, the term "major source" is redefined to include smaller sources, which will have to implement tough technology-based standards.

Apart from these general provisions, the amendments also contain a series of complex provisions relating specifically to ozone, NO_x, CO, and particulates. The ozone provisions are illustrative. The statute divides ozone nonattainment areas into five classes, depending on the severity of the pollution. Only Los Angeles is in the worst class (extreme nonattainment). Compliance requirements are keyed to this classification scheme. For example, marginal areas must achieve attainment within three years, while serious areas have nine years, and Los Angeles is given 20 years. Major sources are also defined differently for the different categories: 100 tons per year in the marginal and moderate areas, but only 50, 25, and 10 tons per year in the serious, severe, and extreme areas. Offset requirements also vary among these areas. The statute requires various specific control measures in different categories. For example, in areas ranked serious or worse, gas stations are required to install special hose-and-nozzle controls on gas pumps to capture fuel vapors. These areas are also required to have more stringent vehicle inspection and maintenance programs. The nonattainment provisions for other pollutants are generally similar but give EPA somewhat more discretion.

Congress has obviously learned a lot about the noncompliance problem in the three decades following the original enactment of the Clean Air Act. It remains to be seen whether this increased regulatory sophistication will be reflected in improved air quality, but the 1990 amendments do seem to promise significant further progress.

c. New Stationary Sources

Section 111 directs the Administrator to promulgate "standards of performance" governing emissions of air pollutants by "new" stationary sources, i.e., sources constructed or modified after the effective date of pertinent regulations. The term "modification" means any physical change or change in the method of operation which increases the amount of any air pollutant. The emission standard must reflect

the degree of emission reduction achievable through the application of the best system of continuous emission reduction which (taking into consideration the cost of achieving such emission reduction, and any nonair quality health and en-

vironmental impact and energy requirements) the
Administrator determines has been adequately
demonstrated.

(If such a standard is not feasible, under § 111(h)
the EPA may issue operating or work practice standards instead.)   In Portland Cement Association v.
Ruckelshaus, 486 F.2d 375 (D.C.Cir.1973), industry
sought judicial review of EPA's standards of performance for cement plants.   The companies contended that EPA had violated the mandate to "take
into consideration" emission cost because it had not
prepared a quantified cost-benefit analysis.   EPA
had estimated that the cost of pollution control was
affordable by the industry and could be passed on to
customers without substantially affecting competition with substitutes such as steel, asphalt, and
aluminum.   The court held that this was sufficient
consideration of economic costs to satisfy the requirement of § 111.

In 1977, the Clean Air Act was amended by
addition of § 317.   It provides that, before publishing notice of a proposal to adopt or revise any
standard of performance under § 111, EPA shall
prepare an "economic impact assessment respecting
such standard or regulation."   This assessment,
which shall be available to the public, must analyze
costs of compliance, potential inflationary or reces-
sionary effects, and effects on competition, consumer costs, and energy use.   However, § 317 expressly
did not "alter the basis on which a standard or
regulation is promulgated" or "authorize or require

any judicial review of any such standard or regulation."

Beginning with the Reagan Administration in 1981, more extensive use of cost-benefit analysis has been required by executive order. Executive Order 12,291 required that "major" regulations satisfy a cost-benefit analysis, unless such an analysis is precluded by statute. Later Presidents have modified the order but continued its basic mandate. The cost-benefit requirement is enforced by the Office of Management and Budget (OMB). OMB's increasingly active role in agency rulemaking has been a source of political controversy and has given rise to legal disputes about whether OMB has violated the statutory procedures governing rulemaking. Congress has repeatedly considered whether to strengthen the role of cost-benefit analysis but has failed to do so.

Under § 172 of the Act, a SIP applicable to any nonattainment area must "require permits for the construction and operation of new or modified major stationary sources." To qualify for a permit, a major source must achieve the "lowest achievable emission rate" (LAER) and satisfy certain pollution "offset" requirements (discussed in section 3 below). Section 171 defines LAER as "the most stringent emission limitation . . . contained in the implementation plan of any state" (unless shown to be unachievable), or "the most stringent emission limitation achieved in practice, . . . whichever is more stringent." Since LAER may not be less stringent than standards of performance for new sources under § 111, LAER must be at least "the best system of continuous emission reduction ... adequately demonstrated," considering cost.

As amended in 1977 by addition of §§ 160–169, the Clean Air Act requires that SIPs include measures to "prevent the significant deterioration" (PSD) of air quality. This requirement applies to areas designated by the states under § 107 as having ambient air quality better than any applicable NAAQS, or for which there is insufficient data to determine air quality. Since classification of areas is pollutant-specific, the same geographic area may be a PSD area for one pollutant but a nonattainment area for another.

No major stationary source may be constructed or modified in a PSD area without a permit, and no permit shall be issued unless (1) the applicant demonstrates that emissions will not contribute to air pollution in excess of the allowable increment or concentration for any pollutant in the PSD area, and (2) the facility's emission limitations reflect "best available control technology" (BACT) for each pollutant subject to PSD regulation. Demonstrations that emissions will not violate applicable increments are to be based on monitoring and diffusion modeling.

About one hundred projects, mostly modifications, pass through the permit process every year. Because PSD has had little effect on plant siting, the technology standards have become the focus of PSD policy. This technology requirement (BACT) has resulted in significant decreases in emissions below the § 111 new source standards. For example, there has been more than a 20% reduction in particulates and sulfur dioxide below new source standards. EPA has implemented a "top down" review process, under which a source must use the most stringent control technology available unless it can demonstrate that use of this technology is infeasible based on "substantial and unique local factors."

A related requirement is intended to protect visibility in national parks because of complaints that haze was seriously impairing their scenic beauty. Section 169A declares as a national goal the prevention of visibility impairment in mandatory Class I federal areas (primarily national parks). Some limited amount of "retrofitting"—that is, upgrading equipment in existing plants—is mandated to help achieve this goal.

If a change at plant is sufficient to constitute a "modification" and trigger new source review, the owner is faced with much more rigorous pollution control requirements under PSD or nonattainment requirements. The Bush Administration used several methods in an effort to restrict the application of these requirements. For example, it classified plants as having major modifications for PSD purposes only if the result was an increase in hourly emissions. Under this approach, changes that allow the plant to operate for additional time periods, and thus increase total emissions, would not be classified as major modifications. The Supreme Court remanded this rule for further consideration in Environmental Defense v. Duke Power, 127 S.Ct. 1423 (2007).

3. OFFSETS AND BUBBLES

As mentioned earlier, § 173 requires permits for the construction and operation of "new or modified major stationary sources" in nonattainment areas. Permits are issued only if "total allowable emissions" from existing sources and new non-major sources are "sufficiently less than total emissions from existing sources allowed under the applicable implementation plan" when the permit is sought, "so as to represent ... reasonable progress." Thus *total* emissions of each pollutant must be reduced even though a new source is added. Under the 1990 amendments, the amount of the reduction varies with the severity of the area's nonattainment problem. New or modified major sources receive credit only for reducing emissions that are allowed under the SIP, not for reductions already overdue.

Section 173 does not require that the source reducing its emissions be owned or operated by the person proposing a new major source. Section 173 refers to "total allowable emissions from existing sources in the region," and EPA guidelines allow offsets based on reductions at sources owned by others. As long as net emissions are reduced, it is immaterial who reduces them. Thus, someone wishing to create a new source could pay another firm to close down a marginal plant, to control it beyond SIP requirements, or to move to another air quality control region. The result is that § 173 creates a private market in emission rights.

Since 1979 the EPA has allowed "banking" of unused emission reduction credits for offset against future new sources. For example, localities may bank reductions that result from firms going out of business. These clean air credits can later be transferred to new firms locating in the community. But who owns offsets that are not used immediately, and how should they be allocated among potential new sources? According to EPA, "the State is free to govern ownership, use, sale, and commercial transactions in banked emission offsets as it sees fit." The offsets might be considered the exclusive property of the parent source that produced them; they might be treated as public property, even though created by private investments; or they might be viewed as privately owned rights that can be made available either to the parent source or to other investors.

The preceding paragraphs were concerned with *inter*-source offsets. The following paragraphs deal with *intra*-source offsets and the so-called "bubble" concept. Just as offsets allow trading between sources, "bubbles" allow trading within a single source. The basic idea is to treat the various components of an industrial complex as a single source for regulatory purposes. Thus, emissions from all stacks are considered only in the aggregate. If only stacks at a single plant are involved, this concept is called "netting." "Bubbles" involve multi-plant facilities under common ownership. In practice, netting is much more common than the use of bubbles.

The bubble policy was the source of conflicting rulings in the D.C. Circuit. That court considered bubbles in a series of three cases. In two cases dealing with § 111 new source standards and non-attainment standards, bubbles were declared invalid. In a case dealing with PSD rules, however, use of bubbles was upheld.

The issue reached the Supreme Court in Chevron, U.S.A., Inc. v. NRDC, 467 U.S. 837 (1984). *Chevron* involved the use of bubbles in state nonattainment regulations. The effect of using a bubble was effectively to allow the firm to offset one emission with a reduction in another emission, without complying with the other requirements of the offset provisions. Nevertheless, the Supreme Court upheld the use of the bubble. Finding nothing in the language of the statute or its legislative history directly on point, the Court concluded that the issue was really one of how to best implement the general policies of the Act. This policy decision, the Court concluded, was best made by the EPA rather than by the judiciary:

In this case, the Administrator's interpretation represents a reasonable accommodation of manifestly competing interests and is entitled to deference: the regulatory scheme is technical and complex, the agency considered the matter in a detailed and reasoned fashion, and the decision involves reconciling conflicting policies. Congress intended to accommodate both interests, but did not do so itself on the level of specificity presented by this case. Perhaps that body consciously desired the Administrator to strike the balance at this level, thinking that those with great expertise and charged with responsibility for administering the provision would be in a better position to do so; perhaps it simply did not consider the question at this level; and perhaps Congress was unable to forge a coalition on either side of the question, and those on each side decided to take their chances with the scheme devised by the agency. For judicial purposes, it matters not which of those things occurred.

Judges are not experts in the field, and are not part of either political branch of government. Courts must, in some cases, reconcile competing political interests, but not on the basis of the judges' personal policy preferences. In contrast, an agency to which Congress has delegated policy-making responsibilities may, within the limits of that delegation, properly rely upon the incumbent administration's views of wise policy to inform its judgments.

Chevron has become the leading case on judicial review of an agency's interpretation of a statute. As this passage makes clear, a subsequent administration would be free to prohibit states from utilizing bubbles in their nonattainment regulations, based on a reappraisal of the competing policies.

4. TOXIC AIR POLLUTION

Prior to 1990, § 112 of the Clean Air Act required EPA to regulate hazardous air pollutants at a level that provided an "ample margin of safety" to protect the public health. This was similar to the standard in the 1972 Clean Water Act governing regulation of toxic water pollutants. As discussed on pages 120–122, implementation of that provision proved impractical, and the Clean Water Act was amended in 1977. The amendment prescribed a list of toxic water pollutants and provided that they were to be subject to effluent limitations based on a BAT standard, with EPA having discretion to impose more stringent limitations based on an "ample margin of safety" standard.

Until 1987, EPA's regulatory approach under old § 112 of the Clean Air Act was similar to that authorized in the 1977 Clean Water Act amendments, even though § 112 did not mention BAT or technological feasibility. However, as to hazardous air pollutants, that approach was found to be unlawful in NRDC v. EPA, 824 F.2d 1146 (D.C.Cir. 1987) (en banc). There the court held that "safe" need not mean "risk-free," and that the EPA Administrator should use his "expert judgment" regarding the level of emissions that would result in an "acceptable" risk to health. Only after this degree of "safety" was assured could the Administrator consider what was an "ample margin," and then he might "diminish" the statistically determined "safe" level of risk by setting the regulatory level at the lowest feasible level.

In 1989, EPA published regulations governing industrial benzene emissions. These were the first toxic air pollutant standards developed under the two-step procedure ordered by the court of appeals. Concerning "acceptable risk" to health, EPA said it would generally presume that a maximum individual risk (MIR) no higher than 1 in 10,000 was acceptable, i.e., a person living very near to the pollution source and exposed to the maximum, modeled long-term concentration of the pollutant 24 hours per day for 70 years should not face an estimated incremental risk greater than 1 in 10,000 of contracting cancer. Concerning "ample margin of safety," EPA sought to provide protection to the greatest number of persons possible—estimated at 99% of all persons within 50 kilometers of all the emission sources—to an individual lifetime incremental risk level no higher than approximately 1 in 1 million.

The Clean Air Act Amendments of 1990 included a totally new § 112, somewhat similar in approach to § 307 of the Clean Water Act. However, the risk management methodology prescribed in the 1987 D.C. Circuit case *NRDC v. EPA* and employed in EPA's 1989 regulations governing industrial benzene emissions was endorsed by Congress and continues to be important under new § 112.

Section 112(b) now contains an initial list of 189 chemicals to be regulated. For each of two catego-

ries of sources, "major" and "area" (non-major),
EPA is to promulgate emission standards that require installation of maximum achievable control
technology (MACT). Standards for 40 of the highest priority source categories were to be issued by
1992. Other standards were to be issued in stages,
with the final deadline being in the year 2000.
Existing sources must comply with MACT standards within three years after issuance, unless EPA
or a state agency grants a one-year extension.

Beyond MACT standards, § 112(f)(2) contemplates subsequent adoption, within 8 years after
promulgation of MACT standards for each category
of sources, of more stringent emission standards
where necessary "to provide an ample margin of
safety to protect public health in accordance with
this section (as in effect before the date of enactment of the Clean Air Act Amendments of 1990) or
to prevent, taking into consideration costs, energy,
safety, and other relevant factors, an adverse environmental effect." If MACT standards applicable
to a "known, probable or possible human carcinogen do not reduce lifetime excess cancer risks to the
individual most exposed to emissions from a source
. . . to less than one in one million, the Administrator shall promulgate standards under this subsection for such source category." Section 112(f)(2)(B)
provides that nothing in § 112 "shall be construed
as affecting, or applying to the Administrator's interpretation of this section, as in effect before the
date of enactment of [the 1990 amendments] and

set forth in [the 1989 industrial benzene emissions regulations]."

C. REGULATION UNDER THE CLEAN WATER ACT

The major sources of water pollution are industrial, municipal, and agricultural. The types of pollutants entering streams, lakes, and oceans include organic wastes, other nutrients, toxic chemicals and other hazardous substances, heated water, and sediments.

Organic wastes decompose by bacterial action. They are commonly measured in units of biochemical oxygen demand (BOD), or the amount of oxygen needed to decompose them. Because fish and other aquatic animals need oxygen, the amount of dissolved oxygen in a water body is one of the best measures of its ecological health. If too much oxygen is consumed in decomposition of organic waste, certain desirable types of fish no longer can live there and are replaced by pollution-resistant fish such as carp. If all the dissolved oxygen is gone, an anaerobic (airless) decomposition process occurs. Rather than releasing carbon dioxide, anaerobic decomposition releases methane or hydrogen sulfide, and the stream or lake turns dark and malodorous.

Discharges of heated water into lakes and rivers ("thermal pollution") also can harm aquatic life. Higher temperatures accelerate biological and chemical processes, reducing the water's ability to retain dissolved oxygen and other gases. The growth of aquatic plants like algae is hastened, and fish reproduction may be disrupted.

Eutrophication, or the "dying of lakes," is a natural process resulting from the addition of nutrients and sediments. Over time, lakes become shallower and biologically more productive, eventually evolving into swamps and finally into dry land. Normally this takes thousands of years, but humans greatly accelerate the process when they add nutrients such as detergents, fertilizers, and human and animal wastes, and allow soil runoff from agricultural and other lands.

Discharges of toxic chemicals, heavy metals, and other hazardous substances can impair aquatic life and render both the water (even after treatment) and fish and shellfish unsafe for human consumption.

Most industrial wastes can be controlled by treatment and production process changes. Some types of wastes, like those from food processing, can be treated efficiently—after pretreatment in some cases—in municipal treatment systems. Such systems receive about half of their wastes from industrial sources and about half from homes, stores, and offices.

Three levels of treatment are employed in municipal treatment plants. Primary treatment is a simple gravity process that separates and settles solids. It provides BOD removal levels of 25% to 30%. Secondary treatment is a biological process that speeds up what occurs in natural water bodies.

Good secondary treatment plants remove 90% of BOD. Advanced waste treatment involves a wide variety of processes tailored for specific treatment needs. They may remove up to 99% of measured BOD, as well as other pollutants. Even after treatment, however, municipal wastes contribute large amounts of phosphate and nitrate nutrients to water bodies. Secondary treatment plants remove an average of 30% of the phosphorous and up to 20% of the nitrogenous materials, although with modifications higher levels of removal are possible.

Another municipal waste problem is street runoff into storm sewers. Where storm sewers are separated from sanitary sewers, runoff enters receiving waters untreated and can carry a variety of wastes, including organic and toxic wastes. Where storm and sanitary sewers are combined, both runoff and raw sewage pass directly into receiving waters when treatment systems become overloaded during storms or thaws.

1. OVERVIEW OF THE CLEAN WATER ACT

Until 1972, the Federal Water Pollution Control Act prescribed a regulatory system consisting mainly of state-developed ambient water quality standards applicable to interstate or navigable waters. The standards for any particular segment of a water body depended upon the uses (e.g., agricultural, industrial, recreational) that the state wanted to facilitate. Enforcement was possible only to prevent an imminent health hazard or when a discharge reduced the quality of the receiving water below the specified ambient level. This system failed for lack of enforcement. Multiple polluters discharging into the same stream or lake presented problems of proof similar to those encountered under nuisance law. As with air pollution, many states were either unmotivated or incapable of taking effective regulatory action.

In 1972 Congress adopted a different approach. The 1972 amendments established a system of standards, permits and enforcement aimed at "goals" of "fishable and swimmable" waters by 1983 and total elimination of pollutant discharges into navigable waters by 1985. Ambient water quality standards were to be supplemented by effluent limitations applicable to all "point sources" ("any discernible, confined and discrete conveyance ... from which pollutants are or may be discharged"). Under § 301, effluent limitations for all point sources except publicly owned treatment works were required to reflect "best practicable control technology currently available" (BPT) by 1977 and "best available technology economically achievable" (BAT) by 1983. Publicly owned treatment works (POTWs) were required to adopt secondary treatment by 1977 and "best practicable waste treatment over the life of the works" by 1983. In addition, all point sources were required to comply with any more stringent limitations established pursuant to § 302 to achieve ambient water quality standards, or pursuant to any other federal or state law.

Special requirements were imposed on some types of sources. Section 306 required that "new" sources in specified categories meet effluent limitations akin to the 1983 BAT standards. Section 307 required that EPA maintain a list of toxic substances and establish separate limitations for them. These limitations were to be based mainly on protection of public health and water quality, rather than on technological feasibility, and were to provide an "ample margin of safety." Section 307 is discussed in more detail on pages 149–151.

Section 402 created a permit system, the National Pollutant Discharge Elimination System (NPDES), under which discharge permits can be issued by EPA or by states with EPA-approved programs. Discharges by point sources, except in compliance with the limitations imposed in permits, were declared unlawful. Permits must incorporate applicable effluent limitations established under §§ 301, 302, 306, and 307, including enforceable schedules of compliance to meet the statutory deadlines. A 1987 amendment prohibits backsliding; with limited exceptions, new permits cannot be less stringent than existing permits for the same facility.

The 1972 amendments contemplated that states would be primarily responsible for enforcement. However, the federal government was not constrained, as it had been under the previous FWPCA, from acting to enforce state or federal standards. Provisions allowing for inspection, entry and monitoring, EPA enforcement suits, and citizen suits were all designed to facilitate enforcement of the new standards. Under § 505, citizens could sue to enforce effluent limitations in state or EPA permits. (As government enforcement action has been hindered by budgetary constraints, citizen suits have become increasingly important.) Citizens also could sue EPA for failure to perform nondiscretionary regulatory duties. Another provision, discussed in Chapter 6, addressed the problem of wetlands protection.

Like the Clean Air Act, the FWPCA was amended in 1977. It was renamed the Clean Water Act. EPA was authorized to grant case-by-case temporary extensions of the 1977 BPT deadline to industrial dischargers that had attempted in good faith to comply. If delays in compliance were caused by lack of federal construction grant funds, the agency also could extend the 1977 deadline until 1983. Another provision, § 301(h), authorized EPA to waive the secondary treatment requirement permanently for POTW discharges into "marine waters" (oceans and tidal rivers) if the sewage would not interfere with public water supplies, aquatic life, and recreational activities.

With respect to the previously established 1983 deadline for industry compliance with BAT effluent limitations, the 1977 modifications were more complex. Different requirements were adopted for three categories of pollutants: (1) "toxic" pollutants, including initially a list of 129 specific chemicals; (2) "conventional" pollutants designated by EPA, including BOD, fecal coliform, suspended solids, and pH; and (3) "nonconventional" pollutants, those not classified by EPA as either toxic or conventional. For toxic pollutants, BAT was to be employed by July 1, 1984 (or for pollutants not on the original list, within three years after EPA adoption of applicable effluent limitations); no exceptions were allowed. Under a surviving portion of the pre-1977 law, EPA may establish even stricter toxic standards, including zero discharge, where necessary either to protect public health with an ample margin of safety or to attain applicable ambient water quality standards. Under the 1987 amendments, stricter standards are also required to control toxic "hotspots," where BAT, new source, and pretreatment standards are insufficient to attain water quality standards.

Previous BAT requirements were also modified. For conventional pollutants, a new standard, "best conventional pollutant control technology" (BCT), was to be achieved by July 1, 1984. In establishing effluent limitations for conventional pollutants, EPA was to consider "the reasonableness of the relationship between the costs of attaining a reduction in effluents and the effluent reduction benefits derived." This "reasonable relationship" factor was not included among those to be considered in formulating BAT limitations for toxic and nonconventional pollutants. Effluent limitations based on the BAT standard were to be achieved for nonconventional pollutants, with a deadline that was ultimately extended to 1989.

Further, under § 304(d)(4), the definition of what constitutes acceptable secondary treatment was relaxed in 1981: "such biological treatment facilities as oxidation ponds, lagoons, and ditches," in which sunlight and algae cause decomposition of the wastes, "shall be deemed the equivalent of secondary treatment" so long as receiving water quality will not be "adversely affected." Clearly, this redefinition, together with the provisions of § 301(h) concerning discharges into marine waters, amounts to a partial retreat—with respect to publicly owned treatment works—from technology-based effluent standards back toward the pre-1972 focus on attainment of ambient water quality standards.

Water quality considerations have continued to play a role in regulating industrial sources. Sections 302 and 303 require stricter effluent limitations when necessary to achieve water quality standards and provide procedures for classifying waters in terms of desired use and needed purity. States have much leeway in determining the type of use, but less in deciding what water quality is necessary for those uses. Section 302 was amended in 1987 to allow modifications of its requirements when there is "no reasonable relationship" between costs and benefits. The most ambitious water quality provision of the 1987 amendments relates to nonpoint source pollution, that is, run-off from agricultural and urban areas. This has proved to be a major yet intractable part of the water pollution problem. Pre-1987 law made an ineffectual effort to grapple with the problem in § 208. The 1987 Act added a new § 319 to address the problem. States were required to identify water bodies in which water quality standards cannot be met without control of non-point source pollutants, and to establish management programs for these water bodies, including "best management practices" for categories of sources.

Although still less significant than technology standards, water quality standards may well attain increasing importance under the Clean Water Act. For example, the Supreme Court upheld the use of state water flow requirements, designed to maintain water quality, in the permit for a hydroelectric project. PUD No. 1 of Jefferson County v. Washington Dept. of Ecology, 511 U.S. 700 (1994). A vociferous dissent by Justice Thomas argued that the Court had allowed the parochial local interest in clean water to overrule the national interest in power generation. The majority not only rejected this argument, but adopted a broad view of the appropriate mechanisms that states could use in defining water quality standards, going well beyond quantitative restrictions on aquatic pollutant concentrations.

Currently, the most controversial water quality issue relates to EPA's power to set total maximum daily loads (TMDLs) under § 303(d). These TMDLs apply not only to point sources (whether or not a BAT standard has been set) but also to other sources of pollution, giving EPA authority to push states well beyond the normal technology-based regime. See Dioxin/Organochlorine Center v. Clarke, 57 F.3d 1517 (9th Cir.1995). Both polluters and state and local governments have vigorously resisted what they consider to be an alarming expansion of water pollution regulation.

To date, technology-based effluent limitations are still the key restrictions on industrial point sources. Section 301(b), as noted above, requires that effluent limitations reflecting different levels of technology—BPT, BCT, and BAT, depending upon the type of pollutant and the deadline for attainment— "shall be achieved" by dischargers. However, the statute does not state explicitly who is to set the limitations, or how. In E.I. du Pont de Nemours & Co. v. Train, 430 U.S. 112 (1977), the issue was whether § 301(b) authorized EPA to establish effluent limitations applicable to *classes* of plants, the class in question being organic chemical plants. The company argued that § 301(b) merely indicated the level of technology to be specially fashioned for each *individual* plant in NPDES permits granted under § 402. Generally, these permits are issued by the states, not by EPA. The critical question was whether the EPA could set effluent limitations by regulation, i.e., by quasi-legislative rulemaking, or whether such limitations had to be established in individualized proceedings by the state officials or regional EPA officials responsible for issuing NPDES permits.

The Supreme Court sided with EPA. After considering the legislative history of § 301, the "impossible burden" of individually considering the unique circumstances of the estimated 42,000 permit applicants, and the judicial deference due EPA's reasonable statutory interpretation, the Court concluded that § 301 authorized both BPT and BAT limitations to be set by regulation. The Court held, however, that some allowance must be made for variations in individual plants, as EPA had done by including a variance clause in the challenged BPT limitations.

2.   CONSIDERATION OF ECONOMIC AND TECHNOLOGICAL FEASIBILITY

The § 301 and § 304 definitions of BPT, BCT, and BAT leave EPA considerable discretion in establishing effluent limitations for different categories of dischargers. We shall review the factors to be considered in implementing BPT, BCT, and BAT standards, in that order. We also shall review relevant provisions of § 306, concerning national standards of performance for *new* sources of water pollution.

a.   BPT

American Meat Institute v. EPA, 526 F.2d 442 (7th Cir.1975) is illustrative of industry challenges to EPA limitations. The BPT regulations there covered slaughterhouses and meat packing. Under §§ 301(b)(1)(A) and 304(b)(1)(B), BPT is based on consideration of total cost in relation to several factors: effluent reduction benefits, age of equipment, production process, engineering aspects of control techniques, and non-water quality environmental impacts. In construing this mandate, EPA relied on legislative history indicating that BPT should reflect "the average of the best existing

performance by plants of various sizes, ages, and
unit processes within each industrial category," except where existing practices are uniformly inadequate. The court approved this interpretation and
sustained the effluent limitations because they had
actually been achieved at some time by one or more
existing processing plants.

The courts have upheld EPA's refusal to consider
water quality in setting BPT limitations. In Wey-
erhaeuser Co. v. Costle, 590 F.2d 1011 (D.C.Cir.
1978), pulp and paper companies challenged the
validity of the BPT regulations for their industry.
Some of their mills discharged effluents into the
Pacific Ocean. The companies urged that because
the amounts of pollutants were small in comparison
to the volume of receiving water, they should not
have to spend heavily on treatment equipment or
increase their energy requirements and sludge levels in order to treat wastes that the ocean could
dilute or absorb. EPA argued that, based on long
experience, Congress in 1972 deliberately ruled out
arguments based on the assimilative capacity of receiving waters. The court agreed with EPA. According to the court, Congress was not only concerned about the lack of enforceability of pre-1972
water quality standards, but also wanted nationwide uniformity to free states from the temptation
of relaxing local limitations in order to woo or keep
industrial facilities. Water quality was to be considered only in setting *more* stringent standards
than those reflected in technology-based effluent
limitations.

Although the statute was silent on the question of variances from BPT standards, the Supreme Court held in *du Pont v. Train*, supra, that EPA's practice of allowing such variances was not only permissible but required. EPA allowed adjustment of the category-wide standards for plants that could demonstrate the existence of "fundamentally different factors" compared with the industry norm. In subsequent cases, the Court clarified the nature of these "FDF" variances. First, in EPA v. National Crushed Stone Association, 449 U.S. 64 (1980), the Court upheld EPA's view that a firm's individual economic inability to comply is not a basis for an FDF variance. Although the relationship between costs and effluent reduction benefits is relevant to setting BPT limits, the extent of an individual firm's financial resources is not a factor in FDF variances. Second, in Chemical Manufacturers Association v. NRDC, 470 U.S. 116 (1985), the Court held that FDF variances are available for toxic pollutants, despite § 301(*l*) of the Act, which prohibited any modification of effluent standards for toxics. The Court explained that an FDF variance is not a "modification" of the effluent standard, but rather a tailoring of the standard to the individual situation of a particular plant. The 1987 amendments added a new subsection, § 301(n), providing for FDF variances from BAT, but was silent about BPT variances.

b. BCT

As amended in 1977, § 304(b)(4)(B) spells out the criteria to be used in establishing BCT effluent limitations.   Concerning cost considerations, the statute provides that BCT shall include: (1) "consideration of the reasonableness of the relationship between the costs of attaining a reduction in effluents and the effluent reduction benefits derived"; and (2) "comparison of the cost and level of reduction of such pollutants from the discharge from publicly owned treatment works to the cost and level of reduction of such pollutants from a class or category of industrial sources."   In 1979 EPA promulgated a BCT methodology that reduced this cost-reasonableness analysis to a single test: a comparison of the marginal costs of going (a) from BPT to BCT and (b) from "secondary treatment" to "advanced secondary treatment" at publicly owned treatment works (the POTW comparison test). EPA analyzed POTW costs and established a figure of \$1.15 per pound as the appropriate marginal cost of advanced secondary treatment at a POTW.   It then screened existing BAT rules for 41 industry subcategories to determine which rules passed the POTW comparison test.

Industry groups challenged the new BCT standards in American Paper Institute v. EPA, 660 F.2d 954 (4th Cir.1981).   They argued that § 304(b) called for a two-part cost-reasonableness test: a cost-effectiveness test and a POTW comparison test. EPA, on the other hand, argued that Congress did not require it to evaluate cost-effectiveness, but only mandated a POTW cost-comparison standard. EPA read the seemingly dual statutory requirements as one, commanding only a consideration of reasonableness. The court rejected EPA's position and invalidated all the BCT regulations. EPA's interpretation of the statute was found to be contrary to its plain meaning, ignoring the mandatory language ("shall") and disregarding the conjunctive ("and"). On the other hand, the court concluded that EPA had not acted arbitrarily or capriciously in choosing advanced secondary treatment as the increment beyond secondary treatment for the POTW comparison test. In 1986, EPA adopted new BCT regulations, adding to the POTW test an industry cost-effectiveness test capping the incremental cost of BCT at 129% of BPT.

A later decision gives additional guidance concerning the role of cost in setting BPT and BCT. In Chemical Mfrs. Ass'n v. U.S. EPA, 870 F.2d 177 (5th Cir.1989), the industry argued that BPT should be governed by a "knee-of-the-curve" test to determine the point at which the marginal cost of removal rises steeply. Increasing the removal of conventional pollutants for the chemicals industry from 96% to 99% would allegedly have cost almost twice as much per pound of pollutant as current treatment methods. CMA argued that this shift went well beyond the knee of the curve and was therefore impermissible. EPA countered that the knee-of-the-curve test could be applied only to assess increases in limitations beyond BPT (that is, for BCT). The Fifth Circuit agreed with the agency:

The BCT provisions were intended to establish an intermediate level between BPT and the stricter BAT limitations for conventional pollutants by adding a cost-effectiveness test for incremental technology requirements that exceed BPT technology. Under BCT, additional limitations on conventional pollutants that are more stringent than BPT can be imposed only "to the extent that the increased cost of treatment [would] be reasonable in terms of the degree of environmental benefits."

The court concluded that cost played a different role in BPT than in BCT. Regarding BPT, the only question is "whether the costs are 'wholly disproportionate' to the benefits." In contrast, cost weighs more heavily in setting BCT. Note that FDF variances are available for BCT under § 301(n), added by the 1987 amendments.

c. BAT

Section 301(b)(2) prescribes BAT effluent limitations for "nonconventional" and toxic pollutants. Section 304(b)(2)(B) directs that BAT "shall take into account" the age of equipment and facilities, the process employed, engineering aspects of control techniques, process changes, "the cost of achieving such effluent reduction," and non-water quality environmental impacts (including energy requirements). There is no requirement of a balancing between the costs and benefits of effluent reduction. Because § 301 mandates compliance with BAT limitations by 1984 for toxic pollutants but fixes no deadline for nonconventional pollutants, EPA's BAT program now is focused on toxics. Effluent limitations and other controls on toxic pollutants under the Clean Water Act are discussed below. Here, we will consider only the availability of variances.

Section 301(c) authorizes the Administrator to grant a variance from BAT upon a showing that modified requirements: "(1) will represent the maximum use of technology within the economic capacity of the owner or operator; and (2) will result in reasonable further progress toward the elimination of the discharge of pollutants." Thus, consideration of individual economic impact, as well as environmental impact, is required. However, § 301(*l*) prohibits variances with respect to pollutants on the toxic pollutant list established under § 307. Thus, § 301(c) variances are available only for nonconventional pollutants.

The 1987 amendments added a new subsection, § 301(n), expressly sanctioning FDF variances for BAT and BCT. Congress ratified the Supreme Court's views about FDF variances by limiting consideration to the factors involved in establishing the effluent limitations "other than cost" and by amending subsection (*l*) to make FDF variances available for toxics. The amendment also seems to ratify lower court decisions rejecting water quality as a factor in granting variances from BPT. Water quality is not a factor in establishing effluent limitations, and the amendments make it clear that the same factors are relevant at the variance stage as at the regulation stage.

Another source of BAT variances (but only for nontoxics) is § 301(g). This subsection allows variances based on water quality considerations. The applicant must show that the modification will not interfere with public water supplies, prevent a balanced population of wildlife and fish, or allow the discharge of toxics posing an unacceptable risk. The 1987 amendments limit § 301(g) variances to a few well-studied nonconventional pollutants.

d. Standards of Performance for New Sources

Section 306 directs the Administrator to establish federal standards of performance for new sources. The term "new source" includes any source the "construction" (but not "modification") of which is commenced after EPA *proposal* of a § 306 standard that will apply to such source. "Standards of performance" must reflect the "greatest degree of effluent reduction which the Administrator determines to be achievable through application of the best available demonstrated control technology, processes, operating methods, or other alternatives, including, where practicable, a standard permitting no discharge of pollutants." In establishing such standards, the Administrator "shall take into consideration the cost of achieving such effluent reduction, and any non-water quality environmental impact and energy requirements."

The ability of owners and operators of individual new sources to comply with industry-wide standards may not be considered. In E.I. du Pont de

Nemours & Co. v. Train, 430 U.S. 112 (1977), the Supreme Court noted that there was no statutory provision for variances and concluded that variances would be inappropriate for a standard intended to ensure national uniformity and "maximum feasible control" of new sources.

3.   TOXIC POLLUTION

As originally enacted in 1972, the Clean Water Act required EPA to publish a list of toxic pollutants and to implement standards for these pollutants providing an "ample margin of safety." For various reasons, implementation of this requirement proved impractical. The agency lacked sufficient information about toxic pollutants and was given too little time to develop such information under the statutory timetable. Furthermore, because of the "ample margin of safety" requirement, the agency believed it had no leeway to consider feasibility. As a result, implementation of the statutory scheme threatened extensive plant closures and severe economic injury to some major industries.

The 1977 amendments to the Clean Water Act were an outgrowth of these problems. Because of the difficulty of implementing the original requirement, EPA had entered into a consent decree with the NRDC governing toxic pollutants. The decree required EPA to issue effluent limitations and new source performance standards for 21 major industries requiring the use of BAT. The 1977 amendments essentially codified this consent decree. Under the present statute, a list of toxic pollutants is specified in § 307(a)(1). Each pollutant on the list is subject to effluent limitations based on the BAT standard. This requirement is contained in § 307(a)(2) and is also incorporated in § 301(b)(2)(A). EPA in its discretion may impose more stringent limitations based on the "ample margin of safety" standard. Section 307 also provides for pretreatment standards for wastes—especially industrial wastes—that are to be introduced into municipal treatment systems rather than being discharged directly into the nation's waterways. These pretreatment standards are intended to prevent introduction of substances that cannot be adequately treated by public facilities or that might damage those facilities.

The Clean Water Act was amended again by the Water Quality Act of 1987. Congress had become concerned that certain waters could not meet applicable water quality standards despite the imposition of BAT requirements. In particular, numerous "toxic hotspots" needed more stringent controls. Section 304(l), added in 1987, established a comprehensive system for toxics control. States were directed to identify, within two years, such "hotspots"—waters where technology-based controls and existing water quality-based controls were not adequate to meet water quality standards because of toxic pollutants, even after implementation of BAT, new source performance standards, and standards requiring pretreatment of industrial wastes discharged into publicly owned treatment plants. The states then were to identify the specific point sources preventing the attainment of standards and the amount of each toxic pollutant discharged by each such source. After these identifications, every state was required to devise an individual control strategy to achieve standards at each "hotspot" within three years after the date of the establishment of the strategy.

Another statute related to water pollution is the Safe Drinking Water Act (SDWA), 42 U.S.C.A. §§ 300f to 300j-26. The Act, as amended extensively in 1986 and 1996, requires EPA to set maximum levels for contaminants in water delivered to users of public water systems. Of special concern are toxic contaminants in water from underground sources. A 1984 report by the Congressional Office of Technology Assessment (OTA) identified more than 200 contaminants in groundwater used for drinking, many of them associated with cancer and damage to the central nervous system, liver, and kidneys. The report documented serious incidents of such contamination by toxic chemicals, including pesticides and wastes leaked from landfills or disposed of in underground injection wells, in at least 34 states.

The SDWA directs EPA to set health-based standards for contaminants in drinking water and to require water supply system operators to come as close as possible to meeting the standards by using the best available technology that is economically and technologically "feasible." Primary enforcement responsibility may be delegated to states that request it, if they adopt drinking water regulations no less stringent than the national standards and implement adequate monitoring and enforcement procedures.

EPA developed a special regulatory program to deal specifically with pesticide contamination of groundwater. The program rests on a combination of state pesticide management plans and federal groundwater quality standards. Most prominent among the federal statutes invoked are the Federal Insecticide, Fungicide, and Rodenticide Act (FIFRA) and the SDWA.

D. ECONOMIC INCENTIVES FOR ENVIRONMENTAL PROTECTION

Preceding portions of this chapter dealt with abatement costs and lack of technology as constraints upon environmental protection. This section examines ways in which government can use economic incentives to promote environmental protection, primarily by increasing the cost of nonabatement to those causing environmental degradation.

Economists view a competitive market as the preferred means of allocating scarce resources in an "efficient" manner, that is, so as to maximize the total value of production. The market mechanism functions correctly, however, only if prices fully reflect the costs and benefits of production to the entire society.   As discussed earlier, two factors that tend to distort the market system are the related problems of "externalities" and "collective goods."   Pollution is a common form of external cost, a spillover effect of production that uses up other resources by degrading them.   Collective goods are commodities that cannot readily be supplied to specific persons without enabling large numbers of other persons to enjoy them as well. One example is the clean air produced by installation of emission control equipment.

Because of the free market's failure to provide adequate incentives, government must intervene to limit external costs and to facilitate production of collective goods.   As discussed at the beginning of this chapter, the basic approaches are (1) *liability*, making damage and injunctive remedies available to injured individuals; (2) *direct regulation*, e.g., emission limitations under the Clean Air Act; (3) *subsidies*, i.e., government payment of some of the expenses of avoiding external costs or producing collective goods; and (4) *charges* for activities generating external costs or failing to provide collective goods.

As we have seen, control of pollution via nuisance actions and direct regulation is not without problems.   Nuisance law proved inadequate to control widespread pollution from multiple sources.   Even if plaintiffs can satisfy standing requirements and sustain the burden of proving material harm attributable to defendants' unreasonable conduct, courts may refuse injunctive relief after "balancing the equities." In addition, nuisance law fails to provide a systematic mechanism for supervising emissions. Direct regulation, by contrast, is systematic. However, it can involve high administrative costs because of the need to conduct economic analyses of entire industries, as well as the need to master the technologies of production and pollution control. As we have seen, the resulting regulatory limits often are challenged in court on the ground that they do not represent "best practicable control technology" or some other statutory standard. Moreover, the economic benefits of delay may be so great in comparison to the costs of timely compliance that regulatory agencies may face widespread noncompliance.

One alternative to the regulatory approach is the use of subsidies. Typical subsidies employed for environmental management have included tax breaks (accelerated depreciation and credits), low-interest loans, and grants for installation of treatment equipment. However, such financial incentives provide only part of the cost of the equipment. They reduce losses, but they do not make installation of abatement equipment profitable. Such subsidies may "sweeten" a regulatory program but cannot replace it. Furthermore, subsidies provide incentives only for investments in equipment. Often the most efficient ways to reduce discharges are to alter production processes, recover materials, produce marketable goods from byproducts, or change the nature or quality of raw materials.

Because of shortcomings in the first three types of public intervention enumerated above, economists and others have shown increasing interest in effluent charges and marketable discharge permits.

1.   EFFLUENT CHARGES AND PENALTIES

An effluent charge system requires payment of a fee or tax on each unit of pollution released into the air or water. Reducing pollution by, say, 90% may be relatively inexpensive for some plants but very costly for others. Rather than a regulatory system with uniform effluent limitations, it may be preferable to have a variable standard that would focus pollution abatement where it costs the least. Each firm would reduce pollution to the point where the cost of removing an additional unit was the same as that for every other firm. With a fixed charge per unit of pollution, each discharger, if acting rationally, would remove pollution until the cost of removing an additional unit was greater than the effluent charge. The larger the charge, the greater the percentage of pollutants any firm would be motivated to remove, though firms with low costs of control would remove larger percentages than would firms with high abatement costs.

Fixing the levels of effluent charges poses some severe problems. Ideally, the legislature or administrative agency should impose on an environmentally damaging activity all of the external or social costs it produces. A polluter then would pay for all of the resources it consumes. But computing total social damages involves enormous difficulties and often is not practical. Other formulas for setting the charges therefore must be considered. One approach is based on the average costs of controlling pollution in various industries. Another is simply to set a charge that in practice provides sufficient incentive to cause polluters to reduce total discharges to socially acceptable levels.

Skepticism concerning the workability of effluent charges stems from concern that fully measuring the effluents actually produced by every source would be too difficult or expensive. While other methods of pollution control, such as direct regulation, do also require some monitoring of discharges, those systems usually do not require *continuous* monitoring for *all* polluters. The necessary technology has only recently become available in certain settings. Obviously the design of charge systems would have to be influenced to some extent by what it is technically and economically feasible to measure, and this may move such systems a considerable distance from the ideal mentioned above.

Despite avowed allegiance to the free market system, private businesses are frequently among the strongest opponents of effluent charges. Many believe they are better off under the present regulatory system than under an effective charge system. Any realistic comparison of the two systems must take into consideration the probabilities of having to comply. Under a charge system, if the problem of monitoring discharges accurately can be solved, a firm is almost certain to have to pay the charge or to spend money to abate its pollution so as to reduce the charge. Under direct regulation, however, some firms decide that, because enforcement is cumbersome and ineffective, they either will never have to pay for expensive controls or can gain the financial advantages of years of delay beyond official deadlines.

Noncompliance penalties under the Clean Air Act are aimed precisely at denying polluters such financial advantages from delay. Section 120, added in 1977, provides that EPA or the state "shall" assess and collect a noncompliance penalty against "every" person who owns or operates (i) a "major" stationary source (other than certain smelters) that violates any applicable implementation plan, (ii) a stationary source that violates an emission limitation, emission standard, standard of performance, or other requirement established under § 111 or § 112, or (iii) a stationary source for which an extension, order, suspension, or consent decree is in effect, and that violates any applicable interim control requirement or schedule of compliance. The amount of the penalty assessed under § 120 shall be equal to "no less than the economic value which a delay in compliance ... may have for the owner of such source," including both capital and operating costs, minus any expenditures actually made for the purpose of bringing the source into and maintaining compliance. Fines under § 120 are in addition to other civil or criminal sanctions that may be imposed under the Act or state or local law.

The Clean Water Act, as a result of the 1987 amendments, provides for administrative penalties of up to $250,000. The amount is to be determined based on a variety of factors, one of which is the degree of "economic benefit or savings (if any) resulting from the violation." These administrative penalties may approximate the noncompliance penalties under the Clean Air Act.

It should be noted that, under a pure effluent charge system, there would be no requirement that a polluter limit its discharges at all. So long as it was willing to pay the charges, it would be in compliance with the law. This is not true with a system involving charges only for discharges in excess of publicly established effluent limitations. Thus, noncompliance penalties render the regulatory system more effective but do not make the standards more economically efficient, unlike a pure charge system. Another attractive aspect of the pure charge system is that a polluter *always* has some financial incentive to reduce his pollution further, down to zero. No such continuing incentive exists under either a pure regulatory system, or under a system imposing effluent charges only on discharges in excess of regulatory limits.

2. MARKETABLE PERMITS

Another system of economic incentives that increasingly has attracted attention allocates discharge rights by means of publicly issued permits, which can be sold to other present or prospective dischargers, or to nondischargers entering the market for speculative or environmentalist purposes. Most trading systems would limit the duration of permits to some specified time, such as five or ten years. The initial permittees can be chosen in several ways. Permits could be allocated among existing polluters (free or for a price), or among broader groups of applicants by auction or lottery.

Once the permits have been allocated initially, they are transferable, and sale prices function as free-market equivalents of officially established effluent charges. Like an effluent charge system, a system of marketable permits provides some continuous incentive for individual sources to improve pollution control methods, since funds could be freed by sale of unneeded permits for the going price. However, permit systems involve two distinct advantages over a charge system. First, a permit system avoids the problems of setting effluent charges at the proper level. The government sets the price of a permit, if at all, only at the time of its initial issuance. If the price were wrongly fixed in relation to market forces, there would be automatic adjustments as permits were resold. The second advantage is that, even if prices were "wrongly" fixed by the government or the market, there nevertheless would be a fixed limit on total permissible discharges. Excessive discharges and damage to the environment would not be legal, as they would be under an effluent charge system (assuming willingness to pay the effluent charges), but could occur only through outright violation of the permit.

Transfers of permits from one geographic area to another—e.g., from one stretch of a stream to another, or from one portion of an air quality control region to another—might have to be regulated by exchange rates, set by the issuing authority so that trading could not cause water or air quality to fall below the prescribed ambient standard at any site. (Otherwise, the permit system would need to be backed up by regulatory standards). For example, if discharges of BOD into stream zone B would be twice as harmful to a critical reach as identical discharges into zone A further upstream, a permit might allow a polluter to discharge either one pound per day into zone B or two pounds per day into zone A. Very fine distinctions between zones and the amounts of discharges authorized would better protect water or air quality, but also would complicate transfers and perhaps impair the marketability of permits.

An ambitious effort to implement a federal marketable permit system is found in the acid rain provisions of the Clean Air Act. Prior to 1990, the Act had proved completely ineffective in dealing with acid rain. Two provisions of the Act, §§ 110(a)(2)(E) and 126, give EPA limited authority to take action against interstate pollution. EPA long declined, however, to implement that authority, and its position was consistently upheld by the courts. EPA's most significant exercise of its § 126 powers did not come until 2000, in response to a complaint from downwind states about nitric oxide emissions. EPA then imposed an emission cap for each upwind state, allocated proportionally among existing sources (except for a small allowance for growth). Sources were then authorized to trade in these emission allowances. EPA's decision was upheld, except for EPA's treatment of certain electricity cogenerators and its calculation of future growth in electricity generation. Appalachian Power Co. v. EPA, 249 F.3d 1032 (D.C.Cir.2001).

During the 1980s, acid rain received increasing attention from environmentalists and the general public. Under the Reagan Administration, however, Congress and the executive were at loggerheads over the issue. The deadlock between Congress and the White House was finally broken with the passage of the 1990 amendments. Title IV of the amendments is devoted to acid rain. It imposes a completely new approach to the problem.

The system is based on a system of allowances that can be banked or sold by emitters. Each allowance is equivalent to one ton of emissions. A utility can emit SO_2 only to the extent permitted by its allowances. The allowances were initially allocated largely on the basis of past emissions and fuel consumption, but there are extra allowances for a variety of purposes. For example, from 1995 to 1999, an extra 200,000 allowances were allocated to power plants in Illinois, Indiana, and Ohio.

A complex set of initial allowances was established to cut SO_2 emissions to 8.9 million tons by

2000. The program was divided into two phases. In Phase I, more than a hundred plants (individually listed in the statute) had to meet a standard of 2.5 pounds of SO_2 per million Btus. The 111 utility power plants in question were those that in 1990 emitted more than 2.5 pounds of SO_2 per million Btus. (For example, generator # 1 at the Colbert plant in Alabama was given a Phase I allowance of 13,570 tons.) The deadline for this standard was 1995, except that plants using scrubbers to meet the standards were given until 1997. These provisions were intended to encourage the use of scrubbers and thereby continue at least part of the market for eastern high-sulfur coal.

Phase II required utilities to reduce emissions by an additional 50%. Large, poorly controlled plants were required to reduce emissions to 1.2 million lbs/mBtu. A complex formula applied to smaller plants. The deadline for compliance was 2000. Total emissions could not exceed 8.9 million tons annually, but for the first ten years, EPA had a half million extra allowances in reserve. A further forty thousand allowances could be given to high-growth states. A four-year extension was available for units that used new clean coal technologies.

In part, the system of allocations embodies the efficiency concerns of economists. The system of allowances seems to have been manipulated, however, in the interests of regional equity, so that utilities that are required to engage in heavy investments will be able to recoup part of their expenses. The initial allocations were large enough that some of these utilities would find it feasible to control emissions more than required to stay within their initial allowances, thereby allowing them to sell excess allowances. At least some of these allowances will have to be purchased by new utility plants in order to operate, helping to defray the cost of controlling emissions from the older plants.

Sulfur dioxide allowances became truly marketable when the Chicago Board of Trade voted to create a private market for them. The federal program seems to have succeeded in reducing the cost of controlling acid rain, aided by some fortuitous economic shifts. A similar market system for CO_2 was created by the Kyoto Protocol. Such a model is likely to be used when Congress adopts climate change legislation.

*

CHAPTER 4

RISK MANAGEMENT AND SCIENTIFIC UNCERTAINTY

This chapter explores some special problems associated with regulation of hazardous and toxic substances. Primary among these is pervasive scientific uncertainty about long-term human effects of exposure to small amounts of such substances. In the face of uncertainty that no party to a regulatory or judicial proceeding may be able to resolve, rules concerning risk assessment, causation, presumptions, burden of proof, sharing of liability, and scope of judicial review become critically important.

A. INTRODUCTION TO RISK ASSESSMENT AND RISK MANAGEMENT

Risk *assessment* is the use of scientific data to define the probability of some harm coming to an individual or a population because of exposure to a substance or situation. Risk *management* is the process of deciding how to deal with a risk that has been determined to exist. Risk management includes taking into account the technical feasibility of reducing risk, in light of social, economic, and political factors.

There are three types of risk assessments. They can address short-term health risks (e.g., food poisoning), long-term health risks (e.g., cancer, a focus of this chapter), and ecological risks (e.g., global warming). These assessments employ a variety of methodologies, ranging from testing rats to doing fieldwork on a mountain stream. The results can be expressed as a safe-unsafe dichotomy or as a quantitative estimate to six decimal places.

EPA uses risk assessment to predict the probability of developing cancer as a result of exposure to a particular agent. Risk assessment of a carcinogen involves four steps: (1) hazard identification, (2) dose-response evaluation, (3) exposure assessment, and (4) risk characterization. Hazard identification is the process of determining whether an "agent" (for example, an industrial chemical) increases a person's risk of developing cancer. Dose-response evaluation reveals how the likelihood of cancer changes with the level of exposure. A risk assessor might estimate, for example, how the probability of lung cancer changes with the number of cigarettes smoked. The third step, exposure assessment, quantifies the amount, or dose, of the carcinogen to which people may be exposed. This may be the amount of a chemical in the air near a factory or the amounts of various foods that an individual consumes each day. After these quantitative inputs to a risk assessment have been determined, the numbers are combined to yield an overall estimate of risk. This risk characterization usually is expressed numerically as the incremental lifetime risk of cancer due to a particular agent at a particular level of exposure. Good risk characterizations should contain not only a final risk number but also a discussion of the uncertainties in and assumptions behind the assessment; unfortunately, such discussion rarely is included.

Separating the assessment of risk from its management is often difficult in practice. One reason is that human or social values, which are supposed to be considered in risk management, also may influence risk assessment. For example, suppose that a chemical is tested on laboratory animals to determine whether it can cause cancer, and that a proportion of the animals exposed does develop tumors. In order to assess the risk of humans contracting cancer from exposure to the chemical—that is, to develop a "dose-response curve"—a number of steps are required, each of which usually entails a substantial degree of uncertainty. Thus, the doses given to the laboratory animals are extremely high, while environmental exposures of humans typically are much lower. To determine the human dose-response curve, one must extrapolate down from the high-dose laboratory data. There are various statistical models for doing this, all of which fit the data, are open to debate, and yield very different predictions. Beyond that problem, it is necessary to extrapolate cancer data from animals to humans, and to deal with uncertainty about the levels of human exposure. All of these uncertainties inherent in risk assessment can combine to produce a very wide range of risk estimates in some cases.

Thus, a National Academy of Sciences report on saccharin some years ago concluded that over a period of 70 years the expected number of cases of human bladder cancer resulting from daily exposure to 120 milligrams of saccharin might range from 0.22 to 1,144,000. Because such a range is of little use to policymakers, a risk assessor may try to narrow it. However, any such narrowing process may be influenced by the scientist's personal and professional experience and values.

Scientists now believe that approximately 85% of all cancers are caused by broad environmental factors, including lifestyle patterns. The rest presumably have a hereditary basis or arise from spontaneous metabolic events. Identifying the environmental factors in cancer has not been easy. Tobacco is thought to be responsible for roughly 30% of all cancers, while a study done for the Congressional Office of Technology Assessment estimated that 35% of all cancer deaths in the United States were caused by dietary factors *other* than chemical additives and pollutants, such as natural carcinogens, excess fats that increase production of carcinogens in the body, and lack of fibers to flush potential carcinogens out of the bowels. The study concluded that less than 8% of cancer deaths resulted from carcinogens in the work place, environmental pollution, food additives, and industrial products.

If indeed almost two-thirds of all cancer deaths are caused by smoking and by dietary factors other than chemical additives and pollutants, while less than one-tenth are caused by carcinogens in the workplace, environmental pollution, food additives, and industrial products, what should be the government's strategy for reducing cancer mortality? As materials in this chapter and Chapter 5 indicate, our regulatory efforts (other than requiring labels warning smokers of health risks) have in fact been directed mostly at the latter four causes.

To date, statistical models that predict chemicals will not cause cancer until humans have been exposed to certain "threshold" levels have failed to gain general acceptance within the scientific community; therefore, in regulating suspected carcinogens agencies usually assume that risk is linear at lower dose levels, i.e., that there is at least some risk associated with any exposure. This conservative "default assumption" is not acceptable, however, in risk assessments of known threshold carcinogens, i.e., where the best available science indicates no threat of cancer from exposure below a certain dose range. See Chlorine Chemistry Council v. EPA, 206 F.3d 1286 (D.C.Cir.2000).

A basic fact about risk management is that there is a difference between a "safe" world and a "zero-risk" world. We all encounter risks of many kinds in our lives. Some, like earthquakes and disease, may be attributable to nature, while others, such as automobile accidents and mishaps at nuclear power plants, usually are attributable to human actions. Hence, in many situations "safety" cannot be absolute but must entail an "acceptable" level of risk, however and by whomever that level may be defined. In some cases the decision may be made by an "expert" risk manager, while in other cases it may be a function of the political process.

Selective aversion to certain risks may entail acceptance of other greater risks. For example, the use of new vaccines entails some risk, but a decision not to use them may be even riskier for the society as a whole. Therefore, the objective of public risk management should be minimization, not elimination, of risk-related costs.

"Public risks" is a term referring to distinctively high-tech hazards. Peter Huber has defined public risks as man-made "threats to human health or safety that are centrally or mass-produced, broadly distributed, and largely outside the individual risk bearer's direct understanding and control." "Private risks," on the other hand, are of natural origin or, if man-made, produced in relatively discrete units, with local impacts more or less subject to personal control. Hence, disease is a natural private risk, automobile accidents are man-made private risks, and effects of new technologies like recombinant DNA are public risks. Many public risks are latent, so that adverse effects do not appear until long after exposure. Such risks also are often diffuse in their impact, spread over many victims, so that the costs to any one victim may be small even though the aggregate costs to all victims may be very large. Two common characteristics of public risks are a potential for catastrophic costs and a low "subjective" probability (lacking a solid actuarial basis) of the catastrophic outcome. Together, these characteristics can produce a "zero-infinity dilemma" for risk managers dealing with problems such as the threat of a Chernobyl-type nuclear accident.

Technical experts tend to rank the risks of various technologies according to their estimates of annual fatalities. William Lowrance has shown that lay persons, on the other hand, tend to consider a greater number of factors in judging the seriousness of risks: involuntary exposure, delayed effects, "dreaded" versus common hazards, irreversible consequences, and others. The general public is more concerned than the experts about risks that have catastrophic potential, that are unfamiliar, uncontrollable, or involuntary, that threaten future generations, that would concentrate fatalities in time or space, that are distinctively threatening as opposed to widespread and shared by the general population, and that have human as opposed to natural origins.

Clayton Gillette and James Krier have analyzed possible reasons for these popular views. With respect to voluntariness, for example, they see underlying concerns about autonomy, equality, and power among individuals in the society. The special dislike for latency and irreversibility is explained by the fact that latency frustrates knowledge, and irreversibility frustrates control; both impair free choice. As for the bias against manmade rather than natural hazards, people are responsible only for artificial risks, not for natural ones, and the government's job is to regulate what people do. Finally, lay persons' "dread" of catastrophic events is related to notions of inequitable distributions of risk within the society or between generations.

There is constant pressure from some economists and politicians for requiring a "marginal cost-benefit, risk-versus-risk" approach in determining which risks to regulate, and to what extent. Advocates of this approach believe that risks should be controlled only where the economic benefits of regulation exceed the economic costs, and then at the level where marginal benefits equal marginal costs. Since limited public resources constrain the number of risks that can be regulated, resources should be devoted to those interventions that will maximize net benefits. Critics of cost-benefit analysis challenge the reliability of monetary valuations of benefits such as lives saved, improved health, and biodiversity preserved. In addition, cost-benefit analysis (done by experts) takes no account of the variations between popular and expert views of the relative seriousness of different kinds of risks, as discussed in the preceding paragraphs.

B. JUDICIAL VIEWS CONCERNING MANAGEMENT OF UNCERTAIN RISKS

1.   EARLY LOWER COURT DECISIONS

A leading case on the problem of scientific uncertainty was Reserve Mining Co. v. EPA, 514 F.2d 492 (8th Cir.1975). Reserve Mining disposed of great quantities of mining byproducts by discharging them into Lake Superior. These materials contained asbestos, a known cause of cancer when inhaled. The district court ordered an immediate halt to all further discharges, which would have required closing the facility. On appeal, the Eighth Circuit considered three issues: (1) whether the ingestion of fibers, as opposed to inhalation, posed any health hazard, (2) whether that hazard was sufficiently great to justify judicial intervention, and (3) what form the remedy should take.

In considering the question of risk, the court was handicapped by a lack of scientific evidence. The district court had directed a study of the tissues of long-time Duluth residents to determine whether asbestos fibers were present. The plaintiffs' principal medical witness had testified that the study should disclose the presence of asbestos if indeed asbestos is absorbed by the body. Nevertheless, the study failed to indicate that Duluth residents had any greater amounts of asbestos in their tissues than did residents of Houston, where the water was free of asbestos fibers. Moreover, animal tests intended to determine whether ingested fibers penetrate into the body were inconclusive and produced conflicting results. On the other hand, strong evidence did exist that workers exposed to asbestos dust suffered from a moderately increased rate of gastrointestinal cancer. One possible explanation, according to expert witnesses, was that asbestos workers first inhaled the asbestos dust and then coughed up and swallowed the asbestos particles.

Taking all of this evidence together, the most the court could conclude was that public exposure to asbestos fibers "creates some health risk." The court was unable to conclude, however, that "the probability of harm is more likely than not."

The next issue to confront the court was whether this showing of harm was sufficient to satisfy the requirements of the Clean Water Act. The Act authorized suit by the federal government to abate discharges in interstate waters where the discharges "endanger ... the health or welfare of persons." (Compare § 504 of the current CWA, concerning "imminent and substantial endangerment"). After careful consideration of the statute, the court concluded that the requirement of a danger to public health was satisfied by the evidence before it.

The final question was the form of the relief. The district court had ordered an immediate halt to discharges. Because of the weakness of the evidence of harm, the cost to both industry and the public of closing the plant, and the company's willingness to spend $243 million to dispose of the materials more safely, the court held that closing the plant was unnecessary. Balancing the equities, the court ordered that Reserve be given a reasonable time to stop discharging its wastes into Lake Superior.

The *Reserve Mining* decision received strong support from the D.C. Circuit's opinion in Ethyl Corp. v. EPA, 541 F.2d 1 (D.C.Cir.1976) (en banc). That case involved § 211(c)(1)(A) of the Clean Air Act, which authorized EPA to regulate gasoline additives whose emission products "will endanger the public health or welfare." EPA determined that lead additives in gasoline presented "a significant risk of harm" to the public health and issued orders limiting the use of such additives. As in *Reserve Mining*, the court was faced with a high degree of scientific uncertainty. The uncertainty was not as to the harmfulness of lead emissions, which were well known to be toxic. Because human beings were exposed to multiple sources of lead, it was difficult to determine whether the incremental increase in the amount of lead in the environment due to gasoline additives had serious health effects. In upholding EPA, the court stressed that assessment of risks involves policy judgments rather than simply factual determinations. Thus, the court accorded substantial deference to EPA's conclusion. As the court explained:

Questions involving the environment are particularly prone to uncertainty. Technological man has altered his world in ways never before experienced or anticipated. The health effects of such alterations are often unknown, sometimes unknowable. While a concerned Congress has passed legislation providing for protection of the public health against gross environmental modifications, the regulators entrusted with the enforcement of such laws have not thereby been endowed with a prescience that removes all doubt from their decision making. Rather, speculation, conflicts, and theoretical extrapolation typify their every action. How else can they act, given a mandate to protect the public health but only a slight or non-existent data base upon which to draw? . . .

Undoubtedly, certainty is a scientific ideal—to the extent that even science can be certain of its truth. But certainty in the complexities of environmental medicine may be achievable only after the fact, when scientists have the opportunity for leisurely and isolated scrutiny of an entire mechanism. Awaiting certainty will often allow for only reactive, not preventive regulation. Petitioners suggest that anything less than certainty, that any speculation, is irresponsible. But when statutes seek to avoid environmental catastrophe, can preventive, albeit uncertain, decisions legitimately be so labeled?

Thus, the court concluded that a rigorous, step-by-step proof of cause and effect should not be demanded where a statute is precautionary in nature, the evidence is on the frontiers of scientific knowledge, and regulations are designed to protect the public health. Hence, EPA may apply its expertise to draw conclusions from "suspected, but not completely substantiated" relationships between facts, from trends among facts, from theoretical projections, and so forth.

This approach was followed in numerous other lower court opinions. For example, in Lead Industries Association, Inc. v. EPA, 647 F.2d 1130 (D.C.Cir.1980), the D.C. Circuit upheld a primary air quality standard for lead that incorporated an "adequate margin of safety." In setting the margin of safety, EPA had given no consideration to feasibility or cost. Moreover, the evidence of harm was unclear. Nevertheless, the court held that feasibility and cost were irrelevant and that EPA had acted properly in setting the margin of safety. As the court explained, use of a margin of safety is an important method of protecting against effects that have not yet been uncovered by research and effects whose medical significance is a matter of disagreement. As the court also explained, "Congress has recently acknowledged that more often than not the 'margins of safety' that are incorporated into air quality standards turn out to be very modest or non-existent, as new information reveals adverse health effects at pollution levels once thought to be harmless." The court also reiterated the need for deference to EPA's expert judgments on these issues. Finally, the court held that the margin of safety requirement could be fulfilled by making conservative decisions at various points in the regulatory process, rather than by determining a safe level and adding a percentage to that as the "margin of safety."

In general, these lower court decisions demonstrated a high degree of deference to EPA's expert judgment. They gave little weight to questions of cost and feasibility when dealing with toxic chemicals. Finally, these courts recognized that administrative action was justified without a showing that harmful effects were more likely than not. Instead, the courts concluded that regulatory intervention was justified whenever a substantial possibility of danger could be found.

2.   SUPREME COURT DECISIONS

The Supreme Court has decided only two toxics cases. Before we consider these cases, it should be noted that they arose in a different context from most environmental issues. Both cases involved protection of workers by the Occupational Safety and Health Administration (OSHA). The cases thus involved a rather special kind of environmental problem, since the environments in question were not used by the general public.

The policy issues presented in OSHA cases are somewhat different from those in normal environmental cases. First, exposure to the risk is arguably more voluntary than is exposure to, say, ambient air pollution. Second, negotiations between the source of the hazard and the possible victims are feasible to a much greater extent than in the normal pollution case. This is especially true when the victims of the hazard, the employees, are represented by a union. Thus, the transaction costs of private settlements are sometimes much smaller here. Third, the possible victims of the hazard have a much greater stake in the economic health of the enterprise creating the hazard than is the case generally in environmental disputes. The option of closing the plant down in order to end the hazard is generally not acceptable to the workers, nor are actions that would seriously jeopardize the prospects for continued employment. For all of these reasons, the balance between protection from risks and economic cost may be different than in the normal environmental case.

Moreover, the statutory scheme is primarily concerned with quite different problems of worker protection. The only provision dealing expressly with toxic chemicals is § 6(b)(5) of the Act, 29 U.S.C.A. § 655(b)(5). This provision requires the agency to set a standard for any toxic material "which most adequately assures, to the extent feasible, that no employee will suffer material impairment of health or functional capacity...." Another section of the Act, § 3(8), 29 U.S.C.A. § 652(8), was thought to be relevant by at least some members of the Court. This section simply defines an occupational safety and health standard as a regulation setting any one of a variety of requirements "reasonably necessary or appropriate to provide safe or healthful places of employment." These provisions provide less guidance than most of the analogous provisions of the Clean Air Act or Clean Water Act. In short, both the statutory context and the policy choices presented in this area are atypical.

The Supreme Court's first encounter with the problem of toxic chemicals was Industrial Union Department, AFL–CIO v. American Petroleum Institute, 448 U.S. 607 (1980). (This decision is generally known as the "benzene case.") The case involved an OSHA regulation governing benzene. Benzene was acknowledged to be a carcinogen, and no safe level of exposure was known. On this basis, the Secretary of Labor had set the permissible exposure level for workers at 1 ppm (part per million), which he considered the lowest feasible level. OSHA estimated the total cost of compliance as including $266 million in capital investments, $200 million in first-year startup costs, and $34 million in annual costs. About 35,000 employees would benefit from the regulation. The Fifth Circuit had struck down the regulation on the theory that the statute implicitly required a cost-benefit analysis by the agency. On review, only one member of the Supreme Court reached this issue; another member of the Court went off on a constitutional ground; and the Court divided 4 to 4 on another statutory issue.

The primary opinion was written by Justice Stevens but was joined in its entirety by only two other Justices, Burger and Stewart, who are no longer on the Court. Justice Powell, also now retired, joined parts of the opinion. This plurality opinion resolved the case on the basis of an interpretation of § 3(8) as a limitation on § 6(b). According to the plurality opinion, § 3(8) requires that OSHA make a threshold finding of a "significant risk of harm" before issuing any regulation. On close examination of the record, the plurality observed that the industry had argued that the regulation would save at most two lives every six years. The Court declined to determine whether the risk level alleged by industry would be considered significant, since the agency itself had made no finding on this issue, which the plurality thought to be a critical requirement of the Act.

The plurality opinion went to some lengths to rebut the dissent's charge that the plurality's approach would prevent effective regulation until deaths had actually occurred. First, the plurality stated that what constitutes a "significant" risk was a judgment for the agency to make and plainly involved policy considerations. Second, the plurality noted that the agency's findings need not be supported by "anything approaching scientific certainty." The agency must be given "some leeway" when its findings are made on the frontiers of scientific knowledge. Thus, the plurality concluded:

[S]o long as they are supported by a body of reputable scientific thought, the Agency is free to use conservative assumptions in interpreting the data with respect to carcinogens, risking error on the side of over-protection rather than under-protection.

In a concurring opinion, Chief Justice Burger was careful to stress the limitations of the plurality opinion:

A holding that the Secretary must retrace his steps with greater care and consideration is not to be taken in derogation of the scope of legitimate Agency discretion. When the facts and arguments have been presented and duly considered, the Secretary must make a policy judgment as to whether a specific risk of health impairment is significant in terms of the policy objectives of the statute. When he acts in this capacity, pursuant to the legislative authority delegated by Congress, he exercises the prerogatives of the legislature— to focus on only one aspect of a larger problem, or to promulgate regulations that, to some, may appear as imprudent policy or inefficient allocation of resources. The judicial function does not extend to substantive revision of regulatory policy.

The Chief Justice noted, however, that "[p]erfect safety is a chimera; regulation must not strangle human activity in the search for the impossible."

Justice Powell was the only member of the Court to reach the cost-benefit issue. He agreed with the plurality opinion's reading of the statute. He also concluded, however, that the Agency was required to give fuller consideration to cost than it had done.

Thus, four Justices, three of whom are no longer on the Court, based their votes on statutory grounds. The decisive fifth vote was cast by then-Justice Rehnquist, now deceased, who reached his decision on constitutional grounds. He concluded that Congress had in fact provided no standard at all concerning the threshold requirements for regulation. He believed that Congress was simply unwilling to decide the relative weights to be given to protection of human life versus economic cost. Because Congress had failed to make this basic policy decision, Justice Rehnquist argued that the statute was an unconstitutional delegation of legislative authority to the agency. This view was out of line with the Supreme Court's decisions over the preceding half century. Not since the Court's unsuccessful attempt to block the New Deal has the Court struck down a statute on this basis. See Whitman v. American Trucking Ass'ns, 531 U.S. 457 (2001), page 106 supra.

Justice Marshall wrote a stinging dissent, joined by Justices Brennan, White, and Blackmun. All have since left the Court. Justice Marshall found it incredible that the plurality could read any substantive meaning into the statutory definition of a health standard as one "reasonably necessary" to provide safe employment. In his view, the relevant section of the statute was plainly § 6, and the meaning of that section was clear: in dealing with any toxic chemical, the Secretary was to set a standard that would *ensure* that no risk would be presented to any employee. Furthermore, Justice Marshall argued that the "plurality's discussion of the record in this case is both extraordinarily arrogant and extraordinarily unfair." In his view, the Court was usurping the agency's power to make factual findings and was mischaracterizing virtually every aspect of the agency's decision. He concluded by accusing the plurality of "an extreme reaction to a regulatory scheme that, as the members of the plurality perceived it, imposed an unduly harsh burden on regulated industries."

This decision clearly left the law in a state of confusion. Four Justices, only one of whom is still on the Court, believed that a "significant risk" finding was required by the statute. Four other Justices, all of whom have now left the Court, disagreed, while former Justice Rehnquist believed that the statute was completely silent on the problem. Moreover, to the extent that the plurality approach represented the law, its meaning was quite unclear. In particular, the test for a "significant risk" was not stated with clarity. Finally, the standard used by the plurality seemed to be set too high. The plurality said a one-in-a-thousand risk "might well" be considered significant. As applied to the general population, such a risk level would mean approximately 300,000 deaths. How many additional deaths would be required before the plurality would find a risk *clearly* significant?

The Supreme Court's second OSHA decision did little to clarify this issue. That case, American Textile Manufacturers Institute, Inc. v. Donovan, 452 U.S. 490 (1981), was decided one year after the benzene case. *Textile Manufacturers* involved a standard regulating cotton dust. Cotton dust is the cause of a disease called byssinosis, more commonly known as "brown lung" disease. The primary issue before the Supreme Court was whether the agency was required to engage in a cost-benefit analysis when issuing its regulation. In an opinion by Justice Brennan, the Court held that no cost-benefit analysis was necessary. According to the Court, all that was necessary under OSHA was a *feasibility* analysis, that is, an analysis showing that performance was economically possible, not an analysis comparing the cost of compliance with the benefits of the regulation. In footnote 30, citing only the Consumer Product Safety Act of 1972, not an environmental law, the Court said, "In other statutes, Congress has used the phrase 'unreasonable risk,' accompanied by explanation in legislative history, to signify a generalized balancing of costs and benefits."

The benzene case was discussed only in two footnotes of *Textile Manufacturers*. The discussion was not very helpful, because the risk issue in *Textile Manufacturers* was easy to resolve. OSHA had expressly found that "exposure to cotton dust presents a significant health hazard to employees." Data relied on by the agency showed that 25% of all industry employees suffered at least low-grade byssinosis, and that even at the level required by the new standard, about half this many employees would suffer from the disease. Thus, the prevalence of the disease "should be significantly reduced" by the new regulation. As the Court said, "It is difficult to imagine what else the Agency could do to comply with this Court's decision in [the benzene case]."

The result of the two OSHA decisions is that, under that statute, consideration of risk and cost is bifurcated: the agency first decides whether there is currently a "significant risk," and then regulates to the extent "feasible."

The implications of these OSHA decisions for toxics regulation under other environmental laws were unclear. The four dissenters in the benzene case clearly endorsed the approach previously taken by lower courts in cases like *Reserve Mining*. The members of the plurality in the benzene case took a more cautious view, but did not squarely reject the then-prevailing approach in the lower courts. One member of the Court, Justice Rehnquist, never spoke to the merits of any of these issues. Eight members of the present Court were not involved in either of these decisions.

3. LATER LOWER COURT DECISIONS

Two court of appeals decisions since the Supreme Court's OSHA cases raised questions concerning the continuing authority of *Reserve Mining* and its progeny. Most importantly, to what extent may the plurality's "significant risk" regulatory threshold in *Industrial Union* now be applied in non-OSHA toxics cases? Also, in light of footnote 30 of the *Textile Manufacturers* opinion, concerning cost-benefit analysis, when may lower courts require agencies to engage in such analysis under other environmental laws?

In NRDC v. EPA, 824 F.2d 1146 (D.C.Cir.1987) (en banc), EPA had refused to set a zero-emission limitation for vinyl chloride, though acknowledging that such a standard seemed to be the only one that would offer complete safety from ambient exposure to this apparently non-threshold carcinogen. Section 112 of the Clean Air Act then required the Administrator to regulate hazardous air pollutants "at a level which in his judgment provides an ample margin of safety to protect public health." Rejecting both plaintiffs' demand for a zero-emission standard and EPA's feasibility/cost-benefit approach, the court held that the Administrator was required to make an initial determination of what was "safe," based exclusively upon his determination of the risk to health at a particular emission level. Citing the plurality opinion in *Industrial Union*, the court of appeals said specifically that "safe" need not mean "risk-free." Rather, the Administrator's decision should be based upon "expert judgment" regarding the level of emissions that would result in an "acceptable" risk to health. Only after this degree of "safety" was assured could the Administrator consider what was an "ample margin," taking into account the inherent limitations of risk assessment and the limited scientific knowledge of the effects of exposure to carcinogens at various levels. At that point he could "diminish" (but not increase) the statistically determined "safe" level of risk by setting the regulatory standard at the lowest feasible level.

The Clean Air Act Amendments of 1990 included a totally new § 112, similar in approach to § 307 of the Clean Water Act, page 150 supra. Under § 112(d), EPA now must establish emission standards for hazardous air pollutants requiring maximum achievable control technology (MACT), while under § 307(a), toxic water pollutants are subject to effluent limitations based on best available technology (BAT) economically achievable. However, under both of these sections, where necessary to protect health, EPA may impose more stringent standards based on an "ample margin of safety." The latter standard is the same as the one involved in the vinyl chloride case, so the decision in that case continues to be relevant.

The other important lower court decision regarding regulation of toxic chemicals is Corrosion Proof Fittings v. EPA, 947 F.2d 1201 (5th Cir.1991). This case was decided under the Toxic Substances Control Act (TSCA, pages 201–208 infra). The factual finding necessary to trigger the regulatory provisions of § 6(a) of TSCA is that there is a reasonable basis to conclude that the chemical substance presents an "unreasonable risk" of injury to health or the environment. Having made such a finding, EPA may by rule apply one or more of seven types of restrictions listed in § 6(a) "to the extent necessary to protect adequately against such risk using the least burdensome requirements." The restrictions range from prohibiting the manufacture or distribution of the chemical (most burdensome) to directing the manufacturer to give notice of the risk of injury (least burdensome). Section 6(c) mandates a hybrid rulemaking procedure, including informal hearings and a limited right of cross-examination. Under § 19(c), a court of appeals must set aside a rule adopted under § 6 if the court finds that the rule is not supported by "substantial evidence in the rulemaking record."

In *Corrosion Proof Fittings*, the court vacated a final EPA rule that would have prohibited the manufacture, importation, processing, and distribution of asbestos in almost all products. The rule was ten years in the making and represented the first time EPA had used its authority under § 6 to place a comprehensive ban on a dangerous substance. The court held that EPA had violated TSCA by not considering adequately the benefits and costs of less burdensome alternatives to a complete ban, by not allowing public comment and cross-examination on methodology adopted at the last minute by EPA to support its benefits calculation, and by not evaluating the toxicity of likely substitute products (some of which were also carcinogens) that would replace asbestos in its various applications.

The court emphasized that TSCA is not a "zero-risk" statute, and that the substantial evidence standard for judicial review under TSCA is less deferential than the arbitrary and capricious standard of the Administrative Procedure Act. The court said that while agency rules have a presumption of validity, "[t]he burden remains on the EPA ... to justify that the products it bans present an unreasonable risk, no matter how regulated," citing the plurality opinion in *Industrial Union*.

With respect to cost-benefit analysis, the court said:

That the EPA must balance the costs of its regulations against their benefits is reinforced by the requirement that it seek the least burdensome regulation. While Congress did not dictate ... an exhaustive, full-scale cost-benefit analysis, it did require the EPA to consider both sides of the regulatory equation, and it rejected the notion that the EPA should pursue the reduction of workplace risk at any cost.   See *American Textile Mfrs. Inst.*, n.30 ("unreasonable risk" statutes require a "generalized balancing of costs and benefits").

The court reacted unfavorably to the fact that EPA's benefit-cost analysis resulted in figures as high as $74 million per life saved.   For example, EPA said that its ban on asbestos pipe would save three lives over 13 years at a cost of $128–227 million; that its ban on asbestos shingles would cost $23–34 million to save 0.32 statistical lives; that its ban on asbestos coatings would cost $46–181 million to save 3.33 lives; and that its ban of asbestos paper products would save 0.60 lives at a cost of $4–5 million.   The court said, "[U]ntil an agency 'can provide substantial evidence that the benefits to be achieved by [a regulation] bear a reasonable relationship to the costs imposed by the reduction, it cannot show that the standard is reasonably necessary.' "

What is the current precedential value of *Reserve Mining* and its progeny, pages 172–177 supra, after the *Industrial Union, Textile Manufacturers*, vinyl chloride, and *Corrosion Proof Fittings* decisions? The approach of *Reserve Mining* and *Ethyl Corp.* still seems to be followed in cases arising under the "imminent hazard" provisions of the Clean Air and Clean Water Acts and of RCRA (pages 228–231, 262–264 infra).   *Lead Industries* involved a CAA regulatory standard ("adequate margin of safety") similar to that in the vinyl chloride case ("ample margin of safety"), and the court in both cases refused to consider feasibility or cost. This approach to implementation of purely health-based statutory standards was upheld by the Supreme Court in 2001, Whitman v. American Trucking Ass'ns, page 106 supra. Thus the cost-benefit approach of *Corrosion Proof Fittings* (and footnote 30 of *Textile Manufacturers*) seems most relevant to TSCA and to FIFRA (page 193 infra), which also regulates "unreasonable risks."

*

CHAPTER 5

TOXIC CHEMICALS, GENETICALLY MODIFIED ORGANISMS, AND HAZARDOUS WASTES

Sections A, B, and C of this chapter examine federal regulation of agricultural pesticides, other toxic chemicals, and products of biotechnology. Sections D-1, 2, and 3 concern regulation of hazardous wastes. Sections D-4, E, and H discuss civil liability for cleanups of waste disposal sites and for personal injuries and property damage caused by toxic chemicals and hazardous wastes. Section F outlines federal requirements that businesses publicly report toxic chemical inventories, usage, manufacture, and releases. Section G analyzes criminal liability under RCRA, the Clean Water Act, and other federal environmental laws.

A. PESTICIDE REGULATION

The earliest toxic chemical problem to receive widespread public attention was that of pesticides, thanks in large part to Rachel Carson's *Silent Spring*. The principal federal statute regulating pesticides is the Federal Insecticide, Fungicide and Rodenticide Act (FIFRA). Congress amended

FIFRA in 1972 by enacting the Federal Environmental Pesticide Control Act, 7 U.S.C.A. § 136, which then was amended substantially in 1975, 1978, 1988, 1990, and 1996. In its present form, FIFRA provides a comprehensive framework for regulating the sale and distribution of pesticides within the United States.

Under the statute, a pesticide may receive EPA approval only if it "will not generally cause unreasonable adverse effects on the environment" when used in accordance with any EPA-imposed restrictions and "with widespread and commonly recognized practice." 7 U.S.C.A. § 136a(5)(D). "Unreasonable adverse effects on the environment" are defined to include "any unreasonable risk to man or the environment, taking into account the economic, social, and environmental costs and benefits of the use of any pesticide." § 136(bb). With few exceptions, FIFRA prohibits the sale, distribution, and professional use of unregistered pesticides. §§ 136a(a), 136j(a)(1).

Because of the explicit requirement of a cost-benefit analysis, FIFRA's "unreasonable adverse effects" standard is unusual among federal environmental statutes: most others employ risk-based standards qualified only by the availability of control technologies. (But see TSCA, pages 201–208 infra.) By disregarding the benefits of the regulated substances, the risk-based statutes provide more protection to health and the environment and less protection to industry than do FIFRA and TSCA.

As part of a registration, EPA must classify the pesticide for either "general" or "restricted" use. § 136a(d). Restrictions relate to such factors as methods of application, qualifications of applicators, amounts to be used, geographic areas of use, and species of targeted pests. EPA may "conditionally" register a pesticide if the pesticide and its proposed use are similar to any currently registered pesticide and use thereof or differ only in ways that would not significantly increase the risk of unreasonable adverse effects. A pesticide containing an active ingredient not contained in any currently registered pesticide also may be conditionally registered for a period reasonably sufficient for the generation of required data if EPA determines that use of the pesticide during such period will not cause any unreasonable adverse effects on the environment and that use of the pesticide is in the public interest. § 136a(c)(7).

Once registered, pesticides are still subject to continuing scrutiny by EPA. § 136d. Indeed, § 6 of FIFRA requires EPA to cancel a pesticide's registration after the first five years in which the registration has been effective (and at the conclusion of subsequent five-year periods if the registration is renewed) "unless the registrant, or other interested person with the concurrence of the registrant, ... requests ... that the registration be continued in effect." § 136d(a). And at any time, EPA may propose cancellation of a registration and initiate elaborate cancellation proceedings if "it appears to the Administrator that a pesticide ... does not comply with [FIFRA] or . . . generally causes unreasonable adverse effects on the environment." § 136d(b).

During the pendency of cancellation proceedings, the registration remains in effect unless EPA "suspend[s] the registration of the pesticide immediately." § 136d(c). But before suspending, EPA must determine that an "imminent hazard" exists—that continued use of the pesticide during the time required for cancellation proceedings "would be likely to result in unreasonable adverse effects on the environment." § 136(*l*). Even then, FIFRA guarantees registrants the right to an expedited administrative hearing on that issue, and the pesticide's registration remains effective during this latter proceeding. § 136d(c)(2). Only if EPA determines that "an emergency exists that does not permit [it] to hold a hearing before suspending" may the agency ban sale of the pesticide in advance of administrative proceedings. § 136d(c)(3).

While commerce in unregistered pesticides is generally prohibited, EPA may permit continued sale and use of existing stocks of pesticides whose registrations have been cancelled, provided that it determines that the sale or use is "not inconsistent with the purposes of this subchapter and will not have unreasonable adverse effects on the environment." § 136d(a)(1).

In a series of opinions arising out of disputes between EPA and the Environmental Defense Fund, the D.C. Circuit has created an extensive case law applying FIFRA. These opinions have established a number of rules concerning the burden of proof in suspension and cancellation proceedings. Once EPA decides to issue a notice of cancellation, a presumption arises in favor of suspension. The suspension decision is analogous to the issuance of a preliminary injunction and calls for a balancing of the equities. Issuance of a notice of cancellation shows that a substantial question of safety exists and requires suspension in the absence of countervailing benefits. (Conceivably, EPA could find that the evidence of risk was just strong enough to justify cancellation proceedings but that the danger was not quite immediate enough to justify suspension.) When EPA does suspend registration, a presumption will arise in favor of cancellation if (a) no benefit is shown or (b) animal tests show that the chemical causes cancer. Moreover, if evidence shows that one mode of exposure is hazardous, a presumption arises that all modes are hazardous until proven otherwise. Thus, for example, if inhalation of a chemical is dangerous, there is a presumption that ingestion of the chemical would also be dangerous.

Although these presumptions were developed on a somewhat ad hoc basis in a series of cases, the cases do have a unifying rationale when viewed as a group. In each case, the court has held that the burden of proof is on the manufacturer once substantial evidence of a health hazard has been shown. Essentially, once EPA has found sufficient evidence of risk to justify initiation of cancellation proceedings, the burden is on the proponent of continued registration to demonstrate that the risk is minimal or that the benefits of use outweigh the risks.

Stricter state and local regulation of pesticide use is permissible, i.e., is not preempted by FIFRA. Wisconsin Public Intervenor v. Mortier, 501 U.S. 597 (1991). However, § 136v(b) of FIFRA provides that a state "shall not impose . . . any requirements for labeling or packaging in addition to or different from those required under this subchapter." In Bates v. Dow Agrosciences LLC, 544 U.S. 431 (2005), the Court authorized a state tort action for mislabeling, brought under Texas law by Texas peanut farmers who alleged that their crops were damaged by a pesticide called "Strongarm." Dow moved to dismiss the case on the ground that FIFRA preempted such state law claims, but the Court held that as long as a state labeling law is "equivalent to, and fully consistent with," FIFRA's provisions, the state action may proceed.

Despite the requirements of FIFRA, supplemented in some situations by stronger state and local regulations, suspensions and cancellations of registered pesticides have been rare. For example, in 1995 it was reported that, of some 10,000 pesticides approved for use in California, fewer than 50 had been banned since 1970. The occasion for this report was the temporary lifting of a suspension by EPA to allow use of the pesticide for one more growing season to exhaust existing domestic supplies of more than 200,000 pounds of the material.

Pesticides in and on *raw* agricultural commodities are regulated under the Federal Food, Drug and Cosmetic Act (FFDCA), 21 U.S.C.A. § 301 et seq. EPA sets *tolerance* levels (regulatory standards) for pesticide concentrations in or on commodities consumed in the United States; the Food and Drug Administration implements those standards, monitoring actual pesticide *content* of commodities, with power to confiscate foods containing either excessive concentrations of registered pesticides or unsafe residues of unregistered pesticides. 21 U.S.C.A. §§ 342, 346a. Under § 346a, EPA is to consider, when establishing tolerances, "the necessity for the production of an adequate, wholesome, and economical food supply" as well as health effects.

When a tolerance has been established for use of a pesticide on a raw agricultural commodity, the FFDCA allows for the "flow-through" of such pesticide residue to *processed* foods, even if the pesticide is a carcinogen. This flow-through is allowed only to the extent that the concentration of the pesticide in the processed food does not exceed the concentration allowed in the raw food. § 342(a)(2)(C). Before 1996, § 409, known as the "Delaney clause," mandated a zero-risk standard for carcinogenic pesticides in processed foods if the pesticide concentrated further during processing or was applied during or after processing. In Les v. Reilly, 968 F.2d 985 (9th Cir.1992), the court refused to imply an exception for "reasonable risks" in the language of the Delaney clause. The court said that the FFDCA unambiguously provided that pesticides concentrated in processed foods were to be treated as food additives, and that if such pesticides induced cancer in humans or animals, they rendered the food "adulterated" and must be prohibited.

The significance of *Les v. Reilly* for toxics regulation in general seems to be that if Congress prescribes a clear and unambiguous risk standard, courts and regulatory agencies may not disregard it in the name of "reason" or of judicial or administrative discretion. This is reminiscent of the Supreme Court's decision in *TVA v. Hill*, the snail darter case under the Endangered Species Act, page 23 supra.

With respect to the FFDCA, however, in 1996 Congress amended the Act to exempt pesticide chemical residues from the Delaney clause. Food Quality Protection Act of 1996, amending FFDCA § 408, 21 U.S.C.A. § 346a. For such residues, the Delaney distinction between "carcinogen" and "noncarcinogen" was replaced with a new distinction between "threshold" and "nonthreshold" toxicants. The "general rule," for threshold toxicants, is that the EPA Administrator may establish a tolerance for a residue in or on a food if she determines that the tolerance is "safe," i.e., "that there is a reasonable certainty that no harm will result from aggregate exposure to the pesticide chemical residue, including all anticipated dietary exposures and all other exposures for which there is reliable information." 21 U.S.C.A. § 346a(b)(2)(A). For nonthreshold toxicants, a tolerance must meet two sets of conditions, one concerning the health risks posed by the residue and a second concerning the economic benefits from use of the pesticide chemical that produces the residue. 21 U.S.C.A. § 346(b)(2)(B).

The 1996 amendments also require that, in establishing a tolerance for a pesticide chemical residue, the Administrator (i) shall assess the risk of the residue based on available information about consumption patterns (exposure) among infants and children, and about their special susceptibility to the residue, and (ii) shall ensure that there is a reasonable certainty that no harm will result to infants and children from aggregate exposure to the residue. 21 U.S.C.A. § 346a(b)(2)(C).

B. THE TOXIC SUBSTANCES CONTROL ACT

Prior to 1976, federal regulation of most toxics consisted of an assortment of specialized provisions, most of them contained in statutes whose main focus was elsewhere. The potential for regulatory gaps was obvious. In 1976, Congress moved to fill these gaps by passing the first comprehensive legislation governing toxic substances. Unfortunately, the statute is hardly a masterpiece of insightful policymaking or incisive drafting.

The aim of the Toxic Substances Control Act (TSCA) was to prevent "unreasonable risks of injury to health or the environment" associated with the manufacture, processing, distribution, use, or disposal of chemical substances other than drugs and pesticides. TSCA's emphasis is on regulating products rather than wastes. Today's policy of *pollution prevention* and of avoiding environmental and health problems by front-end regulation of chemical production and use is the same policy that underlies TSCA.

The Act as a whole must be read in light of the policy section, § 2(b). Three policies are set forth. First, data should be developed on the environmental effects of chemicals; primary responsibility for the development of these data is placed on industry. Second, the government should have adequate authority to prevent unreasonable risks of injury to health or the environment, particularly imminent hazards. Finally, this authority should be exercised so as "not to impede unduly or create unnecessary economic barriers to technological innovation while fulfilling the primary purpose of this Act to assure that . . . such chemical substances . . . do not present an unreasonable risk of injury." (Note the similarity to FIFRA's mandate to balance adverse effects on human health or the environment against economic and social benefits of the use of a pesticide.) Obviously, much depends on the relative weights given to these potentially conflicting goals of protecting technological development and assuring human and environmental safety.

The most important substantive provisions of the Act are found in §§ 4, 5, and 6. These sections concern testing, premanufacturing clearance, and regulation of manufacturing and distribution. We will consider only the main outlines of these provisions, without too much attention to the innumerable exemptions, exceptions, qualifications, and procedural details.

Section 4 relates to testing. It empowers the EPA to adopt rules requiring testing by manufacturers of substances. Such rules must be based on a finding that insufficient data are currently available concerning the substance, and that the substance may "present an unreasonable risk," "enter the environment in substantial quantities," or present a likelihood of "substantial human exposure." There are a variety of complicated procedural devices set out in exhaustive detail in the section. In addition to § 4, the statute contains several other provisions aimed at collection of information.

Section 5 requires a manufacturer to give notice to the EPA before manufacturing a new chemical substance, or manufacturing or processing any chemical substance for a "significant new use." If the substance is covered by a § 4 rule, the § 4 test results must be submitted along with the § 5 notice. For substances not covered by § 4, but listed by EPA as possibly hazardous, the manufacturer is to submit data it believes show the absence of any unreasonable risk of injury. Normally, the next step would be a § 6 proceeding. But if EPA finds that an unreasonable risk may be presented before a § 6 rule can be promulgated, it can issue a "proposed section 6 rule," which will be immediately effective; issue an administrative order prohibiting manufacture; or seek an injunction, § 5(f). Often, of course, EPA will not have sufficient information to make a definite finding about safety. EPA can then make findings similar to those triggering the § 4 testing rules and issue an administrative order prohibiting manufacture or use. (If a timely objection to the order is filed, however, EPA must seek injunctive relief, § 5(e).)

Section 6, unlike § 5, applies to all chemicals, not just to new chemicals or new uses. The finding necessary to trigger § 6 is that "there is a reasonable basis to conclude" that the substance "presents or will present an unreasonable risk of injury to health or the environment." Having made such a finding, EPA may by rule apply any of a number of restrictions "to the extent necessary to protect adequately against such risk using the least burdensome requirements," § 6(a). Obviously, much depends on whether more weight is given to the "protect adequately" standard or to the "least burdensome" standard. In general, § 6(c) directs EPA to use its powers under other statutes in preference to § 6. The effective date of a proposed rule may be accelerated if the EPA finds a likelihood of "an unreasonable risk of serious or widespread injury to health or the environment" before the effective date of the final rule. The requirements for acceleration under § 6(d), it should be noted, are somewhat different from those applicable to new chemicals under § 5(f).

One other provision that deserves mention is § 7, which allows EPA to obtain emergency judicial relief in cases of "imminent hazards." The Act also contains the usual panoply of provisions on civil and criminal penalties, judicial enforcement, judicial review, and preemption.

By 1983, EPA had only begun to put the statutory scheme into operation. It had compiled an inventory of 62,000 "old" chemicals. Using the inventory, an expert Interagency Testing Committee (ITC) had started to identify the riskiest existing chemicals and to designate them as high priority. Under § 4, EPA then was either to propose a testing rule for each such chemical or to decide that testing was not necessary. Of the first 33 priority chemicals recommended by the ITC, EPA concluded that no testing was necessary for about half. Although the agency had *proposed* testing rules for the others, it had not actually adopted any rules. Instead, it had adopted a policy of negotiating voluntary testing agreements with industry, though the agreements were not legally enforceable. NRDC v. EPA, 595 F.Supp. 1255 (S.D.N.Y.1984) held that this practice violated § 4, which directs that where the Administrator has made the findings specified in § 4(a)(1)(A) or (B), test rules "shall" be promulgated and shall identify the specific effects for which testing must be done, the test standards, and the deadlines for test completion and submission of data. This decision resulted in a complete revamping of EPA's procedures for negotiating test rules under § 4 of TSCA. The agency now seeks to make consent agreements enforceable on the same basis as test rules. 40 C.F.R. § 790.

Between 1976 and 2003, EPA issued only about 31 test rules, covering approximately 114 chemical substances and mixtures. See Physicians Committee for Responsible Medicine v. Horinko, 285 F.Supp.2d 430 (S.D.N.Y.2003). In that case, plaintiffs challenged EPA's voluntary testing program designed to generate toxicity data on some 2,800 high production volume (HPV) chemicals. The court denied cross-motions for summary judgment, holding that EPA was not required to promulgate a formal test rule unless it had made a finding, under § 4(a)(1), that the chemicals (A) may present an unreasonable risk to health or (B) may enter the environment in substantial quantities or present a likelihood of substantial human exposure. Although EPA had made no such explicit or formal findings of fact, the court ordered a trial on the question whether EPA had made the requisite "B-track" findings *de facto* for some of the 2,800 chemical substances and mixtures involved in the agency's HPV Challenge Program. Ultimately EPA won a summary judgment because the court held that the Administrator had not made such de facto B-track findings and therefore did not have a nondiscretionary duty to issue a formal test rule. Physicians Committee For Responsible Medicine v. Johnson, 436 F.3d 326 (2d Cir.2006).

Manufacturers sometimes challenge EPA test rules judicially, and the courts review in detail the agency's findings and reasons for demanding tests. See Chemical Manufacturers Ass'n v. EPA, 899 F.2d 344 (5th Cir.1990), in which a rule requiring manufacturers and processors of chemical cumene to perform toxicological testing was remanded for EPA to articulate the standards on the basis of which it found both the quantities of cumene entering the environment from the facilities in question and the potential human exposure to be "substantial."

The requirement that EPA issue a rule before requiring testing distinguishes TSCA from food, drug, and pesticide statutes, which mandate production of safety data prior to marketing. It seems that TSCA essentially establishes a presumption of safety, which EPA must overcome before it may even require further testing of a chemical.

Many of the problems concerning "new" chemicals have related to compliance with § 5's requirement that a "premanufacture notice" (PMN) be submitted to EPA before a chemical is manufactured or imported into the United States. The statute calls for submission of information on chemical identity, proposed use, anticipated production volume, expected byproducts, estimates of the number of people likely to be exposed during manufacture, and methods of disposal. Test results—and therefore tests—are not required unless the company has them on hand. (Other data on environmental and health effects must be submitted "insofar as known ... or reasonably ascertainable.")

If EPA decides that a PMN does not provide sufficient information on which to base the necessary determination of risk, the agency may request

more data. If such data are not provided, EPA can
take no action (thus allowing manufacture), issue
an order for additional information, or take steps to
limit production or use of the chemical.

The most important judicial interpretation of
TSCA to date occurred in Corrosion Proof Fittings
v. EPA, 947 F.2d 1201 (5th Cir.1991), discussed at
length in Chapter 4 supra at pages 188–190. EPA
had adopted a rule, under § 6, that would have
prohibited most uses of asbestos. The court held
that EPA had violated TSCA by not considering
adequately the benefits and costs of *less burdensome* alternatives to a complete ban, by not allowing
public comment and cross-examination on methodology adopted at the last minute to support its
benefits calculation, and by not evaluating the toxicity of likely *substitutes* for asbestos. Substantive-
ly, the court found that EPA had not provided
substantial evidence of an "unreasonable risk of
injury" to human health or the environment. *Corrosion Proof Fittings* raises serious doubts about the
usefulness of § 6 of TSCA to regulate individual
toxic chemicals.

C. REGULATION OF GENETICALLY MODIFIED ORGANISMS

Biotechnology has the potential to address some
of the greatest challenges facing the United States
and the world, including hunger, disease, and environmental degradation. Genetically modified crops
may yield increased agricultural efficiency, im-

proved nutrition, new medicines, and reduced environmental impacts. Genetically engineered animals may create cheaper food, provide organs or tissues for human transplants, and reduce pressures on wild animal populations.

On the other hand, biotechnology could have harmful consequences: threats to human health from new allergens or toxins, injury from incidental releases of genetically engineered pharmaceuticals or industrial compounds into the food supply, and ecological damage and loss of biodiversity from the introduction of invasive species.

Among ecologists the greatest source of apprehension is the potential hazards of introducing non-native organisms into a particular natural environment. Experience has shown that putting a non-native or "exotic" species into a new environment sometimes results in that species displacing native varieties and dominating the environment. GMOs introduced into new environments might have ecological impacts similar to those of exotic species. Theoretically, the GMOs may multiply and exchange genetic material, or hybridize, with other organisms. For example, corn that has been genetically modified to resist pesticides may pass the pesticide-resistant gene on to weeds, creating new ecological and farming problems.

Individual nations have taken different approaches to protecting the environment from possible adverse effects of GMO releases. Denmark and Germany follow a process-oriented approach, which views the technique of genetic engineering itself as a risk. Hence those countries regulate the use of DNA techniques, even if the end-product is not a GMO. On the other hand, the United States has adopted a product-specific approach. Its regulations are concerned not with the use of biotechnology techniques, but with the use of GMO end-products, such as foods or seeds. The GMO end-products are regulated like similar products created by more traditional techniques, under the statutory authority of FIFRA, FFDCA, TSCA, and the Federal Plant Protection Act, 7 U.S.C.A. § 7701 et seq.

The 1986 Coordinated Framework for Regulation of Biotechnology, issued by the U.S. Office of Science Technology Policy, divided jurisdiction over the environmental regulation of biotechnology among several federal agencies. EPA has primary responsibility. It treats biopesticides as chemical pesticides under FIFRA, page 193 supra, and other biotech products as new chemicals under TSCA, page 201 supra.

The Food and Drug Administration reviews genetically engineered food products for food safety under the FFDCA, pages 199–201 supra. The U.S. Department of Agriculture, through its Animal and Plant Health Inspection Service (APHIS), has authority to regulate the release of genetically modified plants, animals, and microorganisms under the Federal Plant Protection Act, which applies to but is not limited to products of genetic engineering.

Under current regulations, APHIS approves *field testing* of transgenic plants through a "notification" process, in which applicants notify the agency that a plant meets general guidelines for not causing unwanted environmental effects. If the agency agrees, the plant can be grown while the company conducts further field testing to rule out adverse environmental effects. There is no public or independent scientific input in this process. Most biotech companies ready to begin *commercial production* of transgenic plants petition for "non-regulated" status, asking APHIS to determine that there is no environmental risk. As part of this process, APHIS conducts a formal environmental assessment that it publishes in the Federal Register, providing the public with a 60-day comment period. A committee of the National Academies' National Research Council has recommended that the public, including scientific peer reviewers, should be more involved in both these processes, and that ecological testing and monitoring should continue after commercial production of a transgenic plant has been approved.

Biotech companies also are developing genetically modified *animals* for human consumption. They include pigs that produce leaner pork chops and less harmful manure, meatier chickens, disease-resistant shrimp, and fast-growing salmon and catfish. It is not clear how, and by whom, releases of such creatures will be regulated. With respect to the salmon, which are expected to be the first such modified animals to be marketed commercially, only the Food and Drug Administration seems to have asserted regulatory authority, which FDA claimed by designating the fish's foreign genes and the growth hormone they produce as a "new animal drug." EPA and the Department of Agriculture bowed out, leaving critics concerned that while FDA may be rigorous in examining food safety, it is not qualified to evaluate the ecological risks posed by releases of transgenic salmon into oceans. For example, according to one study, if wild female salmon preferred to mate with genetically engineered males, and if those matings produced offspring that did not survive well, wild populations could be wiped out—a result known as the "Trojan gene effect." In many species of fish, females prefer larger males as mates, setting the scene for an advantage for growth-enhanced fish.

The New York Times reported (Andrew Pollack, *Without U.S. Rules, Biotech Food Lacks Investors*, N.Y. Times, July 30, 2007, p. 1) that business uncertainty from under-regulation of biotech foods has discouraged private investment in that industry. As a result, the FDA was beginning to "get serious" about drafting new rules to determine whether and how genetically engineered fish, meat and milk can safely enter the nation's food supply So far, contrary to the practice in Europe, the FDA does not require that such foods be labeled as containing GMOs.

In general, it seems that current U.S. regulation of GMOs—relying on three agencies operating under at least three different statutes with overlapping jurisdiction, none designed with GMOs as a primary focus—has resulted in haphazard and incomplete regulatory policy with no clear standards to guide agency decisions on whether a GMO should be permitted to be released into the environment. It would be better to replace the 1986 Coordinated Framework for Regulation of Biotechnology with a new, comprehensive law regulating all releases of transgenic materials. However, such a change is politically unlikely unless the biotechnology industry itself concludes that its own self-interest would be advanced by greater regulatory clarity and efficacy.

D. THE RESOURCE CONSERVATION AND RECOVERY ACT (RCRA)

Enacted in 1976, RCRA was a response to growing public awareness of serious problems related to disposal of hazardous wastes. According to EPA estimates, 290 million tons of hazardous wastes were produced in the United States in 1981. The principal industries generating the wastes were chemicals and petroleum (71%) and metals (22%). The wastes included organic materials from industrial processes (e.g., benzene and PCBs), heavy metals, biological wastes with bacterial and viral contaminants, sludge (the solid or semisolid byproduct of most air and water pollution control methods), and various chemicals.

Before RCRA, many such wastes were stored or disposed of at sites where water contamination could occur, for example, sites located in flood-plains, over aquifers unprotected by impervious rock or soil, and in filled wetlands. Water filtering through such sites can leach chemicals into ground-water, and surface runoff from rain and snowmelt can carry chemicals to nearby streams. In either case, the result may be impairment or destruction of public water supplies.

Congress was confronted with the dual problems of dealing with serious threats posed by many existing waste disposal sites, and regulating future disposal activities so as not to multiply those threats. The lawmakers responded by enacting RCRA in 1976 and, thereafter, the Comprehensive Environmental Response, Compensation, and Liability Act of 1980 (CERCLA).

RCRA was primarily a forward-looking statute. Most of its provisions were aimed at creating a regulatory program to control future waste treatment, storage, and disposal (TSD) activities. However, it also was retrospective, imposing civil liability upon past contributors to TSD facilities that currently present an "imminent and substantial endangerment" to health or the environment.

CERCLA was primarily backward-looking. Its main thrust was to create broad civil liability for cleanup of leaking TSD sites, most of which presumably were expected to antedate the implementation of RCRA's regulatory program. However, CERCLA also was forward-looking. It contained some regulatory provisions, including one requiring that persons in charge of TSD facilities notify EPA of any hazardous substance releases. More importantly, however, strict liability for cleanup of leaking sites provided a strong economic incentive for proper TSD activities by future generators and handlers of hazardous wastes.

1.   OVERVIEW OF THE ACT

The hazardous waste provisions of RCRA are contained in subtitle C, as amended in 1984 and 1986. Section 3001 requires EPA to promulgate criteria for "identifying the characteristics" of hazardous waste, and for "listing" hazardous wastes, which should be subject to RCRA regulation, "taking into account toxicity, persistence, and degradability in nature, potential for accumulation in tissue," and other hazardous traits such as corrosiveness and flammability. The remaining provisions of subtitle C relate to standards and enforcement.

Three sets of standards are required, covering generators, transporters, and disposal sites. EPA has broad authority to prescribe such standards "as may be required to protect human health and the environment." Certain types of standards are required. Section 3002 requires standards for generators of hazardous wastes covering recordkeeping, reporting, labeling, and use of appropriate containers. Section 3002(5) requires use of a "manifest" system to ensure that the hazardous waste generated by the source is ultimately processed on site or at a facility with a § 3005 permit. (A manifest is a list or invoice of cargo for a transporter, identifying the cargo and its intended destination.) The manifest system is incorporated into § 3003, which requires standards for transporters. (Transporters are also subject to recordkeeping and labeling requirements.) As the last phase of this "cradle-to-grave" system for hazardous wastes, § 3004 requires standards covering treatment, storage, and disposal (TSD) facilities. These standards cover compliance with the manifest system and other recordkeeping requirements. More importantly, they also cover TSD methods, as well as location, construction, and operation of disposal sites.

Under § 3004 (as amended in 1984), new landfills and surface impoundments, as well as expansions of existing units, must have double plastic liners, leachate collection systems, and groundwater monitoring facilities unless EPA specifically finds for a particular site that an alternative design or operating practice will be equally effective in preventing migration of hazardous substances into ground or surface water. The 1984 amendments also direct EPA to require the owner or operator of a disposal site to provide assurances of financial responsibility to comply with applicable regulatory standards. Assurances may consist of one or a combination of insurance, guarantee, surety bond, letter of credit, or qualification as a self-insurer.

An important feature of the 1984 amendments is that they shifted the focus of hazardous waste management away from land disposal to *treatment* alternatives. Section 1002(b)(7) now states that "land disposal ... should be the least favored method for managing hazardous wastes." Consistent with this, § 3004 prohibits hazardous wastes from being disposed of on land unless one of two conditions is satisfied: (1) EPA determines, "to a reasonable degree of certainty, that there will be no migration of hazardous constituents from the disposal unit ... for as long as the wastes remain hazardous," or (2) the waste is pretreated to meet standards established by EPA under § 3004(m). Pursuant to this subsection, EPA in 1986 issued regulations requiring that hazardous wastes be treated to levels achievable by application of "best demonstrated available technology" (BDAT).

A permit system established under § 3005 is the key enforcement provision for TSD facilities. EPA is given broad inspection powers, § 3007, and the power to issue compliance orders (with violators subject to civil penalties) or bring a civil action against violators of any requirement, § 3008. Criminal penalties are also available for violation of the permit requirements or falsification of documents, § 3008(d). Finally, RCRA makes careful provision for state regulation. Under a provision modeled on the Clean Water Act, states may assume responsibility for hazardous waste control, § 3006. State laws less stringent than federal requirements are preempted, § 3009.

One federal appeals court has held that where EPA authorizes a state to administer and enforce a hazardous waste program, and the state enforcement agency enters into a no-penalty settlement with a serious RCRA violator, § 3006 bars EPA from "overfiling," i.e., bringing a separate action based on the same violations. Harmon Industries, Inc. v. Browner, 191 F.3d 894 (8th Cir.1999). However, two other appeals courts have rejected *Harmon* and held that EPA's authorization of a state program does not strip the United States of civil or criminal enforcement authority because RCRA contemplates that only the federal regulatory or permitting program is supplanted by the state program. United States v. Power Engineering Co., 303 F.3d 1232 (10th Cir.2002); United States v. Elias, 269 F.3d 1003 (9th Cir.2001), *cert. denied*, 537 U.S. 812 (2002).

The 1984 amendments also provided for regulation of underground storage tanks containing petroleum products and other hazardous liquids such as solvents and pesticides, §§ 9001–9010. EPA regulations provide for detection and correction of leaks in existing tanks and establish performance standards for new tanks. The aim is to avoid groundwater pollution. 1986 amendments established a $500 million Leaking Underground Storage Tank Trust Fund, derived from federal taxes on motor fuels and to be used for correction of releases of petroleum when EPA cannot identify a financially responsible owner or operator of the tank who will undertake action properly.

2. "SOLID" AND "HAZARDOUS" WASTE DEFINED

RCRA's coverage extends to all "solid waste." However, the waste need not be in solid form. Section 1003(27) defines "solid waste" to include any garbage, refuse, sludge, "and other *discarded* material, including solid, liquid, semisolid, or contained gaseous material" (emphasis added), excluding, however, solid or dissolved materials in domestic sewage, irrigation return flows, or industrial discharges from point sources. The statutory exclusions leave large quantities of hazardous materials unregulated by RCRA.

An important issue is the extent to which RCRA covers materials that are *recycled* or held for future recycling. Can such materials be considered "discarded"? In American Mining Congress v. U.S. EPA, 824 F.2d 1177 (D.C.Cir.1987) (*AMC I*), a divided court held that Congress did not intend RCRA to regulate "spent" materials that are recycled and reused "in an *ongoing* manufacturing or industrial process." The majority said that such materials have not yet become "part of the waste disposal problem," but are *"destined for beneficial reuse or recycling in a continuous process by the generating industry itself."* In a dissent, Judge Mikva said that RCRA's definition of "disposal" encompasses more than just "discarding or throwing away." Rather, he said, the definition was "functional": waste is disposed of if it is put into contact with land or water in such a way as to pose the risk to health and the environment that moved Congress to adopt RCRA. "Simply because a waste is likely to be recycled will not ensure that it will not be spilled or leaked before recycling occurs."

Two subsequent decisions of the D.C. Circuit limited the effect of *AMC I*. In American Mining Congress v. U.S. EPA, 907 F.2d 1197 (D.C.Cir.1990) (*AMC II*), the court sided with EPA, saying: "*AMC*'s holding concerned only materials that are 'destined for *immediate reuse* in another phase of the industry's ongoing production process' [emphasis added], and that 'have not yet become part of the waste disposal problem.' Nothing in *AMC* prevents the agency from treating as 'discarded' the wastes at issue in this case, which are managed in land disposal units that *are* part of wastewater treatment systems, which *have* therefore become 'part of the waste disposal problem,' and which are *not* part of ongoing industrial processes."

In American Petroleum Institute v. U.S. EPA, 906 F.2d 729 (D.C.Cir.1990), the court held that even if materials are in fact recycled, they may already be considered wastes at the time of recycling and therefore subject to RCRA regulation. The court overturned an EPA determination that materials utilized in a metals reclamation process ceased to be solid waste when they arrived at a reclamation facility because they no longer were "discarded material." The court said that the materials were discarded before being subject to reclamation, and that they had become "part of the waste disposal problem."

Section 1004(5) of RCRA defines "hazardous waste" to mean a "solid waste, or combination of solid wastes, which because of its quantity, concentration, or physical, chemical, or infectious characteristics may (A) cause, or significantly contribute to an increase in mortality or an increase in serious irreversible, or incapacitating reversible, illness; or (B) pose a substantial present or potential hazard to human health or the environment when improperly treated, stored, transported, or disposed of, or otherwise managed." Under § 3001, EPA is to promulgate regulations identifying the *characteristics* of hazardous waste and *listing* particular hazardous wastes to be regulated under subtitle C, "taking into account toxicity, persistence and degradability in nature, potential for accumulation in tissue, and other related factors such as flammability, corrosiveness, and other hazardous characteristics."

EPA regulations provide two principal ways in which solid waste may be deemed to be "hazardous": by exhibiting one of four hazardous characteristics (*"characteristic* wastes"), or by being identified specifically as hazardous waste by EPA (*"listed* wastes"). 40 C.F.R. § 261.3. EPA has established four general categories of listed wastes (the "F," "K," "P," and "U" lists). On the "P" list are acutely hazardous chemical products. The "U" list includes non-acutely hazardous chemical products. The "F" and "K" lists of waste mixtures and combinations include wastes that meet the criteria for the "P" and "U" lists or one of the four "characteristics" (toxicity, ignitability, corrosivity, and reactivity). Within these lists, EPA has identified hundreds of specific types of wastes as "hazardous."

To prevent generators from evading hazardous waste regulations by diluting or otherwise changing the composition of listed wastes, EPA has adopted two important rules, the *"mixture"* rule and the *"derived-from"* rule. The former provides that a mixture of "listed" hazardous waste with other solid waste is also a hazardous waste. The derived-from rule provides that any solid waste "generated from the treatment, storage, or disposal of a hazardous waste ... (but not including precipitation runoff)" is hazardous waste.

Chemical Waste Management, Inc. v. U.S. EPA, 976 F.2d 2 (D.C.Cir.1989) concerned EPA's treatment standards for *leachate*, which is produced when liquid such as rainwater percolates through wastes stored in a landfill. The derived-from rule provided that leachate derived from hazardous waste was also a hazardous waste. The court held that EPA did not act arbitrarily and capriciously by mandating that environmental media (such as soils) contaminated by hazardous wastes must themselves be treated as hazardous wastes. The court said that the rule on contaminated soil was part of a coherent regulatory framework, "one application of a general principle, consistently adhered to, that a hazardous waste does not lose its hazardous character simply because it changes form or is combined with other substances."

The mixture and derived-from rules do not require that materials that are not really hazardous nevertheless be managed as hazardous waste. The derived-from rule merely establishes a presumption, which can be overcome, for example, by showing that a leachate is nonhazardous. EPA's regulations explicitly exempt a mixture that "no longer exhibits any characteristic of hazardous waste."

Edison Electric Institute v. U.S. EPA, 996 F.2d 326 (D.C.Cir.1993) demonstrates the complexity of formulating and applying rules pertaining to *characteristic* wastes, solid wastes that are not specifically "listed" by EPA as hazardous but that manifest one or more of the four characteristics (toxicity, ignitability, corrosivity, and reactivity) set out in EPA regulations for the purpose of identifying other (non-listed) hazardous wastes. EPA regulations prescribed a testing procedure, the Toxicity Characteristic Leaching Procedure (TCLP), for determining the "toxicity" characteristic of solid waste. The TCLP was based on a scenario involving disposal of toxic waste in an actively decomposing municipal landfill overlying a groundwater aquifer. The test required a waste generator to mix a sample of its waste with an acidic leaching medium and then to test the resulting liquid waste to see if it contained unsafe levels of toxic contaminants identified in the National Primary Drinking Water Standards. In *Edison*, generators of mineral processing wastes and manufactured gas plant wastes challenged EPA's application of the TCLP to their wastes. The court held that the TCLP did not bear a

rational relationship to the wastes in question because EPA had not shown that such wastes had
ever been disposed of in municipal landfills or in
any other manner that would cause them to come
into contact with an acidic leaching medium. The
court remanded to allow EPA to provide a fuller
and more reasoned explanation for its decision to
apply the TCLP to the wastes in question.

3.   THE LAND DISPOSAL BAN

When it amended RCRA in 1984, Congress sought
to discourage land disposal of hazardous waste.
Section 3004(d)(1) provided a staged prohibition on
land disposal of *untreated* hazardous waste unless
EPA "determines the prohibition of one or more
methods of land disposal of such waste is not required in order to protect human health and the
environment for as long as the waste remains hazardous."   In making these determinations, EPA
was directed to take into account the characteristics
of the waste, "the long-term uncertainties associated with land disposal," and the importance of encouraging proper management of hazardous waste
initially.   Sections 3004(d)(1), (e)(1), and (g)(5) limited EPA's discretion by specifying that a method of
land disposal may not be determined to be protec-
tive of human health and the environment "unless,
upon application by an interested person, it has
been demonstrated to the Administrator to a reasonable degree of certainty, that there will be *no
migration* of hazardous constituents from the dis-

posal unit or injection zone for as long as the wastes remain hazardous" (emphasis added).

Congress did not entirely ban the land disposal of wastes unable to meet this standard. It provided an exception for wastes treated to "substantially diminish the toxicity of the waste or substantially reduce the likelihood of migration of hazardous constituents from the waste so that short-term and long-term threats to human health and the environment are minimized." § 3004(m). The statute directed EPA to promulgate treatment standards specifying how waste otherwise subject to the "land ban" could satisfy the standard. Thus, the land disposal ban, in effect, applies to *untreated* hazardous wastes and authorizes EPA to require pretreatment of wastes that can not be shown to be capable of safe disposal on land in untreated form.

To prevent generators of hazardous waste from frustrating the land ban by simply storing waste indefinitely, § 3004(j) prohibits the *storage* of waste subject to the land disposal ban "unless such storage is solely for the purpose of the accumulation of such quantities of hazardous wastes as are necessary to facilitate proper recovery, treatment or disposal." In Edison Electric Institute v. U.S. EPA, 996 F.2d 326 (D.C.Cir.1993), electric power companies challenged EPA's interpretation of this section, making it unlawful to store "mixed" wastes for an indefinite period pending the development of adequate treatment techniques or disposal capacity. The companies contended that the interpretation was inconsistent with the statute and unreasonable as applied to generators of wastes containing both hazardous and radioactive components, for which there were then few lawful treatment or disposal options. EPA's regulations established a burden-shifting scheme for determining when storage would be viewed as "solely for the purpose of the accumulation of such quantities of hazardous waste as are necessary to facilitate proper recovery, treatment, or disposal." Basically, if waste was stored for longer than one year, the owner or operator had the burden of proving that the storage was solely for the purpose of accumulating sufficient quantities for proper recovery, treatment, or disposal. The court concluded that EPA's interpretation of § 3004(j) was consistent with RCRA's status as a "highly prescriptive, technology-forcing statute." The court said that RCRA's "draconian incentives" for the rapid development of adequate treatment and disposal capacity would be significantly diminished if generators could rely on the possibility of indefinite storage. The fact that technology may not be able to keep up with statutory timetables did not mean that the courts were at liberty to ignore them. Any relief would have to come from Congress.

Chemical Waste Management, Inc. v. U.S. EPA, 976 F.2d 2 (D.C.Cir.1992), *cert. denied*, 507 U.S. 1057 (1993), concerned the *extent* to which "characteristic" wastes must be *treated* prior to land disposal. The "NRDC petitioners" (environmental organizations and companies in the business of treating hazardous wastes) challenged EPA's decision not to require the use of "best demonstrated available technologies" (BDAT) in *all* situations. "Industry petitioners" (waste generators) objected to regulations mandating levels of treatment that in some situations went *beyond* removal of the characteristic (ignitability, corrosivity, reactivity, or toxicity) that had led to the waste's classification as hazardous. The court rejected the NRDC claim that some form of technology must be used to treat waste in *all* instances, and that dilution is never sufficient. The court found that RCRA does not bar *dilution* of ignitable, corrosive, or reactive (ICR) wastes, but merely defines the purposes that a method of treatment must achieve. The court also rejected the generators' argument that the moment a waste ceases to meet the regulatory definition of a hazardous waste, EPA loses its authority to regulate that waste any further. The court concluded that, in combination, subsections 3004(g)(5) and (m) provide EPA with authority to bar land disposal of certain wastes unless they have been treated to reduce risks *beyond* those needed to trigger the characteristics themselves. The rationale was that the environmental concerns related to wastes displaying the *toxic* characteristic are different from the concerns for ICR wastes. Toxic constituents can have a *cumulative* impact on land disposal, even where waste is below the characteristic level. On the other hand, treatment that removes the ICR characteristics "fully addresses the environmental concern from the properties themselves."

4. CIVIL LIABILITY: IMMINENT HAZARDS

In addition to EPA's regulatory powers, RCRA also gives EPA authority to seek injunctive relief under certain circumstances. Section 7003 provides:

Notwithstanding any other provision of this chapter, upon receipt of evidence that the past or present handling, storage, treatment, transportation or disposal of any solid waste or hazardous waste may present an imminent and substantial endangerment to health or the environment, the Administrator may bring suit on behalf of the United States in the appropriate district court against any person (including any past or present generator, past or present transporter, or past or present owner or operator of a treatment, storage, or disposal facility) who has contributed or who is contributing to such handling, storage, treatment, transportation, or disposal to restrain such person from such handling, storage, treatment, transportation, or disposal, to order such person to take such other action as may be necessary, or both.

Section 7002, the citizen suit provision, empowers "any person" to commence a civil action against parties whose past or present hazardous waste activities contribute to an imminent hazard, under a standard similar to that of § 7003. The two sections make RCRA important not only for dealing with present hazardous waste disposal activities but also as a complement to CERCLA in securing judicially mandated cleanups of abandoned disposal sites.

In applying the "imminent and substantial endangerment" standard, the courts have required only a relatively low level of danger as a trigger. Further, proof of actual harm is not necessary. Plaintiff need only prove that an existing dangerous condition creates a *risk* of harm to the environment or human health. Compare the decision in Reserve Mining Co. v. EPA, under the Clean Water Act, page 172 supra.

United States v. Waste Industries, Inc., 734 F.2d 159 (4th Cir.1984) is one of several important cases giving an expansive reading to the liability provisions of § 7003. The court noted that this section stands apart from other portions of RCRA defining EPA's regulatory authority, since § 7003 is designed to deal with situations in which the regulatory schemes break down or have been circumvented. Thus, § 7003 has a retrospective dimension—authorizing action against "inactive" sites to which wastes no longer are being added—whereas §§ 3001–3020 are prospective. Section 7003 (like § 7002) authorizes actions against persons who have "contributed" to the "handling, storage, treatment, transportation or disposal" of hazardous waste that may pose an imminent hazard. The court emphasized that inclusion, in § 1004(3), of the word "leaking" as one of the definitional components of "disposal" demonstrated that Congress intended the latter term to have "a range of meanings, including conduct, a physical state, and an occurrence." A person who in the past contributed to a present occurrence ("leaking") can be ordered not only to stop this "conduct" but also to "take such other action as may be necessary," e.g., to reimburse the government for cleanup costs, to monitor for and prevent further contamination, and to restore groundwater.

United States v. Northeastern Pharmaceutical & Chemical Co., Inc., 810 F.2d 726 (8th Cir.1986) held that § 7003 does not require a finding of fault or negligence in order to hold past offsite generators and transporters liable for response costs. Such parties are strictly liable even for acts of disposal that occurred before RCRA became effective in 1976. Persons liable as "contributors" can include *officers and employees* of corporate generators and transporters. Because the remedies available to the government under § 7003 are essentially equitable, defendants are not entitled to jury trials. Presumably the result would be the same in citizen suits under § 7002.

Among the citizen-suit provisions found in various federal environmental laws, § 7002 of RCRA is unique in authorizing suits by private and other non-EPA plaintiffs to abate potential imminent hazards. In Maine People's Alliance v. Mallinckrodt, Inc., 471 F.3d 277 (1st Cir.2006), *cert. denied*, 128 S.Ct. 93 (2007), the court said that "the combination of the word 'may' with the word 'endanger,' both of which are probabilistic, leads us to conclude that a reasonable prospect of future harm is adequate to engage the gears of RCRA § 7002(a)(1)(B) so long as the threat is near-term and involves potentially serious harm." The court ordered the defendant polluter to conduct a multi-million dollar study to learn whether mercury contamination in the lower Penobscot River adversely affected human health or the environment, and if so, to devise a feasible remedial approach.

An important question is whether § 7002 authorizes the courts in citizen suits to exercise their full equitable powers, including the power to order restitution, not merely to issue injunctions. In Meghrig v. KFC Western, Inc., 516 U.S. 479 (1996), the owner of contaminated land cleaned it up and then sued the prior owner responsible for the contamination. The Supreme Court held that § 7002(a)(1)(B) does not authorize a private plaintiff to seek restitution for past cleanup costs where the "imminent and substantial endangerment" does not still exist when the suit is filed. Plaintiff should have sued *before* spending $200,000 to comply with a county order to remove the oil-tainted soil. To obtain reimbursement for out-of-pocket expenditures in such a case, plaintiff would have to bring an action based on CERCLA or common law tort.

E. THE COMPREHENSIVE ENVIRONMENTAL RESPONSE, COMPENSATION, AND LIABILITY ACT

CERCLA, also known as the "superfund" law, was enacted in 1980 and revised by the Superfund Amendments and Reauthorization Act of 1986

(SARA) and the Small Business Liability Relief and Brownfields Revitalization Act of 2002. Its principal purpose is the cleanup of leaking hazardous waste disposal sites.

1. OVERVIEW OF THE ACT

The Act has four basic elements. First, it establishes an information-gathering and analysis system to enable federal and state governments to characterize chemical dump sites and develop priorities for response actions. Section 102 directs the EPA Administrator to issue regulations designating as "hazardous" those substances that, when released into the environment, may present "substantial danger" to the public health or welfare or the environment. (Section 101(14) also incorporates by reference any substance designated by EPA as hazardous or toxic pursuant to § 311(b)(2)(A) or 307(a) of the Clean Water Act, § 3001 of RCRA, § 112 of the Clean Air Act, or § 7 of TSCA. Petroleum and natural gas are expressly excluded.) Section 103 requires owners and operators of hazardous waste sites to notify EPA of the amount and types of hazardous substances to be found there, and of any known, suspected, or likely releases of such substances from the sites. This information is important for EPA's development of a National Priorities List (NPL) of uncontrolled sites, used in planning appropriate responses.

Second, the Act establishes federal authority to respond to hazardous substance emergencies and to clean up leaking sites. Section 104 authorizes the President to provide for "removal" and "remedial" actions consistent with the National Contingency Plan (NCP) referred to in § 105. Removal actions are emergency responses, while remedial actions are intended to provide long-term solutions. Response actions may be carried out by the federal government directly, through contractors, or through cooperative agreements with states. The NCP was originally developed under § 311(c) of the Clean Water Act. Under § 105(a) of CERCLA, a section of the NCP known as the national hazardous substance response plan establishes procedures and standards for responding to releases of hazardous substances. The President is required to employ a Hazard Ranking System in determining the sites or facilities to be added to the NPL. Federal response actions at listed sites are limited to cases in which the responsible parties either cannot be found or do not take the necessary actions.

Third, the Act creates a Hazardous Substances Trust Fund (the "superfund") to pay for removal and remedial actions. However, the special corporate and excise taxes (particularly on petroleum and chemical feedstocks) originally enacted to finance the fund expired in 1995. The superfund continues to operate on interest from unexpended funds, recoveries from private parties required to reimburse EPA for cleanup costs, and money appropriated by Congress from general tax revenues.

Fourth, the Act makes persons who are responsible for hazardous substance releases liable for

cleanup and restitution costs. Section 106 authorizes the Attorney General to seek injunctive relief
where an actual or threatened release poses an
"imminent and substantial endangerment" to the
public health or welfare or the environment. Alter-
natively, the President may issue administrative
orders directing responsible parties to take protec-
tive action. Section 107 provides that generators
and transporters of hazardous substances, as well
as owners and operators of treatment, storage, or
disposal (TSD) facilities, shall be liable for (a) all
costs of removal or remedial action incurred by the
federal or state government "not inconsistent with"
the NCP; (b) any other "necessary" response costs
incurred by any other person "consistent with" the
NCP; and (c) damages to "natural resources" resulting from release of hazardous substances. The
courts have held that § 107 imposes strict liability,
not dependent on fault. Section 107(b) contains
narrow exceptions for releases caused solely by acts
of God or war or acts or omissions of certain "third
parties." As discussed below, liability is usually
joint and several among responsible generators,
transporters, owners, and operators, although § 107
does not expressly say so.

2.   IMPLEMENTING CLEANUPS

In implementation of CERCLA, the guiding policy
is to achieve private-party cleanup, either voluntary
or through enforcement action, if possible. Response actions financed from the superfund are

undertaken only when federal and state governments determine them to be appropriate. An important part of implementation is federal negotiation of cooperative agreements with states, under which they take lead responsibility for cleanup, with later recovery of costs from responsible parties.

Sections 116 and 121, added in 1986, established schedules for response actions and preferences among types of responses. Section 121 establishes a preference (in remedial actions under § 104 or § 106) for treatment that permanently and significantly reduces the volume, toxicity, or mobility of the hazardous substances. Offsite transport and disposal of the hazardous substances or contaminated materials is least favored where "practical [on-site] treatment technologies" are available. Remedial actions are to be "cost-effective," considering total short-term and long-term costs. The actions taken are to attain a degree of cleanup and control of further releases that, at a minimum, "assures protection" of human health and the environment.

Before SARA, both potentially responsible parties (PRPs) and environmental groups often sought judicial review of EPA's proposed remedial actions at particular sites before the cleanups were implemented. Rather than waiting to raise defenses in subsequent cost recovery actions under § 107, PRPs directed early challenges to the selection of remedial actions, claiming, for example, that EPA had chosen unreasonably elaborate or expensive remedies. Environmental groups, on the other hand, had different reasons for seeking pre-enforcement review of proposed remedial actions. They wanted early access to the courts to halt implementation of remedies that, in their view, failed to go far enough in protecting public health and the environment. Before 1986, CERCLA provided little guidance on the propriety of pre-enforcement judicial review. A leading case, Lone Pine Steering Committee v. U.S. EPA, 777 F.2d 882 (3d Cir.1985), held that the courts lacked jurisdiction to conduct pre-enforcement review of EPA's method of cleanup. The court was concerned that such suits would frustrate Congress' intention that EPA act quickly to remedy problems posed by hazardous waste sites.

In SARA, Congress codified in § 113(h) the general denial of access to the courts to obtain pre-enforcement review of remedial action. Congress remained troubled, however, by the effect that the rule might have on citizen groups wishing to challenge the adequacy of remedial action before cleanups were completed. Therefore, Congress created an exception authorizing the filing of citizen suits after a removal or remedial action has been taken under § 104 or secured under § 106. Congress then defined this exception liberally by explaining that such suits can be filed after the completion of "distinct and separate phases" of a remedial action, indicating in the conference report that it is not necessary to wait until the entire action has been completed. The intent was to permit judicial review early enough so that the direction of a multistage cleanup could be modified, if necessary, prior to completion.

3. LIABILITY OF RESPONSIBLE PARTIES

United States v. Monsanto Co., 858 F.2d 160 (4th Cir.1988) was typical of early enforcement suits by the federal government to recover its costs of removing hazardous substances from disposal sites. The four-acre site contained more than 7,000 55-gallon drums of chemical waste, many of them leaking toxic, carcinogenic, mutagenic, explosive, and highly flammable substances. Defendants, who had refused to enter into settlement agreements with the government, included three generators and the two owners of the site. (The owners had leased it to another firm, which then accepted wastes for disposal, perhaps without the site owners' knowledge.) The government moved for partial summary judgment on the issue of defendants' joint and several liability. The court found that each defendant fell within one of the four classes of persons identified in § 107(a) as liable for response costs. Once the requisite nexus with the waste site was established, each class was *strictly* liable unless it could prove under § 107(b) that the release or threat of release of hazardous substances was caused solely by unrelated persons or events.

A *generator* was liable under § 107(a)(3) if the government could prove that:

a. The generator's hazardous substances were, at some point in the past, shipped to the facility;

b. The generator's hazardous substances, or hazardous substances *like* those of the generator, were present at the site;

c. There was a release or threatened release of *any* hazardous substance at the site; and

d. The release or threatened release caused the incurrence of response costs.

The court rejected defendants' contention that plaintiff must prove that hazardous substances traceable to each defendant were released at the site. The court said that to require specific proof of causation would be at odds with the express language of the statute and would frustrate the intent of Congress because of the technological infeasibility of tracing a given generator's substances at the site.

The court also held that *joint and several* liability was appropriate under CERCLA in circumstances of "indivisible" injury. The court expressly approved the rationale and discussion in United States v. Chem-Dyne Corp., 572 F.Supp. 802 (S.D.Ohio 1983), in which the district court said:

If the harm is divisible *and* there is a reasonable basis for apportionment of damages, each defendant is liable only for the portion of the harm he himself caused * * *. In this situation, the burden of proof as to apportionment is upon each defendant * * *. On the other hand, if the defendants caused an entire indivisible harm, each is subject to liability for the entire harm.

The *Monsanto* court found that defendants had failed to meet their burden of establishing a reasonable basis for apportioning liability among the responsible parties:

> To meet this burden, the generator defendants had to establish that the environmental harm at [the site] was divisible among responsible parties. They presented no evidence, however, showing a relationship between waste volume, the release of hazardous substances, and the harm at the site. Further, in light of the commingling of hazardous substances, the district court could not have reasonably apportioned liability without some evidence disclosing the individual and interactive qualities of the substances deposited there.... [T]he defendants still have the right to sue responsible parties for contribution, and in that action they may assert both legal and equitable theories of cost allocation.

The defendants in *Monsanto* also argued that "retroactive" application of CERCLA, to create liability for conduct that occurred prior to the Act's passage, would violate due process. The court rejected the argument, saying that a presumption of constitutionality attaches to "legislative Acts adjusting the burdens and benefits of economic life," and that the burden is on one complaining of a due process violation to establish that the legislature has acted in an arbitrary and irrational way:

"CERCLA operates remedially to spread the costs of responding to improper waste disposal among all parties that played a role in creating hazardous conditions."

Two other leading decisions in agreement with *Monsanto* on the foregoing issues are United States v. Northeastern Pharmaceutical & Chemical Co., Inc., 810 F.2d 726 (8th Cir.1986) (also holding that the federal government could recover retroactively response costs that it *incurred* before enactment of CERCLA), and State of New York v. Shore Realty Corp., 759 F.2d 1032 (2d Cir.1985).

Northeastern Pharmaceutical dealt with several other significant issues. It held that liability under § 107(a)(3) attached not only to a corporate generator but also to an individual corporate officer or employee who personally participated in making arrangements for the disposal of wastes. The statute provides that any person who "arranged" for disposal shall be liable for the government's response costs; there is no requirement that the "arranger" own or possess the waste or the facility from which it is transported for disposal.

It should be noted that § 107(a)(2), prescribing liability for any person who at the time of disposal of a hazardous substance owned or "operated" the disposal facility, also has been applied to senior corporate officers and lower-ranking employees who personally participated in the disposal. See *Shore Realty*, supra, and United States v. Gurley, 43 F.3d 1188 (8th Cir.1994), *cert. denied*, 516 U.S. 817 (1995). On the other hand, a "consultant" who also was the corporate secretary and chairman of the board and owned 85% of the company's stock was held not to be an "operator" because there was no evidence that he personally participated in any conduct that violated CERCLA. Riverside Market Development Corp. v. Int'l Building Products, Inc., 931 F.2d 327 (5th Cir.1991). "Operator" liability also has been imposed on *parent corporations* whose subsidiaries owned disposal facilities. The parent itself, e.g., acting through an agent who is not an officer of the subsidiary, must have "actively participated in, and exercised control over, the operations of the *facility itself.*" United States v. Bestfoods, 524 U.S. 51 (1998).

The *Northeastern Pharmaceutical* court also held that under § 107(a)(4)(A)—which imposes liability for governmental response costs "not inconsistent with the national contingency plan"—the burden of proof of inconsistency with the NCP is upon the defendants, and that all costs incurred by the *government* that are not inconsistent with the NCP are conclusively presumed to be reasonable and recoverable. On the other hand, under § 107(a)(4)(B)—which imposes liability for response costs incurred by "any other person consistent with" the NCP—*non*governmental plaintiffs have the burden of proving that their expenditures were consistent with the NCP. Finally, the court held that defendants do not have a right to a jury trial where the government seeks response costs under § 107, since CERCLA affords essentially equitable relief in the form of restitution.

Shore Realty, supra, held that a state could recover its emergency, or short-term, costs from a corporate site owner (which neither owned the site when hazardous wastes were placed there nor caused the presence or release of the wastes) and from its principal officer and stockholder (as an "operator"), even though the site was not on EPA's National Priorities List. The court held that while NPL listing may be a requirement for the use of superfund money under §§ 104 and 111, it is not requisite to liability under § 107. NPL listing, said the court, is not a general requirement under the National Contingency Plan, since the NPL is a "limitation on remedial, or long-term, actions—as opposed to removal, or short-term, actions—particularly federally funded remedial actions." Nor was the state's recovery barred by its failure to obtain EPA's prior approval of the response action, since the NCP's requirements concerning collaboration in joint federal-state cleanup efforts are inapplicable where a state acts on its own without seeking reimbursement from the superfund.

Section 107(a)(2)(B) also creates a *private* cause of action for recovery of response costs if they are "necessary" and "consistent with" the NCP. Potential plaintiffs include owners of land adjacent to a leaking disposal site, and even the owner of the site itself on which defendant deposited hazardous waste. Although reimbursement of private response costs from the *superfund* requires that they be approved under the NCP and federally certified, § 111(a)(2), private recovery from a generator, transporter, owner or operator under § 107(a)(2)(B) does not require that plaintiff's response actions have been taken pursuant to a governmentally authorized cleanup program. It is sufficient, for example, if the actions were required by a state or local agency and were consistent with provisions of the NCP in effect at the time of the response. NL Industries, Inc. v. Kaplan, 792 F.2d 896 (9th Cir. 1986); Wickland Oil Terminals v. Asarco, Inc., 792 F.2d 887 (9th Cir.1986).

Prior to 1986, there was a division among the courts regarding whether the possible joint and several liability of CERCLA defendants was a matter of federal or state common law. Although SARA was silent on this point, legislative history indicates that Congress intended federal law to control. As Representative John Dingell explained on the floor of the House, "[t]he courts have established, as a matter of federal common law, that the liability of potentially responsible parties at superfund sites is strict, joint and several, unless the responsible parties can demonstrate that the harm is divisible." He said that the reasoning of the court in United States v. Chem-Dyne Corp., page 238 supra, correctly expressed congressional intent.

Because § 107(a) extends liability for cleanup costs to all "owners" of contaminated properties, regardless of the circumstances of their ownership, parties who involuntarily or innocently acquired former disposal sites have been required to pay for cleanup, even when the cost exceeded the value of the land. Several well-publicized cases helped to

focus Congress' attention on this aspect of CERC-
LA's liability scheme.   In United States v. Maryland Bank & Trust Co., 632 F.Supp. 573 (D.Md.
1986), for example, a bank made a mortgage loan of
$335,000 on a piece of land.   The borrower default-
ed, and the bank instituted a foreclosure suit.   After the bank took title to the property, state and
federal authorities determined that it was a contaminated waste site requiring cleanup under CERCLA.
The bank was held liable for response costs of more
than $550,000.

Prompted by the perceived unfairness of such
results, Congress included a new defense in SARA
to protect "innocent landowners."   While
§ 107(a)'s general liability standard for "owners
and operators" was maintained, Congress expanded
§ 107(b)(3)'s third-party exception by redefining
the term "contractual relationship" in § 101(35).
Now, "innocent landowners" who acquire property
involuntarily by inheritance or bequest, or voluntarily without "reason to know" that hazardous
substances have been disposed of there, are not
liable as owners or operators under § 107.

With respect to the "reason to know" limitation,
§ 101(35), after being further amended in 2002 by
the Small Business Liability Relief and Brownfields
Revitalization Act, provides in part:

To establish that the defendant had no reason to
know, the defendant must demonstrate to a court
that—

(I) * * * before [acquiring] the facility, the defendant carried out all appropriate inquiries [due diligence, pursuant to "standards and practices" established by EPA at 40 C.F.R. Pt. 312] into the previous ownership and uses of the facility in accordance with generally accepted good commercial and customary standards and practices; and

(II) the defendant took reasonable steps to stop any continuing release; prevent any threatened future release; and prevent or limit any human, environmental, or natural resource exposure to any previously released hazardous substance.

The Small Business Liability Relief and Brownfields Revitalization Act created two additional exclusions from owner or operator liability. New § 107(q) provides protection for the owner of property "contiguous" to land from which there is a hazardous substance release, and new § 107(r) exempts "bona fide prospective purchasers" so long as they do not impede response actions. Under § 107(q), an owner of land contaminated by a "contiguous property" is not considered to be an owner or operator under § 107(a) if she did not cause or contribute to the release of hazardous substances; takes reasonable steps to prevent further releases and to prevent exposure to hazardous substances released on her own property; cooperates with persons authorized to undertake response actions; and conducted "all appropriate inquiries" within the meaning of § 101(35) concerning "innocent landowners." If a person does not qualify for liability relief as a contiguous landowner because she knew of the contamination at the time of purchase, she nevertheless may qualify for relief as a bona fide prospective purchaser under § 107(r).

Section 107(r) exempts "bona fide prospective purchasers" from owner or operator liability under § 107(a) so long as they do not impede a response action. The purpose of § 107(r) is to facilitate the acquisition, cleanup, and redevelopment of contaminated "brownfields." Section 101(40) defines "bona fide prospective purchaser" as one who establishes that: all disposal on her land occurred before she purchased it; she made "all appropriate inquiry" within the meaning of § 101(35); she exercises appropriate care to prevent any further releases and prevent or limit exposure; she provides full cooperation to persons authorized to undertake response actions; and she is not potentially liable or affiliated with any other person that is potentially liable for response costs.

What about landowners who *know* the contaminated condition of a site when they acquire ownership, who do nothing to aggravate the situation, and who then transfer it to another person after disclosing the condition? Are such "passive intervening landowners" liable under § 107(a)(2) if the contamination spreads within or beyond the site? The answer can depend on the definition of "disposal" in § 107(a)(2) and in § 101(40)(A) concerning bona fide prospective purchasers. Section 101(29) states that "disposal" shall have the meaning provided in

§ 1004(3) of the Solid Waste Disposal Act, which defines it to include "discharge, deposit, injection, dumping, *spilling*, *leaking*, or placing of . . . hazardous waste into or on any land or water" (emphasis added). The courts have disagreed on the question of CERCLA liability for passive intervening landowners. Nurad, Inc. v. William E. Hooper & Sons Co., 966 F.2d 837 (4th Cir.1992) held that § 107(a)(2) imposes liability not only for active involvement in the "dumping" or "placing" of hazardous waste at a facility, but for ownership of the facility at a time when such waste was "spilling" or "leaking." However, United States v. 150 Acres of Land, 204 F.3d 698 (6th Cir.2000) held that "disposal" requires "human intervention," and United States v. CDMG Realty Co., 96 F.3d 706 (3d Cir. 1996) held that "while 'leaking' and 'spilling' may not require affirmative human conduct, neither word denotes the gradual spreading of contamination." Most recently, Carson Harbor Village, Ltd. v. Unocal Corp., 270 F.3d 863 (9th Cir.2001) held that "disposal" does "not include passive soil migration" but "may include other passive migration," including leaking of contaminants out of underground barrels or storage tanks.

Based on § 107(a), which provides for liability of any "person" who fits within one of the four specified classes of potentially responsible parties (PRPs), federal courts have imposed CERCLA liability on corporate "successors"—companies that purchase the stock or assets of hazardous waste disposers. However, the courts have differed on whether state corporate law or federal common law should be applied in defining "successors."

In Louisiana–Pacific Corp. v. Asarco, Inc., 909 F.2d 1260 (9th Cir.1990), the court applied narrow liability rules used in most states: an asset purchaser may be liable only if (1) it expressly or impliedly agreed to assume the predecessor's liabilities, (2) the transaction amounted to a "de facto" merger, (3) the successor is "merely a continuation" of the predecessor, or (4) the transaction involved fraud in an attempt to escape liability. *Id.* at 1263. The court left open the possible application of a more expansive "continuing business enterprise" rule.

Applying "evolving principles of federal common law," the court in United States v. Carolina Transformer Co., 978 F.2d 832 (4th Cir.1992), applied the continuing business enterprise rule (which it called the "continuity of enterprise" or "substantial continuity" rule). The factors which the court considered in holding the purchaser liable under CERCLA were: (1) retention of the same employees, (2) retention of the same supervisory personnel, (3) retention of the same production facilities in the same location, (4) production of the same product, (5) retention of the same name, (6) continuity of assets, (7) continuity of general business operations, and (8) successor's holding itself out as the continuation of the previous enterprise.

Recently, in K.C. 1986 L.P. v. Reade Mfg., 472 F.3d 1009 (8th Cir.2007), another court acknowledged that the viability of the substantial continuity theory of successor liability as a creation of federal common law "has been seriously questioned following the Supreme Court's pronouncement in *Best-foods* [page 241 *supra*] that nothing in CERCLA purports to rewrite the settled rules of state corporation law simply because the cause of action is based upon a federal statute." K.C. 1986 L.P. at 1023. However, the court declined to decide the question because the facts in the record did not satisfy the substantial continuity test.

Both federal and state rules concerning successor liability may be modified by contract. *Indemnification agreements* are often used to address environmental and other liabilities related to the assets and business transferred. Section 107(e)(1) provides that no indemnification agreement shall be effective to transfer CERCLA liability from a PRP under § 107 to any other person, but that "[n]othing in this subsection shall bar any agreement to insure, hold harmless, or indemnify a party to such agreement for any liability under this section."

With respect to *lender* liability, § 101(20)(A) excludes from the definition of "owner or operator" any "person, who, without participating in the management of a . . . facility, holds indicia of ownership primarily to protect his security interest in the . . . facility." Financial institutions and other secured creditors were shocked by the decision in United States v. Fleet Factors Corp., 901 F.2d 1550 (11th Cir.1990), which held that Fleet's activities as a secured creditor might make it liable if it participated in the "financial management of a facility to a degree indicating a *capacity* to influence the [bankrupt debtor] corporation's treatment of hazardous wastes" (emphasis added). The court said that it was not necessary, for liability, that the creditor actually involve itself in day-to-day operations of the facility; it was enough if the involvement with management was "sufficiently broad to support the inference that it could affect hazardous waste decisions if it so chose." Congress then amended § 101(20) by adding a new subsection (E), "Exclusion of lenders not participants in management." The phrase "participate in management" is defined to mean "actually participating in the management or operational affairs" of a facility, and "does not include merely having the capacity to influence, or the unexercised right to control" facility operations. Note the similarity between this treatment of lenders and the treatment of parent corporations under United States v. Bestfoods, page 241 supra.

4. RIGHT OF CONTRIBUTION

Although apportionment of response costs among responsible parties is appropriate under § 107(a) when there is a reasonable basis for division of the harm, joint and several liability is the general rule. The government thus is relieved of the obligation to join all potentially responsible parties (PRPs) and to prove their individual contributions to the hazardous waste site. The burden of proving divisibility of harm is on the defendant seeking to limit its liability. In this situation, the subject of contribution among PRPs is of great importance, especially to those against whom the government initially chooses to proceed for recovery of response costs.

In an action for contribution, one joint tortfeasor that has discharged more than its fair share of the common liability seeks to recover the excess costs from another tortfeasor. Before the 1986 amendments to CERCLA, a few district courts had recognized an implicit right to contribution under CERCLA. They conceived of the area of contribution as one for development of a federal common law. On the other hand, at least one court looked to state law.

SARA amended § 113 to provide explicitly for a right to contribution. Section 113(f)(1) now provides that any person may seek contribution from any other person who is liable or potentially liable under § 107(a), "during or following any civil action under" § 106 or § 107(a). Such claims are governed by federal law. In resolving them, the court may allocate response costs "using such equitable factors as the court determines are appropriate." Factors frequently considered include the relative amounts of waste disposed of by the various generators and transporters; the relative toxicity of the wastes; the degree of involvement by each party in the generation, transportation, or disposal; the degree of care exercised by the various parties; and the degree of their cooperation with public officials to prevent harm to public health or the environment.

The final sentence of § 113(f)(1) says that nothing therein shall diminish the right of any person to bring an action for contribution in the absence of a civil action under § 106 or § 107(a). Despite this savings clause, the Supreme Court in Cooper Industries, Inc. v. Aviall Services, Inc., 543 U.S. 157 (2004), held that a PRP that had conducted a voluntary cleanup under the State's supervision, without any action against the PRP under § 106 or § 107(a), could not maintain an action for contribution against other PRPs under § 113(f)(1). The Court's rationale was that the sole function of the final sentence is to clarify that § 113(f)(1) does nothing to diminish any cause of action for contribution that may exist independently of § 113(f)(1). The Court said that this sentence "does not itself establish a cause of action; nor does it expand § 113(f)(1) to authorize contribution actions not brought 'during or following' a § 106 or § 107(a) civil action; nor does it specify what causes of action for contribution, if any, exist outside § 113(f)(1)."

The *Cooper* decision was criticized by some commentators as discouraging the voluntary cleanups favored by CERCLA and the EPA, especially since several appellate courts previously had held that contribution suits could be brought only under § 113(f). However, in United States v. Atlantic Research Corp., 127 S.Ct. 2331 (2007), the court alleviated the problem by holding that PRPs who do voluntary cleanups can recover at least some of their response costs from other PRPs under § 107(a). Such plaintiff PRPs qualify as "any other person" under § 107(a)(4)(B), and the action is one for recovery of "necessary costs of response incurred," not for contribution. Only a PRP that pays money to satisfy a court judgment or an administrative or judicially approved settlement may pursue § 113(f) contribution.

Several cases have held that a defendant's potential liability under § 107(a) does not preclude a *zero* allocation of response costs to that defendant in a contribution suit under § 113(f). Thus, in Kalamazoo River Study Group v. Rockwell Int'l Corp., 274 F.3d 1043 (6th Cir.2001), where the trial court found that defendant had released less than 20 pounds of PCBs into the river (in contrast to the hundreds of thousands of pounds released by plaintiffs), the appellate court affirmed the lower court's decision not to allocate any response costs to defendant. The court of appeals said that "a defendant's release of what, standing alone, would be a significant amount of such material might have no impact on the total cost of cleaning up a contaminated site."

Allocation of liability in a contribution action can be complicated by the insolvency or unavailability of some PRPs. For example, suppose that each of five generators sent 20% of "the problem" to a disposal site. One of them, E, went out of business many years ago, and the owner and operator of the site is now insolvent. Firm A has paid for the entire $500,000 cleanup, pursuant to an administrative order from EPA, and now brings a contribution action against B, C, and D, the other PRPs. How-

ever, D has only $20,000 of assets. Each of B and C
argues that its liability is limited to $100,000, which
would leave A out of pocket in the amount of
$280,000. Two interrelated issues are presented:
(1) May the court find B and C jointly liable, as they
would be under § 107(a), or only severally liable for
their 20% shares of the total response costs? (2)
May the court allocate some of E's $100,000 "or-
phan share" (and perhaps some of D's unpaid
$80,000) of the response costs to B and C, or, again,
is their liability limited to $100,000 each?

While contribution liability usually has been held
to be only several, a few courts have said that joint
liability may be imposed in appropriate circumstances because § 113(f) expressly provides for allocation based on "equitable factors."   Browning-
Ferris Industries of Illinois, Inc. v. Ter Maat, 195
F.3d 953 (7th Cir.1999). With respect to the second
issue, one court has said, "Under § 113(f)(1), the
cost of orphan shares is distributed equitably
among all PRPs just as cleanup costs are."   Pinal
Creek Group v. Newmont Mining Corp., 118 F.3d
1298 (9th Cir.1997). In the hypothetical case
above, by finding joint liability or by apportioning
the orphan shares of E and perhaps D, a court could
allocate to each of B and C one-fourth or one-third
of E's $100,000 share of the response costs, and
perhaps also one-third of the $80,000 of D's share
that D will not be able to pay. Otherwise, A would
be left in a much less favorable position than B and
C, simply because EPA moved against A alone rather than against all three of them.

5. MEASURE OF DAMAGES

Another important matter is the kinds of costs for which PRPs may be held liable. Section 107(a) defines in general terms the costs and damages recoverable under CERCLA. It mentions "costs of removal or remedial action" incurred by the federal or state government, "other necessary costs of response" incurred by any other person, and "damages for injury to, destruction of, or loss of natural resources, including the reasonable costs of assessing such injury, destruction, or loss." Before SARA, there were numerous disputes about recoverability of contractor costs, enforcement costs, and even interest. SARA attempted to remedy this problem by expanding the list of recoverable costs and damages to include virtually every conceivable expense associated with superfund cleanup activity. The costs of health assessments and health effects studies now are recoverable, as are enforcement costs and costs related to indemnification agreements with response action contractors. However, private plaintiffs may not recover compensation for lost property value or individual medical monitoring. Price v. U.S. Navy, 39 F.3d 1011 (9th Cir. 1994). Nor may they recover reimbursement for their attorneys' fees. Key Tronic Corp. v. United States, 511 U.S. 809 (1994).

Under § 107(f), CERCLA liability for injury to *natural resources* is owed to the United States government, to any state for resources "within the State or belonging to, managed by, controlled by, or

appertaining to such State," and to any Indian tribe
in specified situations. The statute creates no private cause of action for natural resource damage.
Authority to recover is in the President or the
"authorized representative of any State," who
"shall act on behalf of the public as trustee of such
natural resources." Sums recovered shall be used
by the trustee only to "restore, replace, or acquire
the equivalent of" the natural resources injured,
destroyed or lost. "Natural resources" are defined
by § 101(16) to mean land, fish, wildlife, biota, air,
water, groundwater, and other such resources belonging to, or managed or held in trust by, the
United States, a state or local government, a foreign
government, or an Indian tribe.

How are the recoverable damages to be measured? Section 301(c) directs the President to promulgate regulations for "the assessment of damages
for injury to, destruction of, or loss of" natural
resources:

   (2) Such regulations shall specify (A) standard
   procedures for simplified assessments requiring
   minimal field observation, including establishing
   measures of damages based on units of discharge
   or release or units of affected area, and (B) alternative protocols for conducting assessments in
   individual cases to determine the type and extent
   of short- and long-term injury, destruction, or
   loss. Such regulations shall identify the best
   available procedures to determine such damages,
   including both direct and indirect injury, destruction, or loss and shall take into consideration

factors including, but not limited to, replacement value, use value, and ability of the ecosystem or resource to recover.

The "standard procedures" are referred to as "Type A" rules, and the "alternative protocols" as "Type B" rules.

The President assigned responsibility for promulgating the regulations to the Department of Interior. In 1986, the Department belatedly published final regulations containing both Type A and Type B assessment rules. Both were challenged in court by state governments, environmental organizations, and industry groups. The Type A rules were upheld in State of Colorado v. United States Dept. of Interior, 880 F.2d 481 (D.C.Cir.1989). However, major portions of the Type B rules were found to violate CERCLA in Ohio v. United States Dept. of Interior, 880 F.2d 432 (D.C.Cir.1989).

The most significant issue in the *Ohio* case concerned the validity of a provision that damages for despoilment of natural resources should be "the *lesser* of: restoration or replacement costs; or diminution of use values" (emphasis added). The court held that, under CERCLA, the Department of the Interior was not entitled to treat use value and restoration cost as having "equal presumptive legitimacy" as measures of damages to natural resources. Primary among the statutory provisions cited by the court was § 107(f)(1), which states that natural resource damages recovered by a government trustee are "for use only to restore, replace, or acquire the equivalent of such natural resources," and that the measure of damages "shall not be limited by the sums which can be used to restore or replace such resources." The court concluded that Congress intended a "distinct preference" for restoration cost as the measure of damages.

6. SETTLEMENTS

CERCLA § 122(a) directs that "[w]henever practicable and in the public interest," settlement agreements should be sought in order to expedite effective remedial actions at superfund sites and to minimize litigation. Among the tools authorized by § 122 to facilitate cost allocations, reduce transaction costs, and otherwise promote settlements are (1) de minimis settlements, expedited settlements for small-volume waste contributors; (2) nonbinding preliminary allocations of responsibility (NBARs) for cleanup costs, developed by EPA for PRPs; (3) mixed-funding agreements to share cleanup costs, permitting use of a combination of federal, state and PRP funds; (4) covenants not to sue, protecting PRPs who settle from future liability to the United States related to the hazardous substance release addressed by a remedial action; and (5) alternative dispute resolution, the use of neutral third parties to help resolve liability and cost-allocation problems.

Section 122(g), concerning de minimis settlements, was amended in 2002 by the Small Business

Liability Relief and Brownfields Revitalization Act. New subsection (7) provides for conditional expedited settlements between the United States and de minimis PRPs who demonstrate an "inability or a limited ability to pay response costs." In determining ability to pay, EPA shall consider whether the PRP can "pay response costs and still maintain its basic business operations."

Section 122(d)(1)(A) provides that whenever the President enters into a settlement agreement with a PRP with respect to remedial action under § 106, except as otherwise provided in § 122(g) concerning de minimis settlements, "the agreement shall be entered in the appropriate United States district court as a consent decree."

In addition to § 122, another CERCLA provision of great significance to settlements is § 113(f)(2), concerning *contribution*:

> A person who has resolved its liability to the United States or a State in an administrative or judicially approved settlement shall not be liable for claims for contribution regarding matters addressed in the settlement. Such settlement does not discharge any of the other potentially liable persons unless its terms so provide, but it reduces the potential liability of the others by the amount of the settlement.

F. MANDATORY REPORTING
OF CHEMICAL HAZARDS

The Emergency Planning and Community Right-to-Know Act (EPCRA) was enacted by Congress with the 1986 amendments to CERCLA. The two general objectives of EPCRA are to support emergency planning by local governments with regard to chemical hazards, and to provide citizens and local governments with information about potential community-based chemical hazards. Congress included three provisions to implement these objectives. The first concerns governmental emergency response planning. The second addresses emergency notification of chemical releases by private industry. The third requires compilation and reporting of information concerning chemical properties, manufacturing, usage, and releases.

The first provision requires each state to establish a state emergency response commission and local emergency planning committees. The latter must have emergency response plans that include, among other things, identification of local facilities at which any statutorily designated "extremely hazardous substances" are present; methods and procedures for reporting any release of such a substance; public notification procedures; and evacuation plans.

The second component requires the owner or operator of a "facility" to give notice of a hazardous substance release to the state emergency response commission and the local emergency planning committee. The notification must contain specific information, including data about the chemical released, the estimated quantity, the time and duration of the release, any known or antici- pated acute or chronic health risks, and advice regarding appropriate medical attention or precau- tions for exposed individuals.

The final provision requires owners and operators of certain facilities to inform citizens about chemi- cals located in their communities by submitting to state and local authorities information about toxic chemical inventories, usage, manufacture, and re- leases.

All information collected under EPCRA is avail- able to the public. Facilities' annual Toxic Release Inventory (TRI) reports have given the public un- precedented pictures of the industries that put it at risk and have given the industries a strong incen- tive to protect or repair their reputations by reduc- ing their releases.

G. CRIMINAL LIABILITY

Almost every federal environmental statute im- poses criminal liability. Congress has made virtual- ly all "knowing" and some "negligent" violations of pollution control standards, limitations, permits, and licenses subject to criminal as well as civil sanctions. These statutes rarely define thresholds indicating when violators' conduct justifies adding criminal to civil penalties. Congress also has crimi- nalized both the failure to report releases of hazardous substances and the filing of false reports, e.g., CERCLA § 103(b) and EPCRA § 325(b).

1.   KNOWING VIOLATIONS

The legal issue that arises most frequently in environmental criminal cases is the extent of the "knowledge" that defendants must be shown to have had in order to justify convictions. For example, § 3008(d) of RCRA—one of the environmental criminal provisions most often used by federal prosecutors—prescribes fines and imprisonment for any person who:

(1) *knowingly* transports or causes to be transported any hazardous waste identified or listed under this subchapter to a facility which does not have a permit under this subchapter . . . ;

(2) *knowingly* treats, stores, or disposes of any hazardous waste identified or listed under this subchapter—

(A) without a permit under this subchapter . . . ;

(B) in *knowing* violation of any material condition or requirement of such permit . . . [emphasis added].

In United States v. Laughlin, 10 F.3d 961 (2d Cir.1993), defendant appealed from a judgment convicting him of knowingly disposing of hazardous waste without a permit in violation of § 3008(d)(2)(A). The trial court had instructed the jury that the government was required to prove

that defendant knowingly disposed of creosote
sludge and knew that it "had the potential to be
harmful to others or the environment or, in other
words, it was not a harmless substance like uncon-
taminated water." On appeal, defendant contended
that the word "knowingly" in subsection (2) applied
not only to the prohibited act—treatment, storage,
or disposal of a hazardous waste—but also to the
fact that the waste had been identified or listed as
hazardous under RCRA and the fact that his corporate employer lacked a permit. He urged that the
jury should have been instructed that the government was required to prove, as essential elements of
the violation, that he was aware of RCRA regulations applicable to creosote sludge and knew that
the employer had not obtained a permit to dispose
of the sludge. In rejecting defendant's contention,
the court invoked what is known as the "public
welfare offense" doctrine:

> When knowledge is an element of a statute
> intended to regulate hazardous or dangerous sub-
> stances, the Supreme Court has determined that
> the knowledge element is satisfied upon a show-
> ing that a defendant was aware that he was
> performing the proscribed acts; knowledge of reg-
> ulatory requirements is not necessary. See Unit-
> ed States v. International Minerals & Chem.
> Corp. [S.Ct.1971] (in prosecution for knowingly
> violating a hazardous materials regulation, Gov-
> ernment was not required to prove that defen-
> dant was aware of regulation, but only that he

was aware of shipment of the hazardous materials).

Similarly, in United States v. Sinskey, 119 F.3d 712 (8th Cir.1997), the court affirmed defendant's conviction under the Clean Water Act. Defendant challenged jury instructions given with respect to CWA § 309(c)(2)(A), which among other things punishes anyone who "knowingly violates" § 301 or a condition or limitation contained in a permit that implements § 301. The trial court had instructed that in order for the jury to find defendant guilty of acting "knowingly," the proof had to show that he was "aware of the nature of his acts, perform[ed] them intentionally, and [did] not act or fail to act through ignorance, mistake, or accident." The court of appeals held that the government was not required to prove that defendant knew that his acts violated either the CWA or the corporate employer's NPDES effluent-discharge permit, "but merely that he was aware of the conduct that resulted in the permit's violation."

This interpretation comports not only with our legal system's general recognition that ignorance of the law is no excuse ..., but also with Supreme Court interpretations of statutes containing similar language and structure. In United States v. International Minerals & Chemical Corp., ...[t]he Court [noted] that where "dangerous or ... obnoxious waste materials" are involved, anyone dealing with such materials "must be presumed" to be aware of the existence of the regulations.

The court in *Sinskey* distinguished United States v. Ahmad, 101 F.3d 386 (5th Cir.1996), in which a convenience store owner had pumped out an underground gasoline storage tank into which some water had leaked, discharging gasoline into city sewer systems and nearby creeks. At trial, defendant asserted that he thought he was discharging water, and that CWA § 309(c)(2)(A) required proof not only that he knew he was discharging something, but also that he knew he was discharging gasoline. The Fifth Circuit reversed his conviction. The *Sinskey* court said that *Ahmad* "involved a classic mistake-of-fact defense, and is not applicable to a mistake-of-law defense such as that asserted by Sinskey."

2.   NEGLIGENT VIOLATIONS

In United States v. Hanousek, 176 F.3d 1116 (9th Cir.1999), *cert. denied*, 528 U.S. 1102 (2000), defendant appealed his conviction for "negligently" discharging a harmful quantity of oil into a navigable water of the United States, in violation of CWA §§ 309(c)(1)(A) and 311(b)(3). Defendant contended that the trial court had erred by failing to instruct the jury that the government had to prove that he acted with *criminal* negligence, as opposed to ordinary negligence. In his proposed instruction, defendant defined criminal negligence as "a gross deviation from the standard of care that a reasonable person would observe in the situation." However, the district court had instructed the jury that the government was required to prove only that defendant acted negligently, which that court defined as "the failure to use reasonable care." In affirming the conviction, the court of appeals said:

If Congress intended to prescribe a heightened negligence standard, it could have done so explicitly, as it did in [§ 311(b)(7)(D), which] provides for increased civil penalties "[i]n any case in which a violation ... was the result of gross negligence or willful misconduct." ...

In light of our holding in [United States v.] *Weitzenhoff* [35 F.3d 1275 (9th Cir.1993)] that the criminal provisions of the CWA constitute public welfare legislation, and the fact that a public welfare statute may impose criminal penalties for ordinary negligent conduct without offending due process, we conclude that section [309(c)(1)(A)] does not violate due process by permitting criminal penalties for ordinary negligent conduct.

3. RESPONSIBLE CORPORATE OFFICERS

Congress has explicitly incorporated the category of "responsible corporate officer" into the definition of a liable "person" in the criminal provisions of the Clean Air Act and Clean Water Act. In United States v. Brittain, 931 F.2d 1413 (10th Cir. 1991), a prosecution under the Clean Water Act for unlawful discharges of raw sewage into a stream, the individual defendant contended that he was not a "person" subject to criminal prosecution under the statute.   The court suggested that a responsible corporate officer (RCO) would not have to personally direct, or commit, a violation of the statute to be criminally liable.   The court said:

> Under this interpretation, a "responsible corporate officer," to be held criminally liable, would not have to "willfully or negligently" cause a permit violation.   Instead, the willfulness or negligence of the actor would be imputed to him by virtue of his position of responsibility.

However, since the individual defendant in *Brittain* did, in fact, have actual knowledge of the illegal conduct, and directed that it occur and be concealed from the authorities, the court's analysis of the extent to which knowledge may be imputed to a corporate officer, by virtue of his position alone, was dicta.   Federal prosecutors have not followed this dicta in subsequent prosecutions.

In United States v. McDonald & Watson Waste Oil Co., 933 F.2d 35 (1st Cir.1991), the president of the company was convicted under RCRA § 3008(d)(1) of knowingly transporting and causing the transportation of hazardous waste to a facility which did not have a permit.   In reversing the criminal conviction, the court said:

> We agree . . . that knowledge may be inferred from circumstantial evidence, including position and responsibility of defendants such as corporate officers, as well as information provided to those defendants on prior occasions.   Further, willful blindness to the facts constituting the offense

may be sufficient to establish knowledge. However, ... a mere showing of official responsibility ... is not an adequate substitute for direct or circumstantial proof of knowledge.

The United States Department of Justice has followed this decision in its subsequent environmental prosecutions.

In United States v. Iverson, 162 F.3d 1015 (9th Cir.1998), defendant was the founder, president, and chairman of the board of a chemical blending company. The company shipped its chemical in drums, which were returned for cleaning and reused. The cleaning process generated a wastewater regulated by the CWA, but the company failed to obtain a discharge permit and resorted to various illegal disposal methods. Although defendant "officially" retired prior to the events that led to criminal charges against him, he continued to receive money from the company, to be listed as president in documents that it filed with the state, and to give orders to employees, including the employee responsible for the drum-cleaning operation. Defendant sometimes was present when drums were cleaned, and he told employees involved that if they got caught, the company would receive only a slap on the wrist.

In affirming Iverson's conviction, the court of appeals approved the trial court's instruction that the jury could find him liable as a "responsible corporate officer" if it found, beyond a reasonable doubt, (1) that he knew that pollutants were being discharged to the sewer system by company employees, (2) that he had the "authority and capacity to prevent the discharge," and (3) that he failed to prevent the ongoing discharge. The court rejected defendant's argument that a corporate officer is "responsible" only when he "in fact exercises control over the activity causing the discharge or has an express corporate duty to oversee the activity."

In United States v. Ming Hong, 242 F.3d 528 (4th Cir. 2001), *cert. denied* 534 U.S. 823 (2001), defendant Hong avoided any formal association with Avion (which operated a wastewater treatment facility) and was not identified as an officer of the company. Nevertheless, he controlled its finances and played a substantial role in its operations. Hong knew that the company's newly acquired treatment system was designed only as a final step in the process of treating wastewater and was not adequate for use with otherwise untreated wastewater. Despite this inadequacy, and with Hong's knowledge, Avion used the system as the sole means of treating wastewater. When the system became clogged, employees discharged untreated wastewater directly into the municipal sewer system in violation of Avion's CWA discharge permit. Applying the RCO doctrine, the court upheld Hong's conviction under § 309(c)(1)(A) for negligent violation of CWA pretreatment requirements.

4.   PROSECUTORIAL DISCRETION

As noted at the beginning of this section on criminal liability, Congress generally has not defined thresholds indicating at what points violations of environmental laws or regulations are serious enough to justify adding criminal to civil penalties. Those judgments are left to enforcement officials in the executive branch. Since 1991 the Department of Justice has had an announced policy of encouraging corporations to develop and implement *voluntary environmental compliance and disclosure programs* as a means of mitigating exposure to criminal prosecution.

Most cases come to federal prosecutors by referral from EPA (which often learns of the problems from tips by "whistleblowers," present and former employees of companies that are knowingly and willfully violating environmental requirements). In 1994, EPA issued a guidance on the exercise of investigative discretion by its criminal investigators. The guidance established specific criteria that EPA investigators are to consider before initiating a criminal investigation. Case selection is based on two general measures, "significant environmental harm" and "culpable conduct." These measures, in turn, are divided into several factors that serve as indicators that a case is suitable for criminal investigation. The factors identified as possible indicators of environmental harm are (1) actual harm, (2) threat of significant harm, (3) failure to report environmental releases, and (4) a trend or common attitude toward noncompliance within the regulated community. Culpable conduct is based on (1) a history of repeated violations, (2) deliberate misconduct, (3) concealment of misconduct or falsification of records, (4) tampering with pollution monitoring or control equipment, or (5) conducting pollution-related activities without necessary permits or approvals.

In a policy statement issued in 2000, EPA said that it generally does not focus its criminal enforcement resources on entities that voluntarily discover, promptly disclose, and expeditiously correct violations, unless there is potentially culpable behavior. Other important factors in avoiding criminal prosecution are lack of repeat violations and willingness to cooperate with enforcement officials. However, even if EPA does not recommend prosecution of a disclosing corporate entity, the agency may pursue prosecution of culpable individuals.

5. STATE PRIVILEGES FOR ENVIRONMENTAL AUDITS

Approximately twenty states have enacted laws making information gathered through voluntary environmental audits *privileged*, or protected from disclosure, in various types of enforcement proceedings. Thus, the information is not accessible to third parties, including the government, absent a waiver or court order. About half of the laws also provide *immunity* from criminal, civil, or administrative prosecution and penalties with respect to violations that are disclosed voluntarily.

The laws typically define an environmental audit as a systematic review of a facility's practices to determine noncompliance with certain environmental laws. Most specify a variety of documents that may be considered parts of such reports and to which the privilege extends. These include field notes, records of observations, findings, opinions, suggestions, conclusions, drafts, memoranda, photographs, maps, charts, graphs, and surveys. Most of the laws prohibit persons who participated in audits from disclosing, testifying, or being compelled to testify about the audit reports or underlying facts. Included among participants are those who were made privy to audits, those who did any of the work, and those who provided estimates for corrective work resulting from the audit.

The federal EPA and Department of Justice strongly oppose state privilege and immunity laws, fearing that federal officials may have to step in and expend federal resources to pursue enforcement actions in cases that would be a state responsibility absent restrictions preventing the states from acting. EPA has threatened to withdraw or refuse delegations of authority to implement federal environmental laws and programs for states whose environmental audit laws interfere unduly with the states' enforcement capabilities. EPA and the Department of Justice also take the position that they are not bound by state privilege or immunity laws in federal enforcement proceedings.

H. COMMON LAW REMEDIES

While Congress and state legislatures have been enacting regulatory statutes aimed at preventing future problems and cleaning up current hazards, state and federal courts have been faced with increasing numbers of tort actions seeking compensatory and punitive damages, and occasionally injunctions, for injuries allegedly caused or threatened by toxic substances. These cases have presented the legal system with a wide range of novel issues and sometimes strained the system to its limits.

A variety of causes of action may be available to private plaintiffs, frequently neighboring landowners, injured or threatened by hazardous waste sites. Such causes of action include nuisance, negligence, trespass, strict liability, emotional distress, enhanced risk of future illness, and medical monitoring. Branch v. Western Petroleum, Inc., 657 P.2d 267 (Utah 1982) (all except enhanced risk and medical monitoring); Ayers v. Township of Jackson, 525 A.2d 287 (N.J.1987) (emotional distress, enhanced risk, and medical monitoring).

Governmental plaintiffs may seek abatement of hazardous conditions by challenging them as public nuisances. In Village of Wilsonville v. SCA Services, Inc., 426 N.E.2d 824 (Ill.1981), the court compelled defendant, the owner and operator of a state-licensed hazardous waste landfill located above an abandoned coal mine, which created a possibility of subsidence, to remove all wastes deposited there because they constituted a "prospective nuisance."

In toxic waste damage actions, the plaintiff's first problem is to establish that defendant's conduct

meets the requisite liability standard. Although
many toxic tort plaintiffs have brought actions under products liability theories holding manufacturers strictly liable for defective products, the liability
standard is less clear in cases not involving manufacturers. The generally accepted liability test for
hazardous waste releases is stated in the Second
Restatement of Torts. Under this test, liability
exists despite the exercise of due care if an activity
was "abnormally dangerous." To determine
whether an activity is abnormally dangerous, a
court must weigh the probability and severity of
foreseeable harm, whether the activity is unusual or
is in an inappropriate location, and other factors.
Restatement (Second) of Torts § 520 (1977). Thus,
fault plays a role in the Restatement assessment. A
few courts have rejected this fault element, however, and have begun to move beyond the abnormally
dangerous test. In State, Dept. of Environmental
Protection v. Ventron Corp., 468 A.2d 150 (N.J.
1983), the court imposed strict liability for harm
caused by toxic substances escaping from a landowner's property.

Proposed Final Draft No. 1 (2005) of the Restatement (Third) of Torts, Liability for Physical Harm
(Basic Principles), Chapter IV, § 20, provides that a
defendant who carries on abnormally dangerous
activity is subject to strict liability for resulting
physical harm. An activity is defined as "abnormally dangerous" if it creates a foreseeable and
"highly significant" risk of physical harm even
when reasonable care is exercised, and if the activi-

ty is not one of common usage. A reporter's comment to § 20 states that a risk of physical harm can be highly significant for either of two reasons: because the *likelihood* of harm is unusually high, or because the *severity* of the harm could be enormous.

Even if the defendant's conduct meets the requisite legal standard for liability, several possible barriers may prevent recovery. Statutes of limitations used to create major difficulties in some states. For example, a New York trial judge in 1983 dismissed 54 of 91 personal injury actions by residents of the infamous Love Canal. The judge held that the actions were barred by New York's statute of limitations because they were filed more than three years after *exposure* to the toxic chemicals. The statute of limitations problem has also received great attention in the asbestos cases.

Approximately forty states have rejected the "exposure" rule in favor of the "discovery" rule, taking the position that the period of limitation does not begin to run until plaintiff discovers her illness. For the remaining states, § 309 of CERCLA was adopted in 1986. It provides that in any action brought under state law for personal injury or property damages "which are caused or contributed to by exposure to any hazardous substance ... released into the environment from a facility," the limitation period for the action shall commence on "the date plaintiff knew (or reasonably should have known)" that the injury or damages were caused or contributed to by the hazardous substance.

Another problem is establishing a link between the defendant and the release of the substance. For example, many hazardous waste generators may have shipped similar materials to the site in question. It may be very difficult to establish whose containers leaked or in what quantities. A similar issue has arisen in products liability cases. In Sindell v. Abbott Laboratories, 607 P.2d 924 (Cal.1980), *cert. denied*, 449 U.S. 912 (1980), the plaintiff's mother was administered the drug diethylstilbesterol (DES) during pregnancy. Although DES was routinely given to prevent miscarriage, it now is known to cause a rare form of cancer in some daughters of women who took the drug. After developing such cancer, the plaintiff sued eleven of the more than two hundred manufacturers of DES. Although plaintiff was unable to identify the manufacturer of the particular DES that her mother took, the court held that she had stated a cause of action against all manufacturers of the drug using an identical formula. Resting this holding on a broad social policy, the court noted that the defendants were "better able to bear the costs of injury resulting from the manufacture of a defective product." The *Sindell* court then adopted a novel theory of liability by making each defendant liable for a share of plaintiff's damages, based on its share of the DES market. A similar approach could be applied where a plaintiff's illness can be traced to releases from a waste disposal site but not to any specific contributor to the site.

Sindell and related theories address the problem of linking the defendant to the chemical exposure.

An even more difficult problem is that of linking the exposure to plaintiff's injury. As we have seen, toxic chemical regulation involves matters at the boundaries of scientific knowledge. This scientific uncertainty causes severe problems for government regulators, but even more serious problems result for private plaintiffs who must establish a defendant's liability by a preponderance of the evidence.

In considering compensation, it is important to keep in mind that there are really two causation problems. One is the problem of establishing that the chemical involved is *capable* of causing the type of harm from which the plaintiff suffers. This is often difficult because the causation of diseases like cancer is poorly understood. For this reason, medical theory is often unhelpful in filling in gaps in the factual picture. Facts themselves are hard to come by. Many toxic substances are relatively novel, and, given the long latency periods associated with cancer, sufficient evidence concerning health effects is not likely to be available for the foreseeable future. Animal studies, although useful, generally involve much higher doses that are difficult to extrapolate to low doses over prolonged periods; there is also the question of whether extrapolation of results between species is valid. Epidemiological studies are helpful but often inconclusive regarding the level of risk created by a toxic substance.

The other problem relating to proof of causation is that of establishing, given that the toxic substance in question *can* cause harm of the type suffered by plaintiff, that the plaintiff's harm *did* in fact result from such exposure. A chemical may increase the prevalence of a disease enough to leave no doubt that *some* members of the exposed population were injured by that chemical. Others, however, may have suffered injuries from independent sources, and the two groups may be impossible to distinguish. The statistical association between exposure and illness may be too weak to justify a finding that a particular plaintiff's disease is causally linked to an exposure to a hazardous substance.

Despite the novelty of tort litigation over toxic causation, clear patterns have evolved in some areas. Litigation about Agent Orange, a defoliant and herbicide used by American forces in the Vietnam war, has provided perhaps the most extensive judicial discussion of toxic causation. See In re Agent Orange Products Liability Litigation, 597 F.Supp. 740 (E.D.N.Y.1984). Numerous lawsuits were filed against the manufacturers by veterans, their families, and others who contended that Agent Orange had caused various illnesses. Ultimately the litigation was consolidated in the Eastern District of New York. The weakness of the plaintiffs' causation evidence persuaded Judge Weinstein to approve a $180 million settlement, which was considered highly favorable to the defendants.

As Judge Weinstein explained, the evidence concerning the possible dangers from Agent Orange would have been enough for a court to uphold an administrative order limiting its use. Emphasizing the distinction between preventive regulatory measures and compensatory legal actions, however, the judge noted that "[in] the latter [case], a far higher probability (greater than 50%) is required since the law believes it unfair to require an individual to pay for another's tragedy unless it is shown that it is more likely than not that he caused it." The key flaw in the plaintiffs' case was that government epidemiological studies showed no statistical link between Agent Orange exposure and significant health effects. Hence, Judge Weinstein agreed that a settlement was in the best interests of the class.

In companion cases, involving opt-outs or individuals never included in the class, Judge Weinstein was forced to rule on the merits of the plaintiffs' claims. In these cases, he granted summary judgment for the defendants despite plaintiffs' tender of expert testimony linking Agent Orange with health effects. The epidemiological studies played a key role in these decisions: "The numerous epidemiological studies . . . are sufficient to shift the burden to plaintiffs of showing that a material fact exists as to causation." Judge Weinstein ruled the plaintiffs' expert testimony inadmissible, and then granted summary judgment because the plaintiffs had no admissible evidence to counter the defendants' epidemiological studies.

The D.C. Circuit has permitted recovery solely on the basis of expert clinical assessments despite a lack of statistical evidence. In Ferebee v. Chevron Chemical Co., 736 F.2d 1529 (D.C.Cir.1984), the court stated that a cause-effect relationship need not be clearly established by animal or epidemiological studies before a doctor can testify that, in his opinion, such a relationship exists: "As long as the basic methodology employed to reach a conclusion is sound, such as use of tissue samples, standard tests, and patient examination, products liability law does not preclude recovery until a 'statistically significant' number of people have been injured or until science has had the time and resources to complete sophisticated laboratory studies of the chemical." A few courts have followed *Ferebee*'s broader view of admissibility.

However, cases like *Ferebee* must be viewed with caution. In Daubert v. Merrell Dow Pharmaceuticals, Inc., 509 U.S. 579 (1993), the lower courts had ruled that expert testimony that plaintiffs wanted to present to the jury could not be admitted because it did not rely on epidemiological studies and was not "generally accepted" in the scientific community. The Supreme Court remanded, ruling that the "general acceptance" test applied by the lower courts, see Frye v. United States, 293 F. 1013 (D.C.App.1923), has been supplanted by a broader and more flexible inquiry under the legislatively enacted Federal Rules of Evidence: "[I]n order to qualify [under Rule 702] as 'scientific knowledge,' an inference or assertion must be derived by the scientific method" and must have been tested, said Justice Blackmun. While publication in a journal subject to peer review is not essential, it is a "relevant" factor for a judge to consider in assessing whether a method or technique is valid. The Court "recognize[d] that in practice, a gatekeeping role for the judge, no matter how flexible, inevitably on occasion will prevent the jury from learning of authentic insights and innovations. That, nevertheless, is the balance that is struck by Rules of Evidence designed not for the exhaustive search for cosmic understanding but for the particularized resolution of legal disputes." The Court rejected plaintiffs' argument that Congress intended to permit juries to resolve scientific disputes through the adversarial process in the same manner as they resolve disputes about economic theories or other complex subjects.

On remand in *Daubert*, the court of appeals again held that plaintiffs' proffered expert testimony was inadmissible. The court emphasized plaintiffs' failure to show either that the testimony grew out of research conducted by the expert prior to and independently of the litigation, or that the research had been subjected to peer review. Daubert v. Merrell Dow Pharmaceuticals, Inc., 43 F.3d 1311 (9th Cir. 1995).

In 2000, Rule 702 was amended to codify principles growing out of *Daubert*. Now it provides that a qualified expert may testify if "(1) the testimony is based upon sufficient facts or data, (2) the testimony is the product of reliable principles and methods, and (3) the witness has applied the principles and methods reliably to the facts of the case."

A basic principle of personal injury law has been that plaintiffs must show "harm" in the form of physical injury in order to recover monetary damages. The so-called "latency" problem is that toxic exposure may result in diseases whose symptoms are not evident for many years. Should plaintiffs exposed to toxic hazards and placed at significant risk of disease, but perhaps not yet showing clinical symptoms of physical injury, be entitled to some kind of legal remedy?

Ayers v. Township of Jackson, 525 A.2d 287 (N.J. 1987), distinguished four kinds of claims related to potential future harms from exposure to toxic chemicals:

(a) Plaintiff has an existing physical injury that may worsen or develop into a more serious illness;

(b) Plaintiff has no existing injury or disease but is at an increased risk of developing a particular disease, such as cancer, in the future;

(c) Plaintiff, because of her susceptibility to the disease, suffers present emotional distress, usually fear or anxiety, which may or may not be accompanied by physical symptoms;

(d) Plaintiff, again because of the enhanced risk of future serious illness, incurs or should incur present and future expenses for medical monitoring or surveillance of the possible development of the disease.

The prevailing rule for cases (a), (b) and (c) is that claims based on "enhanced risk" or "mental distress" are not compensable unless plaintiff can establish that the probability of the future disease is greater than fifty percent.

With respect to cases in category (d), In re Paoli R.R. Yard PCB Litigation, 916 F.2d 829 (3d Cir. 1990), held that a "medical monitoring" claimant must show (1) that she was significantly exposed to a proven hazardous substance through the negligent action of defendant, (2) that as a proximate result of exposure she suffers an increased risk of contracting a serious latent disease, (3) that the increased risk makes medical examinations reasonably necessary, and (4) that monitoring and testing procedures exist which make early detection and treatment of the disease possible and beneficial.

In most medical monitoring cases plaintiffs have sought or courts have awarded a traditional lump sum of monetary damages. In some cases, however, litigants have pursued or courts have preferred periodic payments of surveillance expenses out of a court-supervised trust fund or similar mechanism. Not all jurisdictions recognize a cause of action for medical monitoring. See Hinton ex rel. Hinton v. Monsanto Co., 813 So.2d 827 (Ala. 2001), in which the court said, "Alabama law has long required a manifest, present injury before a plaintiff may recover in tort. . . . Here, the plaintiff has not alleged a present injury."

Advances in molecular biology and genomics are likely to transform traditional conceptions of risk and injury. New technologies will enable us to identify an expanding progression of biological effects between chemical exposure and fully developed disease. Courts may be moved to reconsider where in the exposure-disease continuum remediable harm has occurred as new biological markers are able to show that bodily integrity has been compromised well before the appearance of classic symptoms.

CHAPTER 6

PRESERVATION OF NATURAL AREAS

Cleaning up the air and water is clearly an important goal of environmental law, as is protecting the public from toxic chemicals. There is, however, another strand of federal environmental law that seeks different, though related, goals. Indeed, this strand predates the federal anti-pollution effort. The reference, of course, is to the goal of preserving wilderness and other natural areas.

Several statutes that we have already considered incorporate this goal. For example, § 101(b) of NEPA requires the government to "fulfill the responsibilities of each generation as trustee of the environment for succeeding generations," to "assure for all Americans safe, healthful, productive, and esthetically and culturally pleasing surroundings," and to "preserve important ... natural aspects of our national heritage...." 42 U.S.C.A. § 4331(b). Much litigation under NEPA relates to whether such factors have been adequately discussed in environmental impact statements. As we will see, the Clean Water Act also contains protections for wetlands, and the Clean Air Act contains specific provisions relating to the protection of parks and wilderness areas.

285

In this chapter, we will be concerned primarily with direct restrictions on land development or resource use in natural areas. The effect of these restrictions is to prevent individuals who wish to do so from using certain areas for economically profitable purposes. This chapter explores the statutory and constitutional implications of these restrictions. We begin by considering government restrictions on the development of privately owned land. We next consider efforts to protect coastal waters and then turn to restrictions on resource development on publicly owned lands. We close with a brief discussion of protection for endangered species, a policy that applies in different ways to all of these geographic areas.

A. PRESERVATION AS A GOAL

Before considering these legal restrictions on development, an understanding of their rationale is helpful. A century ago the idea of preventing the development of "useless" wilderness areas might have been widely regarded as completely irrational. Obviously, individuals who share this judgment will regard the legal mechanisms under discussion here as incomprehensible at best and perhaps perverse at worst. What are the arguments in favor of protecting natural areas?

Because the alternative land uses typically are economically profitable, it is useful to begin by examining this question from an economic perspective. As we saw in Chapter 3, economists typically regard the free market as the ideal means of determining resource allocation. It has been argued that this model should be extended to wilderness areas, so that, for example, the Grand Canyon would be sold to the highest bidder. If the highest bidder was the Sierra Club, the Canyon would be saved; if the highest bidder was a power company, the Canyon would be dammed. Any attempt to defend wilderness preservation must confront and attempt to refute this position.

Several economic arguments can be made in favor of wilderness preservation. As we saw earlier, the market mechanism breaks down when public goods or externalities are present. Arguably, both are involved in wilderness preservation. Individuals may consider preservation of wilderness worthwhile even though they have no present plans to use the wilderness. These individuals may be considered as having a so-called "option demand" for wilderness. That is, they would be willing to pay to preserve the option of using the wilderness in the future for themselves and their descendants. More broadly, some individuals who have no desire to use wilderness at any time may nevertheless have a preference for the preservation of wilderness as an ethical value. These individuals' preferences arguably make wilderness preservation a public good. The reason is that if the wilderness is preserved, these individuals cannot be excluded from enjoying the resulting satisfaction of their preferences. Furthermore, externalities are also present. Many biologists would suggest, on the basis of studies of prior ecological changes, that widespread changes in undeveloped areas are likely to have unforeseen negative consequences there and elsewhere. For example, development of estuaries or marsh areas may indirectly affect wildlife and marine life, thereby impinging on the interests of hunters and fishermen. The existence of these externalities provides a basis for preserving wilderness areas that is not unlike the basis for preventing pollution.

Moreover, temporal externalities also exist, for many of the affected individuals belong to future generations. Some economists have argued that these intertemporal effects may be quite large. The amount of wilderness is limited by present supplies; indeed, the future amount of available wilderness probably will be even less than that existing today. As the supply decreases, the price individuals would be willing to pay to use any one piece of wilderness will tend to increase. Moreover, preservation of wilderness seems to be a "normal" good—that is, a good that is in greater demand as income rises. If we assume that economic growth will continue, the result will be higher individual incomes and therefore a higher demand for wilderness. Hence, future generations may have a stronger demand for wilderness areas than current generations do. Ignoring the preferences of future generations could result in greatly distorted resource allocation. Thus, from the perspective of neoclassical economics, a strong argument can be made against leaving decisions about wilderness to the market.

As a descriptive science, economics can tell us only the consequences of a decision, not its desirability. Society must make a value judgment about those consequences. Today's society clearly has made a judgment in favor of preserving wilderness. This can be seen in the various environmental statutes considered in this chapter. It can also be seen in more direct measurements of public opinion in various opinion polls, which show consistent support for wilderness preservation.

With this background in mind, we will turn to the problems raised by attempting to prevent individuals from developing privately owned lands.

B.   RESTRICTIONS ON DEVELOPMENT OF PRIVATE LAND

Much environmentally significant land, particularly in wetlands and coastal areas, is in the hands of private individuals. We will not attempt to survey the various state laws restricting the development of this land. Instead, we will focus on the constitutional issues. We will first consider the extent to which attempts to regulate development of private land may violate the taking clause of the Constitution. We will then turn to the public trust doctrine and some related doctrines legitimizing restrictions that might otherwise be constitutionally dubious.

1. THE TAKING PROBLEM

The Fifth Amendment provides that private property shall not "be taken for public use, without just compensation." This provision applies only to the federal government. The Fourteenth Amendment, which imposes constitutional restrictions on the states, does not contain similar language. The Supreme Court, however, has construed the Fourteenth Amendment as imposing the same requirement by implication from its due process clause. Consequently, courts have not distinguished between the federal and state governments for purposes of taking clause analysis.

The earliest relevant taking case is Hadacheck v. Sebastian, 239 U.S. 394 (1915). *Hadacheck* involved a Los Angeles city ordinance making it unlawful to operate a brickyard within certain portions of the city. Hadacheck owned a brickyard in one of those areas. He had purchased the land when it was well outside the city limits and far from any residential district. He alleged that he had had no reason to anticipate that the area would ever be annexed to the city, that much of the property had been excavated for clay, that the land was worth $800,000 if used for brick-making purposes but no more than $60,000 for any other purpose, and that the ordinance would force him out of business. He also made two additional allegations that were rejected by the state courts: (1) that the operation of his business did not have detrimental effects on adjoining property, and (2) that the real purpose of the ordinance was to give brickyards located elsewhere in the city a monopoly. The Supreme Court decisively rejected the attack on the ordinance, which it found a valid exercise of the police power:

It is to be remembered that we are dealing with one of the most essential powers of government, one that is the least limitable. It may, indeed, seem harsh in its exercise, usually is on some individual, but the imperative necessity for its existence precludes any limitation upon it when not exerted arbitrarily. A vested interest cannot be asserted against it because of conditions once obtaining. To so hold would preclude development and fix a city forever in its primitive conditions. There must be progress, and if in its march private interests are in the way they must yield to the good of the community.

Hadacheck was decided at a time when the Supreme Court was much more willing than it is today to strike down state statutes regulating economic activities. Yet even in that pro-business period, the Court firmly upheld the *Hadacheck* ordinance.

Hadacheck might seem to suggest that the impact of a regulation on private individuals is irrelevant to determining constitutionality. The theory of the case seems to be that if a statute is otherwise legitimately within the police power—that is, if it is reasonably related to the public health, welfare, or morals—then individuals who suffer severe losses because of the regulation have no remedy. Less than a decade after *Hadacheck,* the Supreme Court drew back from this conclusion in Pennsylvania Coal Co. v. Mahon, 260 U.S. 393 (1922). This case involved a Pennsylvania statute making it unlawful for coal companies to cause the subsidence of any public building, street, or private residence. The Mahons were bound by a covenant to permit a coal company to remove all the coal without liability. The effect of the statute was to annul this covenant. Pennsylvania law recognized three separate property rights: the right to use the surface, ownership of the subsurface minerals, and the right to have the surface supported by the subsurface earth. The coal company claimed that the statute operated as a taking of the second and third rights, both of which belonged to it under its deed with the Mahons. In perhaps the most important single decision under the taking clause, Justice Holmes held that the statute was indeed a taking. The heart of the opinion is to be found in the following famous passage:

> Government hardly could go on if to some extent values incident to property could not be diminished without paying for every such change in the general law. As long recognized, some values are enjoyed under an implied limitation and must yield to the police power. But obviously the implied limitation must have its limits, or the contract and due process clauses are gone. One fact for consideration in determining such limits is the extent of the diminution. When it reaches a certain magnitude, in most if not in all cases there must be an exercise of eminent do-

main and compensation to sustain the act. So the question depends upon the particular facts. The greatest weight is given to the judgment of the legislature, but it always is open to interested parties to contend that the legislature has gone beyond its constitutional power.

In applying this test, the Court stressed that the statute made coal mining in certain areas commercially impractical and thus had "very nearly the same effect for constitutional purposes as appropriating or destroying it." The Court concluded that so long as "private persons or communities have seen fit to take the risk of acquiring only surface rights, we cannot see that the fact that the risk has become a danger warrants the giving to them greater rights than they bought." Justice Brandeis filed a strong dissent.

At the very least, *Pennsylvania Coal* makes it clear that *Hadacheck* cannot be taken to its logical extreme. That is, cases exist in which there is a legitimate public purpose for regulation but the regulation falls too heavily on a single individual, who must be compensated under the taking clause. As the Court says in *Pennsylvania Coal*, this is a matter of degree and therefore difficult to predict in advance.

The next case made it clear, however, that even the physical destruction of property may sometimes be permissible without compensation. In Miller v. Schoene, 276 U.S. 272 (1928), the Court upheld a Virginia statute authorizing the state entomologist to order the destruction of ornamental red cedar trees. The purpose of the statute was to prevent the transmission of a plant disease to neighboring apple orchards. The Court held that the existence of cedars was incompatible with the existence of the apple trees, so that the state was forced to choose which form of property to preserve. As the Court said, "[W]hen forced to such a choice the state does not exceed its constitutional powers by deciding upon the destruction of one class of property in order to save another which, in the judgment of the legislature, is of greater value to the public."

For the next fifty years, the Supreme Court paid little attention to takings issues. In the late 1970s, however, the Court's attention returned to this area. Penn Central Transportation Co. v. New York, 438 U.S. 104 (1978) involved a New York historic preservation ordinance. Briefly, under the ordinance a special commission was empowered to designate buildings as landmarks, subject to administrative and judicial review. After designation, the exterior of a building had to be kept in good repair, and exterior alterations had to be approved by the Commission. Development rights lost because of the landmark designation could be transferred to nearby plots of land, thereby allowing additional development on those plots beyond the usual restrictions of the applicable zoning and building codes. Penn Central owned Grand Central Terminal, a designated landmark. A plan by Penn Central to build a multistory office building perched above the terminal was rejected by the Commission.

Penn Central then brought suit claiming that its property had been taken without compensation. It conceded, however, that the transferable development rights had some value and that the company could still earn a reasonable return on its initial investment.

The opinion of the Court by Justice Brennan begins by reviewing the factors that had shaped prior decisions. The Court conceded that it had been unable to develop any "set formula" for determining when compensation was required. Instead, it referred to the prior cases as involving "essentially ad hoc, factual inquiries." The Court did, however, point to several relevant factors. The most important were (1) whether the regulation had "interfered with distinct investment-backed expectations," and (2) whether the government had physically invaded the property or had simply enacted "some public program adjusting the benefits and burdens of economic life to promote the common good." In reviewing the specific regulation before it, the Court concluded that the ordinance was "expected to produce a widespread public benefit applicable to all similarly situated property." The Court then held that the regulation passed the *Pennsylvania Coal* test because it did not deprive the company of all use of the property, but instead allowed continuation of a past use and, more importantly, permitted the company to obtain a "reasonable return" on its investment.

Since *Penn Central*, taking cases have been a regular part of the Court's docket. A year after

Penn Central, the Supreme Court decided two additional significant taking cases. The first case, Andrus v. Allard, 444 U.S. 51 (1979), involved a statute prohibiting commercial transactions in certain "artifacts" such as eagle feathers. The plaintiffs owned bird feathers when the statute was passed and were subject to prosecution for selling them. In rejecting a taking claim, the Court stressed that the plaintiffs retained the rights to possess, donate, and devise the feathers. The Court noted that the feathers could conceivably be exhibited for profit, but then went on to add that a loss of future profits, unaccompanied by any physical property restriction, "provides a slender reed upon which to rest a takings claim." The second case, Kaiser Aetna v. United States, 444 U.S. 164 (1979), involved a private fishpond that the owners connected to the ocean and converted into a "marina-style subdivision community." Although the government did not initially object to this project, it later contended that the marina was subject to a right of public access. The Court held that belatedly imposing this right of access would constitute a taking.

In 1987, the Supreme Court decided three important taking cases. One related to remedies. In First English Evangelical Lutheran Church of Glendale v. County of Los Angeles, 482 U.S. 304 (1987), the Court significantly strengthened the remedy available to a property owner whose land has been "over-regulated." Under *First English*, the land owner is entitled not only to an injunction against enforcement of the ordinance, but also to damages for the temporary restriction on development between the ordinance's passage and the injunction invalidating it. Thus, governments may become liable for substantial damage awards if they misjudge the location of the blurred and wavering line between valid regulations and invalid takings.

The other two 1987 cases increased the uncertainty about the difference between regulation and taking. In one case, Keystone Bituminous Coal Ass'n v. DeBenedictis, 480 U.S. 470 (1987), the Court upheld a statute strikingly similar to that struck down in the old *Pennsylvania Coal* case. This time, the Court found that protection of surface land from subsidence was a valid public purpose and that the mining companies could still earn a fair return on their holdings, since only a small percentage of the coal had to be left in the ground to support the surface. The Court was sharply divided, however, with four dissenters insisting that *Pennsylvania Coal* was controlling.

In the final case in this trilogy, the Court found a taking based on quite a different analysis. Nollan v. California Coastal Commission, 483 U.S. 825 (1987) involved an owner's effort to construct a bungalow on his beachfront property. As a condition of approval, the California Coastal Commission required him to record an easement giving the public lateral access to the beach from adjacent beach property. In an opinion by Justice Scalia, the Court held that this requirement was a taking. The Court assumed that the commission could have simply forbidden construction of the bungalow, but held that any conditions on approval had to be "reasonably related" to problems created by the new construction. The four dissenters accused the majority of substantially raising the level of scrutiny applied to land-use regulations. The dissent also pointed out that the permit condition was not alleged to diminish the value of the owner's investment in the land.

The Court fleshed out the *Nollan* test in Dolan v. City of Tigard, 512 U.S. 374 (1994). Like *Nollan, Dolan* involved conditions on a building permit: a requirement that in order to expand a hardware store, the owner dedicate a floodplain area and the adjacent 15 feet to a public "green-space" and bicycle path. The court upheld the conditions to the extent that they limited development in this part of the land but found it difficult to see why the owner was also required to give up her control over access to the greenway. Applying a test of "rough proportionality," the Court concluded that the city had failed to provide any quantitative evidence that the bikeway would offset the increased traffic demand from the store expansion. Later precedent indicates that the nexus and proportionality tests apply only when the government conditions a permit on the grant of a property interest such as an affirmative easement. These requirements do not apply when the government merely restricts the use of property.

None of these cases involved the core question raised by Justice Holmes in *Pennsylvania Coal*: When does a diminution in value become so great as to become a taking? In Lucas v. South Carolina Coastal Council, 505 U.S. 1003 (1992), the Court held that a *complete* destruction of land value is normally a taking. *Lucas* involved a taking claim by the owner of two beachfront residential lots, who could not build on the property at all because of a state law protecting fragile breaches. Although dicta in a number of previous cases had suggested that a 100% loss of property value would be a taking regardless of the government's regulatory justification, *Lucas* was the first square holding to that effect. Justice Scalia's opinion for the Court sets some limits on this rule: it does not apply when the land use would be a common law nuisance or otherwise in excess of the owner's common law rights; it does not apply to personal property; it may not apply to regulations that are not specifically directed to land use. In a concurring opinion, Justice Kennedy argued for a more fluid balancing approach, while Justices Blackmun and Stevens sharply dissented.

Not surprisingly, landowners have made aggressive use of *Lucas* claims. More recent decisions, however, have not been in their favor. In Palazzolo v. Rhode Island, 533 U.S. 606 (2001), the Court found that there had been no total taking because the owner was left with the right to build a residence on part of an eighteen-acre tract. (More favorably for property owners, however, the Court rejected the argument that the taking claim was completely foreclosed by the fact that the owner acquired the property after the regulation was in place). Another extension of *Lucas* was attempted in Tahoe-Sierra Preservation Council, Inc. v. Tahoe Regional Planning Agency, 535 U.S. 302 (2002). There, the landowners argued that a moratorium was a "total temporary taking," since it prohibited all use of the property for a designated time period. In an opinion by Justice Stevens, the Court rejected this application of *Lucas* and held that the more flexible *Penn Central* test applied. The majority characterized *Lucas* as carving out an exception for the " 'extraordinary case' in which a regulation permanently deprives property of all value," while "the default rule remains that, in the regulatory taking context, we require a more fact specific inquiry."

Obviously, the Court has not steered a steady course in construing the taking clause, and the theoretical foundations for the endeavor remain mysterious. At this point, however, it is possible to discern a fairly clear pattern in the results of the cases. The Court seems to divide land-use regulations into three categories.

First are the access mandates. Such a regulation mandates that a landowner open up his land to the public or allow it to be physically occupied by a third party. Such regulations are much like condemnation of an easement and not surprisingly are considered virtually per se takings. *Kaiser Aetna* is an illustrative case.

Second are use limitations. A regulation may restrict the landowner's use of the property so greatly as to impose a severe economic loss. Assuming that the land use would otherwise have been lawful, the regulation is a taking if it renders the land completely valueless. The Court has never precluded the possibility that a partial use restriction might be severe enough to constitute a taking even if the government is pursuing a bona fide public policy. Notably, however, in the 80 years since *Hadacheck*, the Court has never found such a partial taking if the government was pursuing a bona fide public policy. So perhaps Holmes's reference to a sufficiently great diminution in value actually means the complete destruction of value. If so, *Lucas* represents the rare case of a taking due to diminution of value.

The third category involves tie-ins between use restrictions and access mandates. The government may require the landowner to allow public access (normally a taking) in order to escape from land-use restrictions (normally not a taking). Here, the Court requires that the access requirement relate to the proposed use of the land and be "roughly proportionate" to the problems created by the new use.

This three-part scheme provides a tidy account of the cases. Taking law has been so doctrinally unruly, however, that it would be unwise to count on future consistency. Perhaps the Court will find that some public access requirements are not takings, after all, or that some partial use restrictions are takings. In the meantime, however, this scheme does at least put the cases into some coherent order.

One response to the taking problem has been to attempt to limit the kinds of interests that can claim the status of property rights. By preventing certain kinds of economic interests from rising to the status of property rights, a court can avoid any taking problem. The court can simply say that whatever was taken was not property and thus not subject to the taking clause. In the next section, we will consider several of the doctrines that have served this function.

2. THE PUBLIC TRUST DOCTRINE

Both the federal and state governments possess certain quasi-property rights stemming from their regulatory powers over waterways. These rights have become important in the environmental context because they serve to justify government regulations in coastal and wetland areas that might otherwise be challenged under the taking clause.

At the state level, these quasi-property rights are defined by the public trust doctrine. The leading case concerning this doctrine is Illinois Central Railroad Co. v. Illinois, 146 U.S. 387 (1892). This case involved the validity of a land grant to the Illinois Central Railroad. In 1869, the Illinois legislature had given the railroad certain submerged lands under Lake Michigan. (When the bill was introduced, it had conveyed these lands to the City of Chicago, but somehow before final passage the grantee had been changed to the railroad.) Four years later, the State repealed the prior statute.

Illinois then filed a quiet title suit to establish its ownership of the submerged lands. It should be noted that if the 1869 statute was valid, the statute reclaiming ownership of the lands could hardly avoid attack as a taking since it would have seized title to private property.

The Supreme Court, however, avoided any such constitutional problem by holding that the original grant of land to the railroad was invalid, so that the railroad never had anything except at most a voidable title to the property. The 1869 Act was invalid because it violated the public trust in which the property was originally held by the state, as the following passage explains:

> That the State holds the title to the lands under the navigable waters of Lake Michigan . . . we have already shown, and that title necessarily carries with it control over the waters above them whenever the lands are subjected to use. . . . It is a title held in trust for the people of the State that they may enjoy the navigation of the waters, carry on commerce over them, and have liberty of fishing therein freed from the obstruction or interference of private parties. . . . The trust devolving upon the state for the public, and which can only be discharged by the management and control of property in which the public has an interest, cannot be relinquished by a transfer of property. The control of the state for the purposes of the trust can never be lost, except as to such parcels as are used in promoting the interests of the public therein, or can be disposed of

without any substantial impairment of the public interest in the lands and waters remaining.

Thus, private property interests in land subject to the public trust are severely limited. To the extent that private individuals can hold title to this land at all, that title is necessarily subject to the requirements of the trust. As the Supreme Court later made clear, the public trust extends not only to navigable waters but also to all waters affected by the tides. Phillips Petroleum Co. v. Mississippi, 484 U.S. 469 (1988).

The evolution of the public trust doctrine is well illustrated by three cases from California. In a 1928 case, Boone v. Kingsbury, 273 P. 797 (Cal. 1928), the California Supreme Court upheld a statute authorizing oil drilling in offshore tidal areas. The court held that this form of development was a justifiable exercise of the public trust. The court stressed the public interest in encouraging "citizens to devote waste and unused lands to some useful purpose." As an example of such useless lands, the court referred to a prior case involving a salt marsh. By 1971, the court's attitude had changed completely. In Marks v. Whitney, 491 P.2d 374 (Cal.1971), the court gave a much more expansive reading to the public trust doctrine. The court stressed that in administering the trust, the state is not bound by traditional classifications of land uses. Instead, the state can give recognition to the need to preserve lands in their natural state, so they can serve as "ecological units for scientific study, as open space, and as environments which provide food and habitat for birds and marine life, and which favorably affect the scenery and climate of the area." As a result, the court held that a neighboring landowner could sue to prevent tidelands from being filled and developed. Such a suit could be brought even if lands had already been reclaimed with or without prior authorization from the state, since neither reclamation nor prior authorization "*ipso facto* terminate the public trust nor render the issue moot." Later, in National Audubon Society v. Superior Court of Alpine County, 658 P.2d 709 (Cal.1983), the same court held that the public trust doctrine limited "prior appropriation" rights over use of water, so that Los Angeles was not automatically entitled to the full use of its water rights where the result would be to completely dry up a lake. Given the almost sacrosanct place of prior appropriation rights in western water law, this was a notable expansion of the public trust doctrine.

The public trust doctrine is not the only property law concept that has been used to uphold restrictions on private land development. In an innovative decision, the Oregon Supreme Court held that fencing private beach land violated an access right of the public deriving from longstanding custom. State ex rel. Thornton v. Hay, 462 P.2d 671 (Or. 1969). Opinions such as this, or such as those applying the public trust doctrine, should not be seen simply as a means of finding a loophole in taking law. Rather, they are best seen as attempts to adjust the technicalities of taking and property law to the realities of modern life. As a realistic matter, certain activities involve longstanding public interests and therefore must reasonably be expected to be subject to broad government regulation. Given the long history of public control over waterways, no individual claiming to own legal title to a public waterway can really have a reasonable expectation of uninhibited use of his "property." Thus, the kinds of firm expectations that taking law was intended to protect simply cannot arise in some contexts.

3. THE NAVIGATIONAL SERVITUDE

Like the states, the federal government has a quasi-property interest in navigable waters. The federal interest is called the navigational servitude. The operation of the servitude is illustrated in United States v. Rands, 389 U.S. 121 (1967). The issue in *Rands* was whether a condemnation award for land along the Columbia River should include that portion of its market value attributable to potential use as a port site. The court held that no individual can own a property interest in the use of navigable waters, for such use is always completely subject to government control: "Thus, without being constitutionally obligated to pay compensation, the United States may change the course of a navigable stream, or otherwise impair or destroy a riparian owner's access to navigable waters, even though the market value of the riparian owner's land is substantially diminished." Indeed, later in the opinion, the Court referred to the "constitutional power of Congress *completely* to regulate navigable streams to the *total* exclusion of private power companies or port owners" (emphasis added).

The *Rands* case may have been somewhat limited by Kaiser Aetna v. United States, 444 U.S. 164 (1979). That case, discussed in the previous subsection, involved the private improvement of a pond that originally was incapable of being used for navigational purposes. As a result of the improvements, the pond was to be used as a private marina. The Court acknowledged that the strict logic of *Rands* and similar cases might allow the government to require public access to the marina, converting it into a public aquatic park. But, the Court concluded, the facts in the *Kaiser Aetna* case were too far removed from previous cases involving navigable waterways. For one thing, the pond was unlike the sort of "great navigable stream" that had previously been held "incapable of private ownership." The Court also stressed the government's consent to the marina project:

We have not the slightest doubt that the Government *could have refused to allow such dredging* on the ground that it could have impaired navigation in the bay, or could have conditioned its approval of the dredging on petitioners' agreement to comply with various measures that it deemed appropriate for the promotion of navigation. But what petitioners *now* have is a body of water that was private property under Hawaiian law, linked to navigable water by a channel dredged by them with the consent of the respondent.... In this case, we hold that the "right to exclude," so universally held to be a fundamental element of the property right, falls within this category of interests that the Government cannot take without compensation.... [Emphasis added.]

This was obviously a guarded holding. Thirty years later, *Kaiser Aetna* seems to have found its place as a narrow exception to the *Rands* rule.

It is important to note that the navigational servitude applies only to waters meeting the traditional test of navigability. While statements of the traditional test vary, the central concern behind these tests relates to potential use for navigational purposes. On the other hand, federal regulation has not been limited to this class of waterways. The courts have held, with strong support in the legislative history, that the Clean Water Act extends beyond traditional navigable waters. The reason, obviously, is that the purity of navigable waterways cannot be maintained unless other bodies of water that directly or indirectly connect to those navigable waters are also cleaned up. To the extent that Congress has extended its jurisdictional net beyond the traditional navigable waterways, however, it can no longer claim the protection of the navigational servitude as a defense to taking claims. Thus, at least some applications of the Clean Water Act might be found to limit the use of certain parcels of land so drastically as to constitute takings.

Perhaps the most significant exercise of congressional authority is § 404 of the Clean Water Act. Section 404 requires permits for the discharge of dredged or fill material. In an important early district court opinion, the permit requirement was applied to man-made canals and mangrove wetlands that are periodically covered by tides. The discharges, which ultimately would have resulted in converting these areas into dry land, were held to violate the Act. United States v. Holland, 373 F.Supp. 665 (M.D.Fla.1974).

The Supreme Court has supported much, but not all, of this expansion of federal jurisdiction. In United States v. Riverside Bayview Homes, Inc., 474 U.S. 121 (1985), the Court upheld a regulation defining the Corps' permit authority broadly. The regulation at issue gave the Corps jurisdiction over any area flooded or saturated often enough to support "vegetation typically adapted for life in saturated soil conditions." But in *SWANCC*, supra page 62, the Court overturned a regulation that asserted federal jurisdiction over all wetlands used by migratory birds. *SWANCC* has left the lower courts in some confusion over whether federal jurisdiction still extends to some isolated wetlands, or whether it applies only to navigable waters, their tributaries, and adjacent wetlands.

The Court revisited the issue in Rapanos v. United States, 547 U.S. 715, (2006), but only added to the confusion. A plurality opinion by Justice Scalia restricted the Corps' authority to include "only those relatively permanent, standing or continuously flowing bodies of water 'forming geographic features' that are described in ordinary parlance as 'streams[,] ... oceans, rivers, [and] lakes.'" 126 S.Ct. at 2225. In Justice Scalia's view, "*only* those wetlands with a continuous surface connection to bodies that are 'waters of the United States' in their own right, so that there is no clear demarcation between 'waters' and wetlands, are 'adjacent to' such waters and covered by the Act." *Id.* at 2226. This test would have been a radical truncation of federal jurisdiction. Justice Kennedy's separate opinion required the government to establish a significant nexus between a wetland and navigable waters. The dissenters would have upheld the Corps' broad claims of jurisdiction over wetlands. Because Justice Kennedy cast the pivotal vote, lower courts seem to be turning to his test for guidance, sometimes augmented by the plurality's test in the view cases where that test is broader.

Because both the federal and state governments have legitimate interests in regulating the use of water bodies and adjacent lands, a cooperative effort is clearly indicated. A beginning has been made toward such cooperation. The Clean Water Act provides for delegation of the permit system to state governments, subject to certain safeguards. In addition, another statute, the Coastal Zone Management Act (CZMA), 16 U.S.C.A. §§ 1451–1464, attempts to encourage state governments to implement land-use plans for coastal areas. The incentive is financial; the requirements are essentially procedural. Congress was less concerned about controlling the eventual form of state regulation than about encouraging the states to engage in some structured form of regulation of coastal areas. The CZMA is discussed in more detail below.

C. PROTECTING COASTAL WATERS

Disputes over the exploration and development of offshore oil and gas deposits have multiplied ever since the disastrous 1969 blowout and spill in California's Santa Barbara channel, which killed birds and marine organisms, damaged beaches and seafront properties, and impaired fishing and recreational activities over a large area. The disputes most frequently have arisen in connection with federal leasing of tracts in the outer continental shelf (OCS). The United States government, rather than the states, exercises sovereign rights over the seabed and subsoil of the continental shelf beyond three miles from the coastline. United States v. Maine, 420 U.S. 515 (1975); Outer Continental Shelf Lands Act (OCSLA), 43 U.S.C.A. § 1331 et seq. Acting primarily through the Department of the Interior, the government leases OCS areas to private firms through a competitive bidding process prescribed by OCSLA. Leasing and the resultant exploration, development, production, and transportation of OCS oil and gas also are subject to the mandates of NEPA, the CZMA, and the Clean Water Act.

The process leading to production and transportation of oil and gas from OCS lands involves several stages at which environmental considerations are to be taken into account. OCSLA charts a path that begins with promulgation of a five-year leasing program and continues through lease sales and exploration to development, production, and sale of the recovered minerals. 43 U.S.C.A. §§ 1344, 1337, 1340, 1351, and 1353. To ensure that the Secretary of the Interior takes into account all relevant policy considerations and the views of all interested persons, the Act provides for participation by Congress, affected state and local governments, other federal agencies, and the public.

Section 18 of the Act, 43 U.S.C.A. § 1344, requires the Secretary to establish a five-year OCS leasing program, consisting of a schedule of proposed lease sales indicating as precisely as possible the size, timing, and location of leasing activity. Section 18 also establishes a mechanism for state governments to offer suggestions and comments. The Secretary must submit the proposed program and any comments received to Congress and the President at least sixty days before he approves it, indicating why any specific recommendation of a state government was not accepted.

Following approval by the Secretary, a leasing program is subject for sixty days to judicial review exclusively in the D.C. Circuit, upon suit by any person who participated in the administrative proceedings related to the program and is adversely affected or aggrieved by it. 43 U.S.C.A. § 1349. The court of appeals must consider the matter solely on the record before the Secretary, and his findings are conclusive if supported by substantial evidence.

After a five-year OCS leasing program has been approved by the Secretary of Interior and survived judicial review, later steps toward production of oil and gas include the proposal and conduct of lease sales by the Secretary, and proposal by lessees of exploration plans and then development and production plans. OCSLA requires at all these stages that the Secretary consider environmental factors and the views of other federal officials, state and local governments, and the public.

Related to federal action under OCSLA, there has been extended controversy over the requirements of the Coastal Zone Management Act. CZMA seeks to achieve sound use of coastal land and water resources by providing monetary assistance to states to develop and administer management programs consistent with standards prescribed in §§ 305 and 306. Approval of a state management program by the Secretary of Commerce triggers "federal consistency" provisions in § 307(c). As originally enacted, this provision required federal agencies, permittees, and licensees to show that their proposed developments in or "directly affecting" coastal zones, including the OCS, would be consistent with the state program. In certain instances the consistency requirement is qualified by the phrase "to the maximum extent practicable" or "unless [found by the Secretary of Commerce to be] consistent with the objectives of this title or otherwise necessary in the interest of national security."

As a rider to the 1990 Omnibus Budget Reconciliation Act, Congress amended § 307(c)(1) of the CZMA to read as follows:

Each Federal agency activity within or outside the coastal zone that affects any land or water use or natural resource of the coastal zone shall be carried out in a manner which is consistent to the maximum extent practicable with the enforceable policies of approved State management programs.

Subsection (B) provides for federal exemption if the federal activity is found by the President to be "in the paramount interest of the United States."

So far, we have considered the process leading up to issuance of leases. Suppose environmental problems arise later. Leases issued by the Secretary of Interior contain provisions intended to protect against damages from oil spills. The Act confirms that Congress intended to exercise both the proprietary powers of a landowner and the police powers of the legislature in regulating leases of publicly owned resources. Safeguards are not limited to those provided by lease covenants; the Secretary may prescribe at any time rules and regulations that he finds "necessary and proper" for the "conservation of natural resources." 43 U.S.C.A. § 1334(a)(1). Rules in effect at the time a lease is executed are incorporated statutorily into the terms of the lease, and the Secretary may obtain cancellation of the lease if the lessee breaches any such rule. However, violations of rules issued after the lease has been executed do not enable the Secretary to cancel the lease; the property rights of the lessee are determined only by those rules in effect when the lease is executed.

When a spill occurs, the issue is no longer regulation but liability. Several federal laws impose liability for oil spills. OCSLA amendments of 1978 established liability for cleanup costs and damages resulting from OCS activities and created the Offshore Oil Spill Pollution Fund. The amendments apply to offshore facilities and to vessels carrying oil from such facilities. Strict liability for cleanup costs and damages is imposed jointly and severally on the owner and operator, subject to monetary caps. These caps, however, are not applicable if an incident is caused by willful misconduct or gross negligence, or by knowing violation of federal safety regulations. The Fund, which is derived from a fee of three cents per barrel imposed on the owner of oil obtained from the OCS, is liable for all losses not otherwise compensated.

Until 1990, the broadest liability for spills was imposed by § 311 of the Clean Water Act. It made vessels strictly liable for cleanup costs incurred by the government unless the owner proved that the spill was solely a result of an act of God, an act of war, an act or omission of a third party, or negligence by the federal government. These exceptions from liability were narrowly construed. Section 311 placed limits on liability. For the Exxon Valdez, the limit would have come to $32 million. However, the limits were not applicable if the government could show that the discharge was due to "willful negligence or willful misconduct within the privity and knowledge of the owner." At this writing, a punitive damage award against Exxon is under review by the Supreme Court.

The Oil Pollution Act of 1990, 33 U.S.C.A. § 2701 et seq., replaced the liability provisions of § 311. Section 1002 imposes liability on "each responsible party" for removal costs, damage to natural resources, damages "for injury to, or economic losses, resulting from destruction of, real or personal property," and lost profits "due to the injury, destruction, or loss of any real property, personal property, or natural resources, which shall be recoverable by any claimant." "Responsible parties" are defined in § 1001(32) to include the owners and operators of vessels, on-shore facilities, or pipelines. Defenses to liability are modeled on CERCLA § 107, which is discussed in Chapter 5. Like § 311, the new statute provides for unlimited liability if the spill is caused by gross negligence, willful misconduct, or a safety violation. The statute also tracks CERCLA in establishing an oil spill trust fund ($1 billion), granting the President federal response authority, and requiring the President to issue regulations governing the measurement of damages for injury to natural resources.

Measuring damages for injuries to natural areas poses interesting issues. This matter was raised in Commonwealth of Puerto Rico v. SS Zoe Colocotroni, 628 F.2d 652 (1st Cir.1980). The government of Puerto Rico was seeking to recover for injuries to an area of coastal mangrove wetlands. The court rejected a commercial or market-value test as the basis for recovery. The proper measure of damages, it said, was the reasonable cost to restore or rehabilitate the environment to its pre-existing condition. Applying this standard, the court rejected a plan to remove all the oil-impregnated mangrove plants and replace them with containerized plants as too costly and destructive to the remaining natural environment. The court also rejected an abstract calculation of six cents per marine animal killed. The case was remanded for the taking of testimony on a plan that "would have a beneficial effect on the ... ecosystem without excessive destruction of existing natural resources or disproportionate cost."

Section 1006(d)(1) of the 1990 Oil Pollution Act now provides that the measure of natural resource damages is:

(A) the cost of restoring, rehabilitating, replacing, or acquiring the equivalent of, the damaged natural resources;

(B) the diminution in value of those natural resources pending restoration; plus

(C) the reasonable cost of assessing those damages.

These costs are to be assessed with respect to the restoration plans promulgated by federal or state trustees. Section 106(e) requires the President to issue damage assessment regulations; damage determinations pursuant to those regulations enjoy a rebuttable presumption of correctness.

D. PROTECTION OF PUBLIC LANDS

1. PUBLIC LANDS POLICY

Although few individuals in the eastern half of the United States are aware of this fact, the federal government owns vast amounts of land. The percentage of federally owned lands, excluding Indian reservations, in the western states ranges from about 30% in Washington to almost 90% in Nevada. The average is close to 50%. Thus federal land policy is of critical importance to the western states.

Land policy is also of great importance to a number of important economic interests. The public lands contain much of the nation's commercial forest land, as well as large amounts of minerals such as copper, mercury, and nickel. In addition, federal lands account for a significant share of the nation's production of oil. Thus, the federal lands have tremendous economic importance.

Of course, the public lands also have tremendous importance to conservationists. In perhaps the single most important conservation action of the previous century, Congress in 1980 set aside vast tracts of land in Alaska as national monuments, parks, and wilderness areas. Roughly 30 million acres were added to the national parks system alone. Even before this legislation, more than 180 million acres had been reserved for national forests and parks.   It takes little imagination to foresee the possibility of considerable conflict between environmentalists and resource developers.

In order to understand the environmental aspects of public land law, a basic understanding of the non-environmental aspects is necessary as background.   Unfortunately, there is no comprehensive statutory scheme governing federal lands.   The numerous existing statutes are complicated and poorly coordinated.   We will merely attempt to give a basic outline of public land law.

Until the twentieth century, the federal government's main purpose with respect to public lands was to dispose of them as quickly as possible.   This policy was evidenced by several homestead acts that conveyed large portions of land to farmers and ranchers.   The most important survivor from this period is the Mining Law of 1872, 30 U.S.C.A. § 22 et seq.   This act allows private purchase of "all valuable mineral deposits in lands belonging to the United States."   (This statute does not apply to certain important minerals such as oil, gas, coal, and oil shale.)   Any individual who discovers a valuable mineral deposit on public lands can obtain a mining claim for that deposit.   The locater of the minerals acquires a possessory interest in the claim, which is a form of transferable property.   Beginning at the time of location, this property interest gives the holder the right to extract, process, and market the minerals.   The holder of the claim also has the right to obtain outright title to the land on which the claim is located.   The locater is not required to apply for a government patent to the land, but if it chooses to do so, the Secretary of the Interior has no discretion about issuing the patent. The sole purpose of this statute is to promote mining. Thus, this statute gives the federal government little power to control mining.

In 1976, mining activities were finally subjected to some degree of government control. As part of the Federal Land Policy and Management Act, Congress provided that in "managing the public lands" the Secretary "shall, by regulation or otherwise, take any action necessary to prevent unnecessary or undue degradation of the lands." 43 U.S.C.A. § 1732(b). The preceding sentence in the statute makes it clear that this provision is applicable to mining. Until this statute was passed, the federal government was essentially powerless to deal with environmental problems relating to mining, and even today its power is limited. In November 2007, the House passed legislation to end patenting and place a royalty on minerals, but the future of the legislation is uncertain.

State governments may also require permits for mining on federal lands. These permit requirements are not preempted if the state is regulating mining methods to limit environmental damage, as opposed to prohibiting mining altogether in certain locations. See California Coastal Commission v. Granite Rock Co., 480 U.S. 572 (1987). Distinguishing between "environmental" and "land-use" regulations, as the Court attempted to do in *Granite Rock*, may prove difficult in practice.

As mentioned earlier, some important natural resources such as oil have been exempted from the 1872 statute. Under the Mineral Leasing Act of 1920, the Secretary of the Interior was empowered to issue prospecting permits and leases for certain minerals such as oil and gas. Unlike the limited government role under the Mining Act, the government's powers to control mineral leasing are quite broad because of its discretion over the issuance of permits and leases.

Logging is another major resource use. Since 1891, the President has been authorized to set aside land as national forests. See 16 U.S.C.A. § 471. Under an 1897 statute, the purposes of establishing national forests were declared to be water control and "a continuous supply of timber." 16 U.S.C.A. § 475. The motivation for the statute was the fear that forest lands might soon disappear, leaving the United States with a shortage of timber and of watersheds needed to control stream flows. In 1960, Congress broadened the purposes of the national forest system by passing the Multiple-Use Sustained Yield Act, 16 U.S.C.A. §§ 528–531. This statute provides that national forests shall be administered for various purposes, including outdoor recreation, timber, and wildlife purposes. Because the Act gave the administrator no guidance as to what weight to give these various purposes, the Act was held to leave the administrator almost complete discretion. In 1974 and 1978, Congress called upon the Secretary of Agriculture to establish land management plans for national forests. This legislation also addresses matters such as clearcutting, a logging practice that had previously given rise to considerable controversy. See 16 U.S.C.A. §§ 1601 et seq. In 1976, the Federal Land Policy and Management Act was passed; it calls for similar planning on the 450 million acres administered by the Bureau of Land Management. See 43 U.S.C.A. §§ 1701–1784.

2. WITHDRAWALS

Historically, resource development on public lands was the rule rather than the exception. Most public land law was geared toward encouraging resource development, while preservation was an exception. Thus, preservation of public lands has taken place when either the executive or the legislature took action to withdraw lands from the "normal" development process.

Presidential authority to withdraw land from development was upheld by the Supreme Court in United States v. Midwest Oil Co., 236 U.S. 459 (1915). Because of the encouragement offered by the public land laws of the time, a race among oil companies arose in California to remove as much oil as possible, with each company attempting to pump out the oil before owners of nearby wells could do so. In 1909, the Geological Survey reported that all the oil lands might be in private hands within a few months. This, in turn, might have jeopardized the Navy's fuel supply. In response, the President issued an order "in aid of proposed legislation" withdrawing certain public lands from disposal to the public. The oil companies argued strenuously that the President lacked statutory authority to take this action. The Court held, however, that Congress had been aware of numerous prior instances of similar Presidential actions. Because Congress did not repudiate these previous withdrawals and indeed acquiesced in the practice, Congress was held to have impliedly consented to the executive practice. The Court stressed the need for Presidential flexibility in administering the public lands.

The Presidential power at issue in *Midwest Oil* was confirmed by the Pickett Act. The Act authorized the President "in his discretion" to

temporarily withdraw from settlement ... any of the public lands of the United States ... and reserve the same for water-power sites, irrigation, classification of lands, or other public purposes to be specified in the orders of withdrawal, and such withdrawals shall remain in force until revoked by him or by an Act of Congress.

Such withdrawals did not affect the application of the mining laws to metallic minerals on withdrawn land. Despite the use of the word "temporary," a temporary withdrawal remained in effect until expressly revoked.

In 1976, the Pickett Act was repealed. The power of the Secretary of the Interior to withdraw public lands is now governed by 43 U.S.C.A. § 1714. The goal of this legislation was to give Congress greater control over executive withdrawals. Withdrawals of large tracts of land (more than 5,000 acres) can be made only for 20-year periods, subject to a legislative veto by concurrent resolution of both houses. (The constitutionality of this legislative veto provision is dubious.) The Secretary is authorized to make smaller withdrawals for various periods of time, ranging from five years to infinity depending on the reason for the withdrawal. The statute does provide for emergency three-year withdrawals, which must be made when either the Secretary or the Interior Affairs Committee of either house of Congress determines that "an emergency situation exists and that extraordinary measures must be taken to preserve values that would otherwise be lost." (The grant of power to congressional committees is constitutionally dubious.) This provision was used in 1978 to make an emergency withdrawal of 105 million acres in Alaska. The legislative history shows that the 1976 legislation was intended to eliminate the President's implied withdrawal power under the *Midwest Oil* doctrine. The President does retain withdrawal power under certain other statutes, such as the Antiquities Act, 16 U.S.C.A. § 431, which was used by President Carter with respect to large tracts of land in Alaska.

Congress can also withdraw land from development through legislation. The most important legislative land withdrawal, apart from the 1980 Alaskan Lands Act, was the Wilderness Act of 1964, 16 U.S.C.A. §§ 1131–1136. This statute created the National Wilderness Preservation System. Section 1132 of the Act designates certain lands as wilderness areas and provides for review of other national forest lands to determine the desirability of further legislation adding them to the wilderness system.

The most important effect of wilderness designation is found in § 1133 of the Wilderness Act, which sharply restricts the use of wilderness land. Section 1133 makes the agency administering any wilderness area "responsible for preserving the wilderness character of the area" and for insuring that these areas are devoted to "the public purposes of recreational, scenic, scientific, educational, conservational, and historical use." Except where the Act expressly provides otherwise, no commercial enterprise and no permanent roads are allowed within any wilderness area. Mineral use remained a major exception, with the mining laws having remained applicable to wilderness areas until 1983. One area of uncertainty is the relationship between the Wilderness Act and other previous legislation, since the Act sharply changes the status of these lands but purports not to repeal such previous legislation.

3. PREVENTION OF CONFLICTING PRIVATE USES

In addition to limiting development of public lands themselves, preservation of these lands often requires restrictions on activities on private lands. For example, preserving a water supply for public lands may be critical if they are to fulfill their purposes. Other public lands cannot be effectively used for their intended purposes without clean air and good visibility. In this section, we will briefly consider the statutory and common law doctrines protecting public lands from conflicting uses of adjacent private lands. As we saw in Chapter 2, congressional power under the property clause to regulate the use of private lands has been disputed. This has not proved a major problem with respect to the restrictions we are about to discuss. Restrictions on water use have been considered to be federal property rights reserved when lands were originally granted to private individuals. The restrictions relating to air pollution are part of a general statute clearly authorized under the commerce clause.

To understand the federal government's special prerogatives in water law, it is necessary to recall some basic facts about western water law. In much of the West, water is a scarce commodity. To allocate this commodity, western states generally use a priority system based on order of use together with some kind of filing system. Generally speaking, individuals who first appropriate part of a water supply have priority over those whose appropriation is later in time. Of course there are numerous complications and local variations, but this is the general scheme. The federal government has often failed to comply with the state priority systems. The question that arises is whether the federal government can claim a greater right to the use of water than it is given by state law.

As Cappaert v. United States, 426 U.S. 128 (1976) illustrates, the federal government does indeed have some special prerogatives in water law. *Cappaert* involved an underground pool in the Devil's Hole Cavern in Nevada. The land surrounding Devil's Hole is part of the Death Valley National Monument. In a pool within the cave live the Devil's Hole pupfish. If the water level falls below a certain level in the pool, uncovering a rock shelf, the fish cannot breed. Nearby landowners began pumping operations that resulted in declining water levels in the pool. The Court held that the Presidential proclamation establishing the cave as part of the national monument in effect reserved the necessary underground water to fulfill the purposes of the reservation. One of the purposes of the reservation was preservation of the pool and the fish that live within it. Thus, although it had not obtained any property interest in the groundwater under state law, as a matter of federal law the government was entitled to insist that sufficient underground water be left to maintain the pool level.

Some of the limits of the implied reservation doctrine became clear in United States v. New Mexico, 438 U.S. 696 (1978). The question in that case was whether the creation of a national forest reserves water for recreation and wildlife-preservation purposes. In an opinion by then-Justice Rehnquist, the Supreme Court held that the sole purposes of creating national forests were to preserve timber supply and watersheds. Although a secondary purpose of preserving wildlife may later have developed, according to the Court such a secondary purpose did not suffice to trigger the implied-reservation doctrine. The Court's opinion showed great sensitivity to states' rights in the water law area. Four Justices dissented, arguing that the congressional desire to "improve and protect" the forests included a desire to preserve the wildlife that inhabit those forests.

The implied-reservation doctrine has deep historical roots. A more recent protection for federal lands is to be found in the Clean Air Act. Section 162, 42 U.S.C.A. § 7472, designates major national wilderness areas and parks as Class I areas. These Class I areas are subject to special protection under the PSD (prevention of significant deterioration) provisions of the Act. As we saw in Chapter 3, air in Class I areas must be kept cleaner than would otherwise be required by the national air quality standards. To implement this clean air requirement, the Act contains special permit provisions and requires changes in state implementation plans.

Under § 165 of the Clean Air Act, 42 U.S.C.A. § 7475, a facility can receive a permit even if its emissions would violate the Class I limits, if the manager of the affected federal lands certifies that there will be no adverse impact on the federal lands. If the federal land manager refuses to issue the permit, the state governor may request a limited Presidential exemption. On the other hand, even if a facility does meet the Class I requirements, it may be denied a permit if it will have an adverse impact on visibility or other "air quality-related values" in a Class I area. Another significant provision of the

Clean Air Act is found in § 169A, 42 U.S.C.A. § 7491. This section is designed to maintain high visibility in mandatory Class I areas. To some degree, retrofitting is required in the interests of improved visibility, although major weight is given to the cost factor.

E. PRESERVING ENDANGERED SPECIES

We close this book with the subject of biodiversity. Protection of endangered species raises the full panoply of issues we have discussed in this book: the division of labor between courts, agencies, and legislatures; the meaning and strength of environmental values; and the necessity or avoidability of trade-offs between environment and economic factors. As we will see, it also raises questions about the rights of governmental and private property owners.

Endangered species receive particularly strong protection under U.S. law. The Endangered Species Act (ESA), 16 U.S.C.A. § 1531 et seq., stems from the formative period of U.S. environmental law in the 1970s. Section 4 requires the Secretaries of Commerce and Interior to determine whether any species is endangered and to designate critical habitat, based on the best scientific data available 16 U.S.C.A. § 1533. Section 7, entitled "Inte agency Cooperation," requires consultation to sure that agency actions do not jeopardize endangered species—the "consultation" has t out to be less important than the "do not jeopardize." 16 U.S.C.A. § 1536. Section 9 goes on to forbid "taking" any endangered species. 16 U.S.C.A. § 1538.

As we saw in Chapter 1, the Supreme Court's decision in *TVA v. Hill* strongly supported a broad interpretation of the ESA by requiring an injunction against an almost-completed multimillion dollar project. The Court's opinion stressed the nearly absolute priority Congress had placed on preserving endangered species. In response to *TVA v. Hill*, Congress amended the ESA to provide an escape hatch in the form of a special committee (commonly called the "God committee"). This committee can override § 7 if there are no reasonable alternatives to the agency action, the benefits clearly outweigh those of compliance with the statute, and the action is in the public interest and has at least regional significance. 16 U.S.C.A. §§ 1536(e), (h). The committee has hardly ever intervened, so the net effect of the amendment was to leave § 7 about as strong as it had been previously.

Section 7, which prohibits the government from jeopardizing any endangered species, has also received strong support from the courts. For example, in National Wildlife Federation v. Coleman, 529 F.2d 359 (5th Cir.1976), the court enjoined construction of an interstate highway that would cross a critical habitat of the Mississippi Sandhill Crane. The court was also concerned about the effect of the highway in encouraging development in the area, placing the crane at further risk. The court emphasized that § 7 "imposes on federal agencies the mandatory duty to insure that their actions will not either (i) jeopardize the existence of an endangered species, or (ii) destroy or modify critical habitat of an endangered species."

Section 7 has not lacked for controversies, most notably in the Northwest, where efforts to protect the spotted owl led to substantial logging restrictions, and where salmon protection is becoming equally controversial. But under § 7, at least the government is only restricting its own activities or the use of its own lands or funds. Section 9 has been even more hotly resented by private landowners, who may be deprived of the right not only to destroy animals causing them economic losses, but also to modify areas of critical habitat needed by the endangered species. Not surprisingly, the concept of "property rights" has been fervently invoked in support of these claims.

In Babbitt v. Sweet Home Chapter of Communities for a Great Oregon, 515 U.S. 687 (1995), the Court confirmed that habitat destruction may violate § 9 of the ESA. Section 9 is a ban on "taking" endangered species; "taking" in turn is defined to encompass any effort to "harass, harm, pursue, hunt, shoot, wound, kill, trap, capture, or collect." 16 U.S.C.A. § 1532(19). The Secretary of the Interior had defined "harm" by regulation to encompass "significant habitat modification or degradtion where it actually kills or injures wildlife significantly impairing essential behavioral terns, including breeding, feeding, or shelter

As construed by the government, the regulation required a clear showing of proximate cause. The question before the Court was whether this was a permissible reading of the statute. In a careful opinion by Justice Stevens, the Court concluded that the agency's interpretation of the statute was valid, relying on the broad statutory reference to "harm" and the legislative purpose of reversing the trend toward extinction.

Justice Scalia wrote a scathing dissent. The crux of the dissent was his assertion that the word "take," as applied to wildlife, is "as old as the law itself," and means "to reduce those animals, by killing or capturing, to human control." "It should take the strongest evidence," he said, "to make us believe that Congress has defined a term in a manner repugnant to its ordinary and traditional sense." Scalia's reading of the statute may not be impermissible, but under the *Chevron* doctrine (discussed in Chapter 2), he had the burden of showing that the agency's contrary interpretation was not merely wrong but unreasonable.

Scalia's textual argument seems overstated. It would be peculiar to say that Mrs. O'Leary's cow didn't "harm" the people of Chicago when it kicked over the lantern that started the Chicago fire. Similarly, as a matter of ordinary English usage, someone who destroys the breeding grounds used by members of an endangered species or eliminates their food supply surely harms them. Thus, rather than being based on the plain language of the text, the dissent seems to be more motivated by concern over the rights of property owners.

Developers have complained bitterly about federal restrictions on private lands. Besides raising commerce clause and taking claims, which so far have been unsuccessful, they have also exerted considerable political pressure. In part to mollify these objections, widespread use has been made of habitat conservation plans (HCPs), under which development of some tracts is allowed in return for mitigation measures and development restrictions on other tracts. Many of these HCPs involve small parcels, but about five percent are over 100,000 acres, and a couple are over a million acres. Ideally, HCPs provide the opportunity for long-term, comprehensive ecosystem planning, but critics complain that they are sometimes just an excuse for nonenforcement of the ESA. HCPs have also been applauded as a model of collaborative environmental governance, a possible new direction in environmental protection.

As always in environmental law, the only thing that can be confidently predicted about the future is that it will remain interesting, as our society continues to struggle with implementing the goal of environmental protection while respecting other important social values. The emergence of the climate change issue may usher in a new era of environmental activity.

As we have seen, environmental regulation involves difficult trade-offs. Partly as a result of the need to accommodate these trade-offs, environmental law has evolved into a complex and highly technical body of rules. In the midst of this complexity, it is easy to lose sight of the law's fundamental underlying goal for the past several decades. At least since the late 1960s, our society has had a firm commitment to the protection of environmental quality. It is the questions of "at what cost?" and "how fast?" that continue to divide us and to cause analytical difficulties. But the basic commitment has now passed the test of time. Despite its imperfections and frustrations, environmental law is here to stay.

INDEX

References are to Pages

---

†